COOKING
WITH THE
SEASONS

To
Dena

May all the
Seasons give
you the joy of
sharing the good
friends
Bon Appetit
[signature]

COOKING
WITH THE
SEASONS

A Year in My Kitchen

Monique Jamet Hooker and
Tracie Richardson

℘ BOUNTY PRESS ℘
E1171 Victory Ridge Road
De Soto, WI 54624

Originally published in 1997 by Henry Holt® and Company

Hardbound CIP Data:

Library of Congress Cataloging-in-Publication Data
Hooker, Monique Jamet.
Cooking with the seasons: a year in my kitchen /
Monique Jamet Hooker and Tracie Richardson.-1st ed.
p. cm.
Includes index.
ISBN 0-8050-4866-9
1. Cookery, American. 2. Menus. I. Richardson, Tracie . II. Title.
TX715.H7854 1997 97-403
641.5973-dc21 CIP

First Edition 1997

ISBN 0-9820640-0-4

Printed in the United States of America

To my two sons, Daniel and Philip (P. K.),
who are my joy, supporting cast, and best tasters.
My deepest gratitude goes to my husband and best friend, Philip,
for his support and critical foresight, but mostly for being there.
M. J. H.

For my daughters, Jessica and Alexandria, who are
learning the lessons of family with grace.
T. R.

Contents

Acknowledgments

My very American husband, Philip, and I come from diverse backgrounds that are both rich in culture and tradition. I am very grateful for his sense of curiosity, which helped me re-create my past, and for his support and admiration of this project. His understanding of the most delicate details of life at Kerbiquet, in Brittany, as it unfolded for him through the twenty-five years of our marriage, helped shape the book.

This book began as a scrapbook and collection of memories of my growing up for our two sons, Daniel and P. K. I hope a record of all the stories and anecdotes of my childhood will help them carry forward the traditions they also grew up with. I thank them for having so many questions for their father and me as we sat around the dinner table and talked about both of our homes.

This book would not have been possible without Tracie Richardson. Tracie joined my class as a student of professional cooking. We both realized her love for food was best served by choosing a pen over a whisk. She urged me to sit down and put this book together, and from this began a long relationship nurtured by tea on the front porch and hot cider in front of the fire. I am appreciative of her everlasting pushing and setting of deadlines, as it is because of her that this book is here for all to read and enjoy.

Thank you to all our friends for sharing our table at the drop of a hat; to every student I've taught in the last twenty-eight years who believed in my philosophy of simple seasonal cooking; to my peers in the industry for their help and support throughout the years; to our editor, Beth Crossman, who understood the vision of seasonal cooking; and to Theresa Park, our agent, for her passion for the book and the time she took to guide us.

Most of all, I would like to thank my three brothers and six sisters for helping shine the light on what it was like for all of us growing up on the farm so long ago.

Monique Jamet Hooker

I first met Chef Monique Hooker three years ago, when I studied under her at the Culinary and Hospitality Institute of Chicago. I quickly learned that a love of food and entertaining does not necessarily translate into the makings of a great chef. It was apparent my skills at the word processor far outstripped my skills with a knife. For someone who loves to eat—and regularly, at that—writing is a rather risky career choice. When I told Monique of my plans to try writing as a full-time career, she answered with the wisdom I've come to admire her for. "*Chérie,* one must always listen to the heart" was her blessing on me. She then spoke the words that changed both our lives forever. "You know, I have an idea for a book. . . ." From that day forward, we set out on a wonderful journey together in which she became my eyes and I became her voice in a world where people take time to savor the best of life with those they love. My thanks and love to Monique for the many happy hours we spent together as colleagues and dear friends. The journey continues.

Without the following people, this book would still only be a wish: our agent, Theresa Park, who understood everything from the start; our editor, Beth Crossman, whose unfailing patience and instincts were invaluable; my parents, Dwight and Sheila Singleton; and my good friends, Brendan Baber, Elizabeth Hanzel, Tracey Pepper, Greg and Bonnie Sun, and Angela Stewart, who listened and encouraged me every day. Finally, to Kelly Donnell, who nourishes my heart as he shares my table.

Tracie Richardson

Introduction

The Philosophy of Seasonal Cooking

I learned early and well that the hand of the seasonal cook is the link between the good earth and family. This important lesson was taught to me while I was growing up on our family's farm in Brittany. There, my mother's daily call of "*à table!*" was a welcome summons to meals celebrating the bounty of each season. Every season offered foods that naturally complemented each other in taste, texture, and color, so her simply prepared dishes dazzled all our senses. What could possibly taste better than spring trout stuffed with delicate watercress? Is there anything prettier than a ruby-red summer tomato warmed by the sun to a vibrant sweetness, accompanied by basil-seasoned roasted eggplant? What is more comforting than a root vegetable stew bubbling in the kitchen while the tang of autumn traces the air? And who can resist the rich smell of a smoky winter ham, complemented by broth-simmered beans with dried mushrooms and spices?

As important as filling the stomachs of ten growing children, "à table" (coming to the table) also meant filling our hearts with the love of good friends and family. People always seemed to find their way to Maman's table, either for special occasions or just by dropping in around suppertime. Time wasn't marked by the calendar, but by the seasonal dishes that appeared on her table to be consumed with liberal helpings of laughter and conversation. Hers was not great cooking in the classical French tradition, but it was classical in the way Maman's wonderful dishes reappeared each year according to nature's calendar. She used foods within their season to let the best natural flavors come through.

The pleasures of cooking and eating foods seasonally, with family and friends, are rarely practiced in our prepackaged, hurry-up world. But learning how to use foods during their true season can enhance our everyday life by optimizing flavor and encouraging simplicity in the kitchen. When we take the time to sit down to a good meal with people we love, we are living closer to the earth through the food we serve, and we are continuing the cycle of nature.

Today modern technology permits us to grow, ship, and store exotic foods from all over the world, no matter what the time of year. We benefit from enlarging our culinary repertoire, but we also blur the natural seasons until they almost disappear. Cleverly we mix and match ingredients, paying no attention to the harmony of flavor and texture. We're often frustrated with the results and don't understand why a mango soufflé in October tastes off or a fresh tomato in January feels like cotton in our mouth.

Foods used in peak season taste, feel, and look like the season they are grown in. Spring brings lightly colored fruits and vegetables, delicate but crisp. Poultry and meats are tender, needing little cooking time to bring out their flavor. Summer foods are robust and piquant, depending on the sun and warmth to develop their intensity. Animals raised free-range take on the taste of the summer grasses they feed on. In autumn, foods grow closer to the ground, looking for the last gentle warmth of the year. They taste buttery and smooth, reflecting the fall colors with deep oranges, mellow golds, and cranberry reds. Winter is a restful time in nature, giving us a chance to enjoy dishes from food put up during the summer harvest. Winter foods are often flavored with nuts and dried fruits, braised or stewed slowly in rich, hearty sauces. When thought of in this way, cooking becomes a daily art involving all the senses.

The United States is a cornucopia of regional foods waiting to be shared. Cooking seasonally offers a wonderful chance to experience unusual and delicious foods from all parts of the country. In Brittany, we have our own cuisine based on seafood, agriculture, and game—bounty of a region that for centuries was physically isolated from the rest of France. Land and sea are situated side by side in Brittany, so Breton culinary tradition sprang from rich farmlands fertilized with seaweed and from coastal towns awash with the smell of the ocean. Our cuisine is basic, and the flavors are subtle. It is resonant with root vegetables, flavorful meats, and fresh seafood. Much of Brittany's cooking is flavored with cider from the abundant apple and pear crops. However, again and again, traditional recipes will call for prunes or apricots not indigenous to the area, or there will be a hint of rum flavoring in a sauce, or the dishes will electrify the palate with the spices of the Orient. This influx of outside influences was the result of trading what was locally grown for staples from other countries. The excitement of introducing new ingredients into the culinary traditions of a culture is as old as the ancient trade routes themselves.

We do the same thing today, mingling ingredients from other cultures, experimenting with the vast amount of variety available to us. While exciting, the downside to this explosion of choice is that refrigeration and mass transportation have sparked a tendency to demand food only because we can have it, not because it is seasonal or fresh. We would not want to turn back the clock or thumb our noses at global availability, but we need to look once again to the local garden for inspiration and serve food balanced to the season.

Cooking with the Seasons: A Year in My Kitchen is meant to help you adapt your cooking to the seasons according to your geographical area. The recipes are seasonally based on the growing cycles of the Midwest because that is where I've made my home for half of my life. They are inspired by the dishes and techniques I grew up with in Europe, but they are uniquely American because I've adapted the recipes to the range of ingredients available to us here. Because the United States is divided into five major growing areas, each with its own particular seasons, you will find a harvest chart at the end of the book. It covers all the fresh produce used in the recipes and is provided as a guide to help you understand when foods come into season in your area or whether foods shipped from other parts of the country to you are at their local peak season.

The recipes I've created are beautiful to look at and simple to prepare using basic cooking techniques. One of the best things about seasonal cooking is the ability to substitute one ingredient for another, playing on seasonal characteristics of taste, texture, and color. Some of the recipes include variations, but these, like the recipes themselves, are only meant to spark the imagination. You'll soon find that knowing what to do with what you have on hand will become second nature. The roast chicken with braised vegetables served on Sunday will become a quick sauté of vegetables over pasta on Monday and chicken vegetable soup on Tuesday. As today's fare becomes tomorrow's supper, it reflects the same cycle in nature that moves one season into the next.

The harvest chart should be used only as a starting point to seasonal cooking. Visit your local farmers' market and notice what is available throughout the months of the growing season. Look around at what the trees, plants, and animals are doing at different times of the year. Smell how the air around us shifts with the seasons. Listen to your body and pay attention to what it is telling you it wants. Clear and sharp spring air causes the blood to rush, making our taste buds want foods that cleanse and rejuvenate our sleepy winter bodies. In the summer, our appetites respond to the heat and long days with extremes—we want big flavors, but we also want to do little work to produce them. Nature obliges us with an overabundance of full-bodied fruits and vegetables that stand on their own, needing minimal attention from us. Fall comes and with it a need to begin to prepare for nature's long night. As we wait, we want hot soups and braised casseroles to seep through our bodies like a drawn blanket protecting us from the chill of the night air. At last, when winter arrives, the desire to close in and huddle with loved ones against the deep cold is answered by slow-simmering meals that evoke the comfort of a flickering hearth fire. All the language of food needed to understand seasonal cooking is within each of us. We just need to listen to what's being said.

Finally, I hope you enjoy reading about my experiences of growing up on a seventeenth-century château-farm in France. Our daily life and many celebrations may seem to speak with the voice of another era, but it is only the echo of the joy I continue to find à table with my family and friends here. There are many ways of gathering around food, taking that little extra moment to share. Let me show you how, by telling of my childhood in Brittany through recipes that celebrate the best food America has to offer each season. By inviting the seasons into the kitchen, I know you will soon find your own joy à table.

APRIL

*My grandmother, Marie Jamet, drawing spring
water from a well in the courtyard of Manoir de
Kerbiquet, our family farm. The well was first dug
in the mid-1400s and is still in use today.*

For the seasonal cook, April is the first month of the culinary year. It's when we really start feeling the relationship between the earth and ourselves as nature begins to renew itself. The sleeping roots that have been sitting underground all winter gingerly sprout tender green leaves. The rivers fill with spawning fish, and dozens of varieties of birds migrate from the south to their northern nesting grounds. Memories of winter fade away, leaving within us a desire to taste nature itself. The concentrated, sharp taste of wild asparagus no thicker than a twig, the first tart strawberries coming to bloom, and the cool crunch of watercress just after it rains—all these foods call to our own sense of reawakening. April is clear, it's fresh, and its foods are very, very light.

At home we celebrated the coming of spring with a traditional Easter fête. During the year, Sunday afternoons were always set aside for a family meal, but Easter Sunday seemed especially festive because the weather was fine and the long wooden table was moved outdoors to accommodate a large number of neighbors and family, some of whom came from as far away as Paris. Easter was a time to reestablish old friendships and family ties that might have been hibernating during the long winter.

Living in the country allowed us to live close to the earth. When my mother prepared a meal, she always looked to the garden for inspiration and then let the food speak for itself. Dozens of dishes made their appearance on the Easter table from year to year, but they were rarely prepared in the same way twice. It was the textures and tastes of what April had to offer that gave the whole meal a sense of familiarity. Maman's food was never complicated, and the flavors were always clean and honest. Of course, there were many family favorites, the recipes of which were handed down from generation to generation. But country recipes were rarely written down, so the honesty of the food depended on the fact that Maman was cooking by sight, taste, and smell for people she loved.

The highlight of the Easter meal was always Maman's preparation of a delicious *pré-salé* lamb from Brittany, whose distinct flavor comes from the salt grasses of the coastal marshlands where the sheep graze. The day before Easter my father dug a pit in the ground, about eighteen inches deep, with dirt mounded all around it. On Easter morning a fire was built in the pit and fed with coals for about three hours, until a deep bed of hot embers glowed red. Meanwhile, Maman prepared the lamb by removing the loose fat and seasoning the lamb inside and out with salt and pepper. The cavity was stuffed with young onion and garlic bulbs and bundles of thyme. The outside of the lamb was rubbed with oil, garlic, and chopped thyme. The lamb was then spitted on stakes and set three feet above the coals. We all took turns hand-cranking the spit so that the lamb roasted evenly. As the intensity of the coals subsided, the lamb was lowered closer to the pit so it would be surrounded by heat. We took turns constantly basting the lamb with a mixture of oil, garlic, thyme, and crushed black pepper. After about two hours the meat was crusted brown on the outside and pink on the inside and ready to serve.

Today I continue the family tradition of serving lamb on Easter Sunday. I miss the pré-salé lamb from Brittany, but adapting to regional foods is part of feeling at home where you live. I have found an excellent substitution for the lamb of my childhood with naturally raised lamb from the western United States, which I order fresh from my butcher a few days before Easter. The grazing grasses in the West give the meat a less strong taste than the lamb I grew up with, but it is still wonderfully satisfying. And yes, we still occasionally roast a whole lamb in a backyard pit, but a leg of lamb roasted in the oven is every bit as delicious as one that has been pit-roasted, if not quite as dramatic!

While the lamb was roasting, the table disappeared under the weight of a variety of seasonal dishes. Pearly fin de siècle oysters, artichokes braised in sparkling cider, stuffed trout on a bed of sautéed spinach, loaves of bread and cheeses, salads made from baby green lettuce and radishes were staples of the holiday. For dessert, cream puffs and napoleons were our favorite. Not surprisingly, the meal usually lasted into the early evening. People drifted in and out during the day, gossiping and laughing, playing cards or boccie ball while taking breaks from the long table that never seemed to empty of its abundance. Everything was simply prepared and presented, and the mood was happily casual. At the end of the day we felt our appetite was satisfied and our hearts were full, as well.

This idea of drifting in and out is the same approach we need to develop when we go to market. If one day the grocer has fresh thyme and the next he doesn't, so what? Try your lamb rubbed with lavender, or basil, or whatever is at hand in your growing region. Take the recipe and improvise. Play with food colors and combinations. It all comes down to simplicity and motivation. Use your senses to tell you what tastes good, smells good, and appeals to the eye.

APRIL RECIPES

EASTER DINNER

Creamy Sorrel Soup

Muscadet

Roast Leg of Lamb with Garlic

Asparagus with Roasted Garlic and Ham

Lime Fava Beans

Pomerol

Mixed Salad of Spring Greens

Camembert and Blue Cheeses

Cabernet Sauvignon

Paris-Brest Pastry

Champagne Brut

CREAMY SORREL SOUP

Sorrel is best in cool spring and fall weather. Found in the wild, sorrel has a tart taste that inspired a game for us as children. Whoever could eat the most before our eyes teared was the winner! Today cultured sorrel has a more pleasant, lemony flavor. Because heat changes the acid content of sorrel, this creamy soup loses some of its bright color during cooking, turning it a soft green.

6 SERVINGS

2 tablespoons unsalted butter
4 shallots, peeled and chopped
2 pounds sorrel leaves, washed and dried
2 tablespoons flour

6 cups chicken stock (see Basics, page 375)
2 egg yolks
1 cup cream
Salt and pepper

In a large saucepan, melt the butter and slowly cook the shallots until soft but not brown.

Reserving 4 leaves for garnish, chop the sorrel and add to the shallots, stirring gently. Add the flour and stir until the butter is absorbed. Slowly stir in the chicken stock and blend well to prevent lumps from forming.

Bring the mixture to a boil, then simmer for 10 minutes. Purée the soup in a food processor, then reheat. In a small bowl, blend the egg yolks and cream, then slowly add to the soup. To prevent the cream from curdling, stir quickly while adding the cream mixture and do not allow the mixture to boil. Adjust the seasoning with salt and pepper. **Chiffonade** the reserved sorrel leaves.

Ladle soup into bowls and top with chiffonade. Serve at once.

VARIATIONS: The same amount of spinach, watercress, or any green-leaf combination can be substituted for sorrel.

- Adding ¼ pound of spinach to the sorrel intensifies the green color of the soup while maintaining the lemon taste.

- Add ½ pound of sautéed mushrooms prior to puréeing for a more robust flavor.

♥ *Monique's Touch:*

Chiffonade is a delightful garnish technique that can be done to any leafy herb or vegetable. Simply stack up 4 to 6 leaves, then tightly roll them lengthwise. Slice the leaves very thin, then separate into strands. Use in soups, sauces, dressings, or on top of hors d'oeuvres.

SIDENOTE:

In most of the recipes I have not specified the type of cream to use: half and half, light, heavy, or whipping cream. Use your own choice and vary the amount to your taste.

COUNTRY SOUP WITH DANDELION AND WATERCRESS

The feeling of renewal in the air led my siblings and I on long walks through the spring country-side. During April we were always curious to see what surprises the new year would bring. Which tree did the cuckoo build his nest in? Who could find the best mushroom patch? But to me, one of the most beautiful sites was breaking through the woods to the pasture where dandelions grew wild, the young pale green leaves shiny with dew in the morning light. We each always took along a paper bag for gathering dandelions to take home. We made sure to pick enough for Maman to make this wonderful soup.

4 SERVINGS

1 tablespoon unsalted butter or olive oil

1 small onion, peeled and diced

1 small potato, peeled and diced

4 cups chicken stock (see Basics, page 375)

8 ounces dandelion leaves, washed and dried

8 ounces watercress, washed and dried

1 cup cream

Freshly ground nutmeg

Salt and pepper

In a saucepan, melt the butter or heat the oil, then cook the onion over low heat until translucent but not brown. Add the potato and cook until the butter is absorbed. Do not brown.

Add the chicken stock and bring to a boil. Lower the heat to a simmer and cook, covered, until the potatoes are soft but still hold their shape, about 5 minutes. Add the **dandelion** and watercress. Stir gently.

Add the cream in a slow stream, blending constantly. Season to taste with ground nutmeg and salt and pepper. Simmer for 10 minutes before serving.

VARIATIONS: Any leafy green or combination of greens can be used to adapt this soup for monthly availability. Try spinach, arugula, or beet, mustard, or kale greens.

- A waxy variety of potato holds a better shape for chunky soups, but a baking potato will dissolve and give a creamier texture. When done this way, it is possible to eliminate the cream for a lower-fat version of a rich, satisfying soup.

- Dandelion and watercress have strong flavors. To soften their taste, add a couple of tablespoons of freshly chopped dill.

♥ *Monique's Touch:*

Spring **dandelions** have a gentle bite, so they lend themselves to soups and salads. Later in the summer, when the leaves are longer and darker, the milky liquid found inside gives them a bitter flavor. I still like to use dandelions then, but I mix them with other milder greens so that the dandelion flavor is not overpowering.

SIDENOTE:

The word dandelion comes from the French *dent de lion,* literally meaning "tooth of the lion," a fanciful reference to the jagged edges of the leaves. Country folk have long eaten dandelion greens in spring, believing they thin the blood and purge the body after a sleepy winter. Look for young, cool, pale greens prior to blooming that will not have developed the bitterness found in summer dandelions.

TROUT BROTH WITH WATERCRESS

The crisp, fresh taste of young spring trout and watercress is an intuitive combination of flavors. Watercress is abundant in Brittany, growing wild alongside the cold streams where we fished for our supper. Like trout, watercress thrives where water is crystal clear. Each year we knew our family's natural water source remained pure and cold when the watercress could be seen growing at the beginning of April near the spring that fed our well.

6 SERVINGS

1 medium onion, peeled and
   coarsely chopped
1 tablespoon olive oil
1 pound trout trimmings and bones
7 cups water
1 cup white wine or ½ cup dry
   vermouth

2 celery stalks, coarsely chopped
3 sprigs each fresh parsley and thyme
3 garlic cloves, peeled and crushed
1 bunch watercress, stems removed
   and reserved
6 whole peppercorns, cracked
Salt

In a large pot, cook the onion in the oil over low heat until translucent. Add the trout **trimmings and bones,** tossing gently to mix well.

Add the water, wine or vermouth, celery, parsley, thyme, garlic, watercress stems, and peppercorns. Lightly season with salt.

Bring to a boil, then immediately lower to a simmer so the broth will not become cloudy. Skim any fat using a large spoon. Cook for 20 minutes.

At this point, taste the broth. If a stronger concentration of flavors is desired, simmer for 3–4 minutes longer until the broth is slightly reduced. When the flavor is to your liking, pass the broth through a fine strainer lined with cheesecloth. Adjust the seasoning. Divide the watercress leaves into serving bowls. Pour the broth over the watercress and serve.

VARIATIONS: Light broth becomes a filling lunch by taking thin slices of French or sourdough bread spread with a good Gruyère or Brie cheese, then toasting them in the oven. Place the cheese toast in the bottom of the serving bowl and pour the broth over before serving.

♥ *Monique's Touch:*

If I don't have enough **trimmings and bones** left from fish I fillet myself, I ask my fishmonger for bones he would otherwise discard. The bones of any lean fish may be used to make broth. Leftover trimmings of snapper, pike, or halibut work well.

SIDENOTE:

Until the mid-1800s watercress was used by city people only as a garnish. Farmers realized they could create a market for the glossy green leaves by extolling its health benefits. Vendors would hold up bunches while crying out in the marketplace, "I have the clearest spring and health in my body. Two cents a bunch! Two cents a bunch!" Watercress soon found its way into delicious soups and salads and won a place in French culinary history. Store watercress upside down and packed in crushed ice until ready to use.

SEARED SEA BASS WITH TINY FRESH PEAS AND ASPARAGUS

Living in the interior of Brittany did not prevent my family from enjoying the fruits of the sea sixty miles away. Once a week the screech of the fish seller's truck horn announced his stop in our village on the way back from his predawn buying trip. The horn was Maman's signal to gather a basket and money, brush the crumbs from her smock, and head down the footpath from the house to the road. By the time she arrived, usually trailed by several young helpers, the fish seller was opening the back of the truck, where he transported sea bass, scallops, sole, turbot, mackerel, and shrimp on a bed of seaweed. The fish were so fresh, the eyes were still bright, clear, and moist. We watched as Maman carefully selected a few pieces, planning a week's menu in her head as she chose the best. Soon the haggling was done, a chuckle between the fish seller and Maman sealing a bargain well made. Within a few minutes of his arrival, the fish seller was gone, blasting his horn down the road to his next customer.

6 SERVINGS

1½ pounds sea bass fillet or striped bass fillet, cut into 6 pieces
1 cup asparagus tips
½ cup fresh peas, shelled

1 tablespoon unsalted butter
1 tablespoon olive oil
2 tablespoons chopped fresh chives
Salt and pepper

Wipe the fish dry on both sides and season with salt and pepper.

In a saucepan of boiling salted water, blanch the asparagus tips and peas for 3 minutes. Drain.

In a large, hot skillet, melt the butter with the oil until they sizzle. Add the fillets, skin side up, and sauté on high heat for 3 minutes. Turn, lower the heat, and cook for another 3 minutes, or until the fish fillets flake with the touch of a fork. Remove from the pan and keep warm.

Add the asparagus and peas to the pan, and swirl in the juices from the fillets until heated. Arrange the fillets on a serving platter with the asparagus and peas over them. Sprinkle with the chives.

VARIATIONS: Fiddlehead ferns, which sprout in the spring at about the same time as asparagus, may be substituted for the asparagus. Soak the fiddleheads for 5 minutes in enough water to cover, with 1 tablespoon of white vinegar mixed in. Strain, coarsely chop the ferns, and proceed as above.

SALMON TROUT WITH DUXELLE

One of my favorite fish is the salmon trout, a freshwater trout whose flesh is salmon-red and tender on the inside. In the United States it is called brown trout for the dull brown color of its skin. As children, we caught salmon trout by wading up to our knees in the river and quietly placing our hands underneath the fish. On the count of three we grabbed it, and out of the water the fish came, flying onto the bank. To carry home our catch, we speared the fish with a willow branch, happily anticipating dinner to come.

6 SERVINGS

3 tablespoons olive oil
Six 5-ounce salmon trout fillets
1 tablespoon lemon juice
¾ cup white wine

3 cups duxelle
Chopped fresh chives, for garnish
Salt and pepper

Set a large sauté pan over high heat and add the oil. Season the fillets with salt and pepper, and sauté for about 2 minutes on each side. Set aside.

Add the lemon juice and wine to the pan. Simmer for 1 minute to reduce the sauce by half. Add the **duxelle** and swirl the pan to mix.

Place the fillets on serving plates and spoon the sauce over the fish. Garnish with chives before serving. Can be served hot or cold.

VARIATIONS: If salmon trout is not available at the fish market, substitute salmon, halibut, grouper, or any other fillet that looks fresh.

- This recipe is also delicious without mushrooms. Instead of using a duxelle, sauté 1 cup each of parsley and shallots in the pan after the fillets are sautéed. Proceed as directed. Serve with fresh lemon wedges.

♥ *Monique's Touch:*

Duxelle, a mixture of chopped mushrooms, parsley, and shallots, can be used to flavor stuffing, sauces, or soups. It can be made with any type of mushroom. The proportions are always the same: one part mushrooms to one-half part each of parsley and shallots. One teaspoon of butter is used only to start the evaporation process for the moisture in the mushrooms, so it isn't necessary to increase the butter content with larger portions. Mix a large batch all at once and keep a portion on hand fresh in the refrigerator for 2 days. Divide the remaining duxelle in an ice-cube tray and freeze for up to 4 weeks. Individual portions can be removed from the tray and used as needed. Five cubes will yield about 1 cup of duxelle.

SIDENOTE:
Fresh fish can be chosen easily and safely by following these simple guidelines.

Whole fish:
Have the fish seller rinse the fish and then ask to smell it. Only a slight, fresh odor should be present. The gills should be bright red, not gray. The body will feel firm, cold, and moist.

Fillet:
Fillets carry no odor whatsoever. The edges should be moist, not dry, which would indicate overexposure to air or ice. The color should be naturally bright. Once the fish is home, wrap it in airtight plastic and store on ice in the refrigerator if it will be used within a few hours. Otherwise, freeze immediately.

TROUT EN PAPILLOTE
WITH CHIVES

Wrapping foods is a cooking technique as old as cooking itself. For thousands of years lettuce, cabbage leaves, grape leaves, papaya leaves, banana leaves, corn husks, and even seaweed have been used to steam foods, each wrapping producing a special flavor and tenderness in the food. En papillote (in parchment paper) is a delightful way to wrap lean, delicate, quick-cooking fish.

6 SERVINGS

6 small whole rainbow trout, heads
   removed (optional)
2 tablespoons olive oil
6 tablespoons chopped shallots

1½ cups chopped fresh chives
½ cup white wine
Salt and pepper

Preheat the oven to 425°F. Cut 6 papillotes. Divide the oil and lightly oil the inside of each paper.

Season the trout inside and out with salt and pepper. Mix the shallots and **chives.** Stuff each trout with 1 teaspoon of the shallot-and-chive mixture. Divide the remaining shallots and chives into 6 portions and sprinkle on the bottom half of each papillote. Place a trout in each papillote.

Seal the papillote tightly. Oil the top of the paper to prevent drying during cooking. Place the packages on a sheet pan and bake 20 minutes, or until the papillotes puff up round.

Carefully cut the papillote at one end and pour off the juices into a saucepan. Add the wine and simmer for 1 minute. Remove the trout from the papillote and place on a serving platter. Spoon the sauce over and serve.

VARIATIONS: Lean fish fillet like sole, turbot, snapper, orange roughy, and salmon work well en papillote. Spread the stuffing on the papillote and place the fillet on top. Close the papillote, then bake as above for approximately 8 minutes per inch of fillet.

- Distinctive flavors can be created by using different herb and spice combinations. For example, spice an orange roughy fillet with fresh ginger and a slice of lemon in place of the shallots and chives.

- For a richer taste, make a simple cream sauce. After pouring off the juices, reduce the liquid slightly and add 1 cup of cream, stirring to mix.

♥ *Monique's Touch:*

Cold weather gives **chives** their strong flavor. When using chives in the early spring, make sure to taste first and adjust the amount you use accordingly. Chive plants grow better if they are snipped often. Snip some now and freeze for later use. They can be used straight from the freezer. Don't ignore the chive's pretty blossom—use it as a garnish or in place of the chive stalk when cooking.

SIDENOTE:

To make a papillote: fold in half a piece of cooking parchment about 2 inches longer than the fish. Starting at the folded edge, cut a half-heart shape, about 1 inch wider around than the fish. When the papillote is unfolded, it is a full heart shape. To fold, start at the top of the half-heart and fold over a small section. Crease the fold and then fold again. Start working around the heart, double folding small sections so that they pleat over each other. Finish off the point with a tight twist. Aluminum foil may be used if parchment paper is not available.

ROAST CHICKEN WITH TARRAGON

One of the pleasures of Maman's spring kitchen was the light licorice scent of tarragon mingling with the aroma of roasting chicken. Roast chicken was served often at our table all year round because the easy roasting technique meant the bird needed no attention from the cook once it was dressed. The herbs Maman used changed with the seasons, but one thing never changed. The comfort my family finds from sharing this dish through the years is timeless.

4 SERVINGS

One 2½-pound chicken
1 tablespoon olive oil
1 tablespoon Hungarian paprika
3 tablespoons chopped fresh
    tarragon

1 tablespoon chopped shallots
½ cup dry white wine
1 cup chicken stock (see Basics, page
    375)
Salt and pepper

Preheat the oven to 425°F. Rinse the chicken inside and out under cold running water. Pat dry. Rub the outside of the chicken with oil and then season lightly with salt and pepper and paprika.

Sprinkle the chicken with 2 tablespoons of the tarragon inside and out. Set the chicken in a metal roasting pan, breast side up. Roast for 20 minutes, then reduce the heat to 375°F. Roast an additional 40 minutes, or until the juices run clear when the joint between the thigh and the breast is pierced with a fork.

Remove the chicken from the pan and keep warm in the oven at 275°F. Do not cover, or the crisp skin will soften.

Place the roasting pan on top of a burner and cook the chicken juices on high heat until the juices and fat separate. Pour off the fat. Add the shallots and sauté for 1 minute. Add the wine and simmer for 1 minute more. Add the chicken stock and the remaining tablespoon of tarragon, swirling the mixture until the juices blend well with the stock. Reduce the sauce by a third, simmering for 2 or 3 minutes. Adjust the seasoning to taste.

Carve the chicken into pieces and serve with the **sauce.** To retain the crispness and juiciness of the chicken, serve at once.

VARIATIONS: Any seasonal herb or spice may be used to vary the flavor of the dish.

- In the fall, wild mushrooms give the sauce a woody fragrance. Add sliced mushrooms along with the shallots.

- To give the sauce a creamy texture and taste, ½ cup of cream or crème fraîche can be added after the chicken stock is reduced.

💜 Monique's Touch:

Leftover **sauce** can be refrigerated. When it's cold, skim the excess solid fat from the surface. The remaining sauce can be used in the next few days to flavor a pasta dish or as a sauce for sautéed meat. It can also be frozen for later use.

SIDENOTE:

Tarragon looks like short grass, with its elongated, narrow leaf. There are two tarragons prominently available. The flavor of French tarragon is more intense than its Russian cousin. Unless tarragon is marked as French, it is most likely the Russian variety. To determine the strength of flavor in tarragon, rub a couple of leaves between your fingers to release the aromatic oil in the tarragon. The stronger the scent, the more intense the flavor will be, so less should be used. This will release the aromatic oil in the tarragon, indicating how much should be used.

POULET PRINCESS

After a clear, cold April rain comes the long-awaited spring mushrooms. My Parisian cousins couldn't wait to visit the country at Easter time, because we always spent pleasant times collecting these treats. Back home we called spring mushrooms petits rosé *because of their slight pink color. You can create the same effect by rinsing the freshest button mushrooms from the market under ice-cold water. Pat dry before using.*

6 SERVINGS

6 chicken breast halves, skinned and
   boned
1 tablespoon unsalted butter
1 tablespoon olive oil
3 cups chopped fresh spinach
3 tablespoons chopped shallots
½ pound mushrooms, thinly sliced
1 cup dry white wine

2 cups chicken stock (see Basics,
   page 375)
½ cup cream
¼ cup water
½ cup lemon juice
18 fresh asparagus tips
4 ounces goat cheese, crumbled
Salt and pepper

Pat the chicken breasts dry. In a heavy skillet, melt the butter with the oil. Sauté the chicken breasts on one side until lightly brown, about 3 minutes. Turn and brown the other side. Remove and set aside.

Add the spinach, cooking until wilted. Remove and set aside.

Pour off the excess fat and add the chopped shallots. Sauté for 1 minute. Add the mushrooms and cook on low heat until most of the moisture is gone.

Turn the heat to high and add the wine, swirling the pan to loosen the brown bits on the bottom. Simmer for about 5 minutes, reducing the liquid by half. Add the chicken stock and simmer for 10 minutes more, to reduce again by half. Add the cream and cook until a syruplike consistency is reached, about 3 minutes. Return the chicken to the pan and cook, uncovered, over low heat for 10 minutes, or until the breasts are firm to the touch.

In the meantime, combine the water and lemon juice in a pot and bring to a boil. Place the asparagus tips in a steamer basket over the water. Cover and simmer until the asparagus tips are crisp-tender, about 3 minutes. Rinse under cold water and set aside.

Top the chicken breasts with the goat cheese and let melt slightly. Adjust the seasoning. Serve the chicken on a platter, covered with the sauce and garnished with the asparagus tips.

VARIATIONS: Veal scaloppine, turkey breast, or sea scallops can be used in place of chicken.

- For added flavor, 1 tablespoon of any chopped seasonal herb may be added to the sauce.

- The cream can be deleted to make a low-fat sauce. In place of the cream, thicken the sauce by blending 2 teaspoons of cornstarch with ¼ cup of cold water. Add to the pan after the chicken stock.

- Chicken breasts with skin and bone still intact may be used. Adjust the cooking time after the breasts are added back to the pan for a total of 20 minutes. The additional time is needed, as it takes heat longer to reach the center of the breast when the skin is left on the chicken.

ROAST LEG OF LAMB
WITH GARLIC

Green pastures dotted with young lambs are always a welcome springtime landscape after the gray winter sky of Brittany. Just as when I was a child, my family today always celebrates Easter and the promise of warm weather to come with a fresh roast leg of lamb, seasoned with tender whole garlic.

8–10 SERVINGS

One 7-pound leg of lamb
4 garlic cloves, peeled and each cut
　into 3 lengthwise pieces
¼ cup olive oil or 2 tablespoons
　unsalted butter, softened

4 tablespoons chopped fresh thyme
3 heads of garlic, loose skin removed
1 cup vermouth
Salt and pepper

Preheat the oven to 425°F. With a small knife, make 6 incisions on each side of the leg of lamb. Insert 1 piece of garlic in each. Rub the lamb with oil or butter and sprinkle with thyme and salt and pepper.

Place the lamb in a shallow roasting pan. Roast, uncovered, for about 20 minutes, or until the meat is brown and crusty. Turn the heat down to 375°F and continue roasting for 1 hour. Place the 3 whole heads of garlic around the lamb and continue cooking for 30 minutes for rare or 50 minutes for medium. When finished, remove the lamb and garlic from the roasting pan. Gently break up the whole garlic into separate cloves. Cover both with aluminum foil to keep warm.

Place the pan on top of the stove over high heat. Bring the juice to a boil so that the drippings adhere to the pan and separate from the fat. Pour off the fat. Add the vermouth and swirl around the pan to loosen the brown bits.

Carve the lamb and serve on individual plates with the sauce ladled over the lamb slices and 2 or 3 garlic cloves on the side.

VARIATIONS: This recipe works just as well with grilled lamb chops or a rack of lamb. Grill the chops for 3 minutes on one side, turn, grill for 5 minutes more. A 6-chop rack should be placed in a preheated 400°F oven for 25 minutes.

SIDENOTE:

The lamb of Brittany is sought after for its tenderness and flavor due to the salt-marsh grazing pastures found around Mont Saint Michel. As lambs age, the flavor of the meat becomes stronger. Size is a good indicator of its age. The best lamb is not more than 6 months old. A tender leg of lamb should weigh around 6 to 8 pounds.

Spring lambs grazing in the pastures of our farm.

SPRING LAMB STEW WITH VEGETABLES

Today's fare is tomorrow's supper, so this stew often appeared on our table the day after Easter. I have learned to roast an extra leg of lamb and freeze the meat to have on hand later. Then in the late spring and early summer, when young vegetables have a more developed yet still delicate flavor, I will make this stew again. Remove the meat from the bone before freezing.

6 SERVINGS

2 tablespoons olive oil
2 pounds cooked lamb from Easter dinner, cubed
1 medium onion, peeled and chopped
3 garlic cloves, peeled and minced
1 dozen baby carrots
2 medium turnips, peeled and diced

3 tablespoons flour
6 cups brown stock (see Basics, page 376)
2 tablespoons chopped fresh thyme
1 pound fresh peas, shelled
1 pound fresh green beans
Salt and pepper

Heat the oil in a dutch oven. Brown the meat, a few pieces at a time, setting it aside as it finishes. Discard the fat from the pan.

Add the onion and garlic, then sauté for 1 minute. Add the carrots, turnips, and browned lamb. Sprinkle the flour in, tossing gently to coat the meat and vegetables. Add the stock and blend well. Add water, if necessary, to bring the liquid even with the contents. Add the thyme and season with salt and pepper. Bring to a boil, then lower the heat to a simmer. Cover and gently simmer for approximately 20 minutes.

Meanwhile, bring a pot of salted water to a boil. Blanch the peas and beans until they change to a bright green color. Drain and rinse under cold water. Place the green vegetables on top of the stew. Cover and simmer for 10 minutes more. Stir to mix before serving.

ASPARAGUS WITH ROASTED GARLIC AND HAM

After fall butchering, our hams and sausages were hung in the chimney to cure. By spring the smoke curling up from winter fires built in our stone hearth always gave the meat a rich, potent taste that varied according to the spices rubbed on it beforehand. Today we turn away from sausage and ham, fearing the fat content and the possible health risks of trace carcinogens in smoke. But as with all foods, moderation is the key. Occasionally treat yourself by using smoked meat as a flavoring instead of a main ingredient.

6 SERVINGS

3 dozen asparagus stalks, scales and
    woody ends trimmed
¼ pound pine nuts
8 ounces ham, coarsely chopped
1 head of garlic, roasted, pulp
    extracted and reserved

1 tablespoon lemon juice
½ cup olive oil
Salt and pepper

Preheat the oven to 350°F.

Bring a large saucepan of lightly salted water to a simmer. Blanch the asparagus for 3 to 5 minutes until crisp-tender. Transfer to a bowl of ice water to cool. Drain and set aside.

In a small pan, heat the pine nuts until lightly toasted. Add the ham and toss until the ham is warmed through. Place the asparagus on a serving platter and sprinkle with the ham-and-nut mixture.

In a mixing bowl, cream together the garlic pulp and lemon juice. Slowly add the olive oil, stirring until well mixed. Adjust the seasoning with salt and pepper. Drizzle the dressing over the asparagus.

VARIATIONS: Instead of garlic dressing, the raspberry vinaigrette used for the June Bridal Salad (page 91) can be substituted for a milder, fruitier taste.

SIDENOTE:

To roast whole garlic heads, remove the loose, dry skin, but do not peel. Cut ¼ inch off the tip of the head. Rub the garlic all over with ½ teaspoon of olive oil and place on a baking sheet in a preheated 350°F oven for about 25 minutes, or until light brown and soft. Cool. Press the pulp out by holding the garlic head by its base. Turn the garlic over a bowl and squeeze the whole head gently until all the pulp is extracted, or divide the cloves and squeeze each one individually. Discard the skin.

SNOW PEA AND RADISH SALAD

This salad is the best of the baby vegetables found in the spring garden. One of the first chores I was given when I was not much more than a baby myself was to help plant the kitchen garden. Radishes were very suitable seeds for little hands to plant, because they didn't need a special place to grow and could be planted haphazardly between the carrot rows. After the radishes began to sprout, I made a daily trip to the garden and reported back to Maman if they were ready to pick. Careful attention was paid to pick the radishes when they were small and tender, about the size of a dime. Radishes left in the ground longer become soft and have a spicier taste.

6 SERVINGS

SALAD:
2 pounds snow peas, ends and
   strings removed
½ pound radishes, thinly sliced

DRESSING:
½ cup basic vinaigrette (see Basics,
   page 381)
¼ cup crème fraîche (see Basics, page
   379)
1 tablespoon goat cheese
Salt and pepper

Bring 2 quarts of salted water to a boil. Blanch the snow peas in the water for 1 minute. Remove and immediately set the peas in a bowl over ice water. Drain as soon as they cool.

Mix the radish slices with the peas in a large salad bowl. To make the dressing, mix the basic vinaigrette with the crème fraîche. Add to the salad, sprinkle with the goat cheese, then toss gently. Season to taste with salt and pepper. Chill until serving time.

SIDENOTE:

In recent years markets have begun offering several types of fresh peas. Until recently, unless one grew them in a private garden, the closest "fresh" pea known was the starchy, mass-produced frozen pea. These three varieties have gained particular favor with consumers.

Snow peas:
Known as *mange tout,* or "eat all," in France, these crisp peas are flat, with no shell. Snap the ends and pull off the strings, then use whole.

Fresh peas:
Cook shelled fresh peas as soon as possible after picking because the natural sugar found in them begins to change to starch if left uncooked.

Snap peas:
These are small, crunchy, and without strings. Cook them as is and eat whole.

ORANGE-SCENTED ASPARAGUS WITH CHICKEN

No matter what the weather is doing outside, for most of us, spring has arrived when the first slender shoots of asparagus make their appearance in the garden or at the market. This lovely dish promises spring to the palate even as the last faint flavor of winter oranges lingers on the tongue.

4 SERVINGS

2 pounds fresh asparagus, tips removed and reserved, stalks cut into ¼-inch pieces

1 tablespoon unsalted butter

8 ounces whole chicken breast, boned and skinned, cut into 8 slices

¼ pound mushrooms

¼ cup dry vermouth

½ cup orange juice

2 cups chicken stock (see Basics, page 375)

Blanch the asparagus tips in lightly salted, boiling water for about 4 minutes until crisp-tender. Plunge immediately into ice water to stop the cooking. Drain and set aside.

In a sauté pan, melt the butter and sauté the asparagus stalks until tender. Set aside. Sauté the chicken on both sides for 3 minutes. Set aside.

Add the mushrooms to the pan and sauté for 1 minute. Add the vermouth and orange juice, then simmer for 2 minutes to reduce the liquid by half. Add the chicken stock and cook over medium-low heat for 5 minutes. Mix in the asparagus stalks and cook for another 2 minutes, or until tender. **Reheat** the asparagus tips.

Arrange the chicken and asparagus stalks on a platter. Garnish with the asparagus tips.

VARIATIONS: Use approximately 1 cup of cubed ham in place of chicken.

- Add ½ cup of cream with the asparagus stems to make a richer sauce. Stir gently.

♥ *Monique's Touch:*

Prior to serving, **reheat** vegetables simply by placing them in a colander and setting the colander on top of a pot simmering with whatever is already cooking. The steam from the cooking liquid will be sufficient to reheat the vegetables in just a couple of minutes.

SIDENOTE:

Americans are most familiar with green asparagus. In Europe the cultivated white asparagus, with its distinctive purple tip, is favored. White asparagus is grown by mounding dirt around the asparagus plant to keep the sun from reaching the stem. While asparagus is found all year round now, the peak flavor months are March through May, when it is also more affordable. Asparagus should be stored upright in the refrigerator, with stem bottoms in about ½ inch of water. If stored out of water, the bottoms of the asparagus become dry and tough, while the stalks lose their crispness.

ARUGULA AND STRAWBERRIES

Often arugula is used more like an herb because the strong tang of the leaves adds zest to a dish. It can also be very expensive, making the cost of using large quantities prohibitive. But the contrast of the peppery flavor of the arugula and the almost buttery flavor of spring strawberries makes this salad worth splurging a little for.

6 SERVINGS

SALAD:
4 bunches arugula, stems removed
1 pint strawberries, hulled and sliced

DRESSING:
1 cup yogurt
2 tablespoons honey
1 tablespoon coarsely ground black
    pepper

In a salad bowl, place the arugula and two thirds of the strawberries.

To make the dressing, purée the remaining strawberries in a blender with the yogurt and honey. Add the dressing to the salad and sprinkle with coarsely ground pepper.

Chill for 20 minutes and toss before serving.

CRÈME CARAMEL

Celebrating the sweetness of a family meal is something even the youngest child can begin to learn early. This simple dessert is a perfect way to let the smallest helper begin to feel the satisfaction of creating a delicious meal that will be shared with loved ones. Crème caramel is also the perfect dessert to serve as winter fades into spring, tying the two seasons together.

4 SERVINGS

1⅓ cups sugar
¼ cup water
2 cups half-and-half
1 vanilla bean or 1 tablespoon vanilla
    extract
2 whole eggs
4 egg yolks

Preheat the oven to 350°F.

In a saucepan, combine 1 cup of the sugar with the water. Stir just until the sugar dissolves, no more. Cook over medium heat until the water evaporates and the sugar turns light brown, about 4 minutes. Remove immediately and pour into a large ovenproof ceramic mold, or divide among 4 individual ceramic molds, tipping to coat the sides with caramel. Turn the mold upside down so caramel will drizzle down.

Heat the half-and-half with the vanilla bean or vanilla extract to just below boiling.

Meanwhile, in a mixing bowl, beat together the remaining ⅓ cup sugar with the whole eggs and the egg yolks until foamy and lemon-colored.

If using the vanilla bean, remove it from the half-and-half. Slowly add the half-and-half to the egg mixture, stirring constantly. Pour the custard into the mold through a fine strainer, which will break down the air bubbles.

Place the mold in a **hot-water bath.** Bake for 35 minutes to 1 hour, until the custard is set and a toothpick inserted in the center comes out dry.

To unmold, run a finger around the inside rim of the dish, applying light pressure along the edge of the custard to pull it away from the side. To serve, invert the mold over a serving plate, follow with a gentle tap to the bottom of the mold. The crème caramel will slip out.

VARIATIONS: Sprinkle leftover caramelized apples or nuts on top of the crème caramel in the fall and winter, or top with tiny spring strawberries.

♥ *Monique's Touch:*

A **hot-water bath,** or bain-marie, is a technique used to cook custards or terrines to assure gentle, even cooking. To set up a bain-marie, line a deep pan large enough to hold the baking dish comfortably with a towel. Set the baking dish on the towel and place in the preheated oven. Carefully pour in enough boiling water to come two thirds of the way up the side of the dish. It is important to pour the water in after the baking dish has been placed in the oven to prevent dangerous spills. Cook as directed.

PARIS-BREST PASTRY

Paris-Brest is traditionally made into the shape of a bicycle wheel to commemorate a bicycle race held between the cities of Paris and Brest. But as children, we liked shaping the paste into a variety of patterns because cream-puff paste will rise in whatever shape it is formed. We liked to make our initials or the numbers for our ages, then cut the pastry in half horizontally and fill it with whipped cream. This was a dessert we did often because it was fun for us and inexpensive to make.

6 SERVINGS

1 recipe puff paste (see Basics, page 386)
½ cup slivered almonds
2 cups heavy cream for whipping
3 tablespoons powdered sugar

2 cups custard cream (see Basics, page 388)
1 pint strawberries, hulled, or any seasonal berry

Preheat the oven to 450°F. Butter and flour a baking sheet. Place an 8-inch cake pan on the baking sheet as a guide, then draw a circle outline in the flour on the baking sheet.

Fit a pastry bag with a ½-inch plain tube tip and fill with puff paste. Pipe a circle of paste on the inside of the guideline and another circle outside the guideline. Pipe a third circle of paste on top of the first two. Make sure to start each circle in a different place, or the pastry will separate during baking. Sprinkle with slivered almonds.

Bake for 15 minutes, or until the pastry is more than double in size. Lower the heat to 400°F and bake for another 10 to 15 minutes until golden brown. Turn off the oven and open the door slightly for 20 minutes. This ensures that the center is completely baked dry, so the pastry will not collapse when removed from the oven.

With a serrated knife, horizontally cut the top third of the wheel off, keeping it in one piece. Remove the top and let cool. The wheel will be hollow inside. **Pre-cut** the top of the wheel into 6 serving pieces.

Whip the cream with the sugar until soft peaks form. To prevent lumps, briefly beat the custard cream to a creamy consistency. Fold the custard cream into the whipped cream.

Fill a pastry bag with the cream mixture and completely fill the bottom section of the hollow wheel. Place the 6 pre-cut portions on top of the cream, following the pattern of the wheel. Sprinkle with powdered sugar. Fill the center of the wheel with strawberries.

To serve, use the pre-cut slices as a cutting guide and cut through the bottom of the wheel. Place each slice on a serving plate, garnished with strawberries.

VARIATIONS: Prior to filling, add powdered praline to the custard cream (see May, Mother's Day Cake, page 60).

- Serve with a custard or berry sauce drizzled over each piece at serving time.

- Extra whipped cream can be piped on top of the custard prior to assembling the wheel, to make the cake higher and, of course, richer.

♥ *Monique's Touch:*

I find it much easier to **pre-cut** the top third of the wheel into 6 serving pieces prior to assembling. This prevents the filling from oozing out the sides while slicing. Because the Paris-Brest is covered with confectioners' sugar, the cuts are not visible, and the dessert still makes a dramatic presentation.

MAY

The best Mother's Day gift:
The entire family gathers in May for the
christening of the five youngest Jamet children.
Maman and Papa are seated (center), and I am
the second child from left, front row.

The renewal of life's rhythms that began last month flows on through the gentle days of May. If there is to be a last whip of winter, we smell it in the crisp, clean wind of April. But May warms the air and brings to our nose the first aromatic sweet scent of flowers and herbs. Back home in the May fields, toddler lambs graze among the perfumed lilac and pristine lily of the valley. They wander off, feeling the pull of independence growth brings. Mother sheep keep the youngsters near, however, knowing they still need close attention and nurturing to grow strong and fine. In the garden the spring seeding is over, and the plants are up. Leafy greens that at the beginning of last month shown pale against the lingering patchy snow change color almost daily now. Spinach, watercress, arugula, the first leaf and Bibb lettuces, all begin to develop deep, rich color, and their flavors lose the acid bite of April as they mature into a smoother texture and taste. Tender young beets, dime-size radishes, and slender shoots of red rhubarb throw a splash of color across the variegated greens. But as with the lambs in the field, careful nurturing is needed now if we are to coax the youthful garden of May into becoming a bountiful provider by the harvest season.

In Maman's *potager,* or kitchen garden, the sound of the hoe scratching the soil was the sound of her taking care of nature, so nature would take care of us later on. There is much work to be done in a garden during May. The soil must be raked every day so wild weeds don't rob the new vegetables of life. Thinning out the seedlings to allow enough growing space for sprouting plants is a repeated chore. An eye to the weather makes sure there is enough water to develop strong roots. If the sky teases us one last time with a cold rain, the plants must be protected and kept warm. A lot of effort went into Maman's garden, but even as she gave the potager a good portion of her precious time, it gave back to her a sense of accomplishment and pride when she leaned against her hoe at the end of a freshly turned row and could see how her work gave the garden a look of being alive again. The reciprocal promise of caring for nature as it cared for her was fulfilled.

Today we have not lost that inner urge to care for the garden so that it might, in turn, replenish us. Look at how many people in the city scurry around searching for a little parcel of land so they can have that special connection to the soil. They don't expect to grow enough to feed the family from it, but there is a need to grow something, even if it's simply a small square of vegetables in an urban community garden or container tomatoes on a high-rise rooftop. People are discovering one bite of a homegrown tomato in August is a touchstone back to a time when they knew the feel of the earth and the true taste of food from the farm, no matter if they have lived in the city all their lives. It is an instinctual sensory memory that never leaves us. The anticipation of reliving the experience spurs us to take up the hoe year after year. The taste of an August tomato will reward us for work and care taken in the May garden.

A garden is one of the ways in which we can still reconnect the cycle of nature to our modern lives. Another is to pay attention to what is going on in our growing region and to give ourselves the best of what is available in late spring. It is time to explore the market for foods that are fresh and new. Go to the farmers' markets and talk with the people who live their lives growing food. Find out what kind of winter they experienced, ask what crops they will be harvesting before the next market, then plan next week's menu around what will be on hand. If you shop at a grocery, ask the produce manager questions that educate him to your needs while you educate yourself about availability. What is coming in this week? Does it come from local growers? How was it grown, organically or with chemicals? As the demand for quality from customers increases, a good grocery will try to meet it.

In May everything is still very young, but gone are the heavy spices of a deep winter meal. It is not quite summer yet, but a fuller flavor replaces the cleansing bitterness of early spring greens. The first herbs—thyme and tarragon—arrive at the store or in our garden. They settle in and develop a pungency that reminds us that summer will be here soon. Even the cooking techniques we prefer to use change now. A dutch oven on top of the stove is an excellent way to cook the tender and flavorful foods of May. It's time to throw open the windows and let the fresh breezes warm your home instead of relying on heat rising from an oven while it slow-braises a winter stew. Roast a fresh Cornish hen in its own juices until half finished, and then lay whole knob onions, fresh pea pods, wild morels, and new potatoes on top. Add a sprig of fresh thyme or tarragon, and let the steam from the bird infuse the vegetables until tender. Simple and light-handed, dutch-oven cooking is a bridge from winter's oven to summer's grill. It is refreshing, nurturing, and brings you closer to the outdoors. It's very much like the month of May itself.

MAY RECIPES

Green Onion and Tarragon Soup

Morel Soup with Sherry

Three Greens Omelet

Soft-Shell Crab with Cilantro

Stuffed Squid with Shrimp

Roasted Fillet of Turbot with Caramelized Onions

Rock Cornish Game Hen en Cocotte

Breast of Chicken on Swiss Chard

Pan-Broiled Lamb Medallions with Chives

Flank Steak with Chervil

Gnocchi with Spring Green Sauce

Warm New Potatoes with Camembert

Mother's Day Cake

Strawberry Tartlets

Strawberry-Rhubarb Compote

MOTHER'S DAY CELEBRATION

Morel Soup with Sherry

Merlot

Sautéed Soft-Shell Crab

Snow Pea and Radish Salad

Mother's Day Cake with Pralines

Sparkling Wine

GREEN ONION AND TARRAGON SOUP

Dishes Maman created were often the result of putting together ingredients culled from the garden when she thinned the vegetables and pruned the herb plants. Green onions are the first onions of the year to come up, and they must be thinned regularly to make room for growth. At the same time, tarragon needs to be cut back during the spring to encourage it to fill out later in the summer. Instead of throwing the onion and tarragon trimmings out, Maman curled her apron up to carry them into the kitchen, where she made a fine green onion and tarragon soup.

6 SERVINGS

1 tablespoon unsalted butter
1 tablespoon olive oil
4 tablespoons chopped shallots
2 dozen green onions, wilted stems
    and roots trimmed, coarsely
    chopped
2 tablespoons chopped fresh
    tarragon

2 tablespoons flour
6 cups warm chicken stock
    (see Basics, page 375)
6 tablespoons crème fraîche
    (see Basics, page 379)
Salt and pepper

In a saucepan, heat the butter and oil together. Sauté the shallots for 1 minute. Add the green onions and tarragon, tossing gently. Add the flour and blend well. Heat for 2 minutes.

Slowly add the warm stock and **blend** until smooth. Season with salt and pepper, and bring to a boil. Lower the heat, then simmer for 10 minutes. Do not cover, so the onions will retain their rich green color.

Strain the soup, reserving 1 cup of the onions. Purée the remaining onions. Add the purée and the reserved onions back into the stock. Simmer until heated through.

If desired, add a dollop of crème fraîche to each bowl before serving.

♥ *Monique's Touch:*

When using flour, cornstarch, or arrowroot to make sauces, soups, and gravies, lumps can be avoided by first **blending** a small amount of water or stock with the starch to make a paste. If a recipe calls for the thickener to be added to a hot liquid base, the room-temperature flour, cornstarch, or arrowroot must be diluted to paste form with a small amount of cold water before stirring into the base. If the recipe calls for heating the starch in a pan first, before adding the liquid, it is best to heat the liquid to boiling in a separate saucepan, then blend a small amount of hot liquid into the starch to make a smooth paste before stirring in the rest of the hot liquid. Remember: If a starch begins cold, add cold liquid to make a paste. If a starch begins hot, add hot liquid to make a paste.

MOREL SOUP WITH SHERRY

Morel soup is often served on Mother's Day because that weekend is the peak time for harvesting the morel, sometimes called the jewel of the mushroom family. The wrinkled cap-shape mushrooms begin pushing up after the first thaw, then quickly disappear when a hint of warm weather brushes past. A morel's taste is faintly reminiscent of its woody autumn cousin, but the nutty perfume is far more subtle. Morels need to be paired with other mild spring foods so their flavor is highlighted and not lost.

6 SERVINGS

1½ pounds fresh morel mushrooms
1 tablespoon cider vinegar
1 tablespoon vegetable oil
2 small onions, peeled and coarsely
    chopped
6 cups chicken stock (see Basics,
    page 375)

2 egg yolks
1 cup cream
3 tablespoons dry sherry
3 tablespoons chopped fresh parsley
Salt and pepper

Soak the mushrooms for 20 minutes, covered, in cold water mixed with the vinegar. Choose 6 nicely shaped small ones and set aside for the garnish. Chop the remaining mushrooms.

In a large saucepan, heat the oil, then add the onions. Sauté until tender but not brown. Add all the mushrooms and toss gently. Add the stock, bring the soup to a boil, and then lower the heat. Simmer for 15 minutes, or until the mushrooms are tender.

Strain the mushrooms, setting aside the 6 whole mushrooms. Reserve ½ cup of the chopped mushrooms and purée the rest. Return the reserved chopped mushrooms and purée back into the stock. Bring to a simmer.

Blend the egg yolks, cream, and sherry together. Add slowly to the soup, stirring constantly. Do not boil after this point or else the egg will scramble. Adjust the seasoning with salt and pepper.

Put 1 whole mushroom in each serving bowl. Fill with soup and top each bowl with chopped parsley.

♥ *Monique's Touch:*

Many foods are designed by nature to be natural hosts for insects. **Soaking** them in a cold-water bath mixed with vinegar will coax out the unwelcome guests. All indigenous foods that might be foraged, such as morels, cattails, wild asparagus, or fiddlehead ferns, should be presoaked before eating. Commercially grown produce is generally pest-free and does not need soaking. However, the tight heads of cauliflower and broccoli sometimes carry insects and can be thoroughly cleaned in this way.

My sister Christiane tilling hay
before seeding the next crop.

THREE GREENS OMELET

As the days of May lengthened, more time was spent working in the fields and away from the house. My sisters and I would carry a basket of food to the workers in the fields at midmorning. While the hot coffee, the bread, and slices of smoked ham were always welcomed by the men, it was my mother's huge omelet tucked under a linen cloth inside the wicker basket that brought the most hearty thanks from hungry workers. We spread a cloth under a shady tree, and everyone took a break. Hot feet dangled in the cool river as we enjoyed this delightful meal before finishing out the morning's work.

1 SERVING

2 eggs

2 teaspoons milk or cold water

1 tablespoon chopped sorrel

1 tablespoon chopped arugula

1 tablespoon chopped fresh chives

1 teaspoon unsalted butter

Salt and pepper

In a mixing bowl, beat the eggs with the salt, pepper, and milk or water. Beat until the egg mixture forms a continuous thread when the fork is lifted out of the bowl. Add all the chopped greens and blend well.

To form the **omelet,** in a 6-inch nonstick sauté pan, melt the butter and let the pan get very hot until the butter fragrance is released but not smoking. Roll the butter over the bottom and sides of the pan. Add the egg mixture and quickly swirl the egg over the pan with a vigorous whirlpool motion. Continue swirling the pan until the eggs are softly set and the top resembles scrambled eggs.

Remove the pan from the heat and, using a spatula, fold over one third of the omelet on top of itself. Slide the omelet to the serving plate, folding the remaining side over.

VARIATIONS: Before folding the omelet for the first time, add cooked, diced new potatoes and onions. Other favorite fillings are tomatoes, spinach, broccoli, mushrooms, and sweet peppers.

- Omelets use up leftovers that are too small to serve on their own. Chop bits of leftover meat or vegetables to use as a filling.

- Omelets can be made with any smooth-melting cheese. Add 2 tablespoons grated Swiss, Gruyère, or Cheddar cheese after the eggs are set. Finish as directed.

♥ *Monique's Touch:*

Omelets have an undeserved reputation for being difficult to master. The truth is, they are fun to make and only require a little practice. To keep an omelet fluffy and not dry, the secret is to swirl and shake the pan to distribute the egg as it cooks. Tilt it in a circular motion so the eggs gather in the middle and take on the look of soft scrambled eggs. Omelets are not pretty as they cook, so don't worry. The uglier it looks, the fluffier the omelet!

SOFT-SHELL CRAB WITH CILANTRO

This is one of the few recipes I have that does not invite substitutions. Blue crabs are a wonderful delicacy indigenous to the Atlantic coastal region. The soft-shell blue is prized in the month of May during their molting season. They are a true seasonal pleasure that should be experienced several times in May. Serve one per person as an appetizer or two per person for a main course.

6 SERVINGS

6 soft-shell crabs	3 tablespoons grated fresh ginger
6 tablespoons flour	3 garlic cloves, peeled and minced
1 teaspoon salt	2 cups white wine
½ teaspoon pepper	1 tablespoon sesame oil
6 tablespoons olive oil	1 tablespoon soy sauce
4 tablespoons unsalted butter	2 tablespoons chopped fresh cilantro
2 tablespoons chopped shallots	Salt and pepper

Pat each crab dry with a paper towel. Combine the flour, salt, and pepper in a shallow container.

Heat the oil and butter in a sauté pan until hot. Lightly dredge each crab in the flour mixture, then place 3 crabs, top side down, in the pan. Do not disturb for 1 minute.

Using a spatula, move the crab around gently to prevent burning, cooking 2 to 3 minutes until golden brown. Turn, cook 4 minutes until golden brown. Repeat with the other 3 crabs, adding more butter and oil, if necessary. Keep the crabs on a warm serving platter.

To the pan, add the shallots, ginger, and garlic, then sauté for 1 minute. Add the wine and reduce the mixture by one third, simmering about 7 minutes. Add the sesame oil, soy sauce, cilantro, and gently toss. Adjust the seasoning with salt and pepper to taste. Pour the sauce over the crabs before serving.

VARIATIONS: Sautéed soft-shell crabs make wonderful sandwiches. Serve hot, cold, or at room temperature on rye or sourdough bread spread with tartar sauce. Add some cole slaw on the side.

- Cilantro should be added sparingly, or its strong taste will overwhelm the delicate crab. As an alternative, use milder parsley or chervil.

STUFFED SQUID WITH SHRIMP

The summer I was fifteen, I took a job in the kitchen of a seaside restaurant. One morning the chef assigned me the task of cleaning one hundred fresh squid that had just come in from the dock. I had never done the job before, but I went to work like I knew what I was doing, cutting off and discarding their ugly little tendrils along with the messy ink sacs. I was determined to impress the chef with the thoroughness of my skills. Several hours later I proudly presented him with all the cleaned and turned squid. He immediately went into a rage and banished me from the kitchen. How was I to know that tendrils were considered a delicacy and the ink was used to make an elegant sauce? The next morning I crept into the kitchen, trying to avoid the chef. There he waited for me with that day's morning chore—cleaning over two hundred more squid.

6 SERVINGS

12 fresh squid, cleaned	½ cup chopped fresh chives
4 tablespoons olive oil	2 tablespoons chopped fresh chervil
6 large shrimp, shelled, deveined, and coarsely chopped	1 cup dried bread crumbs
	½ cup cream
1 small onion, peeled and chopped	1 egg, beaten

Bring a large pot of water to boil. Remove the heads and tendrils from the **squid** body. Turn the bodies inside out. Plunge the squid, heads, and tendrils into the boiling water and cook for 2 minutes. Drain and pat the squid dry. Chop the heads and tendrils coarsely, and transfer to a large mixing bowl. Refrigerate the squid bodies until ready to use.

Heat 1 tablespoon of the oil and sauté the shrimp with the onion. Add the shrimp to the chopped squid. Mix in the chives, chervil, and bread crumbs. To bind the shrimp with the herbs, beat the cream and egg together in a mixing bowl and stir together with the stuffing.

Stuff each squid with the shrimp. Secure the ends of the squid with toothpicks. Heat the remaining 3 tablespoons of oil and sauté the squid until brown on each side, about 10 minutes.

VARIATIONS: Stuffed squid can be served cold as a salad, drizzled with your favorite vinaigrette dressing.

- As a main dish, serve with rice, pasta, or couscous and a fresh tomato sauce.

- Squid can be stuffed with a variety of choices. Leftover cooked fish or vegetables can substitute for the shrimp, making this an unusual way to turn yesterday's fare into tomorrow's supper.

♥ *Monique's Touch:*

Unless the **squid** is turned inside out, the skin will split during cooking. I have found that turning squid before stuffing also keeps the stuffing in place as it heats.

SIDENOTE:

Generally, squid—or calamari, as it is also known—is cleaned and left whole before you purchase it. Final preparation before cooking is minimal. Cut off the tendrils and head directly behind the eyes. Feel for any small cartilage left in the head and pull it out. Turn the squid body inside out. Sometimes a clear and sharp cartilage remains from the initial cleaning, so remove it with a sharp tug. Often black juice will seep out of the squid when the ink sac is punctured, but this is edible and in no way indicates freshness.

ROASTED FILLET OF TURBOT WITH CARAMELIZED ONIONS

This recipe encompasses all the elements needed for seasonal cooking. The young fresh onions, mild tasting this time of year, are paired with turbot, a delicate fish found in northern waters. The onions enhance but do not overpower the turbot. They are both quickly sautéed, then finished in a hot oven. The flavors hold their own, eliminating the need for extensive seasoning or long cooking time.

6 SERVINGS

2 tablespoons unsalted butter
1½ cups pearl onions
1 tablespoon chopped fresh thyme
1 teaspoon sugar
2 tablespoons olive oil

1 leek, washed, tough end trimmed,
    cut into ¼ × 2-inch strips
Juice of 1 lemon
1½ pounds turbot fillet
Salt and pepper

Preheat the oven to 400°F.

In a small saucepan, melt the butter, then sauté the onions until brown. Add the fresh thyme and sugar. Season with salt and pepper, cover, and cook over low heat for 30 minutes, or until the onions are soft and caramelized.

Meanwhile, heat ½ teaspoon of the olive oil in an ovenproof sauté pan and sauté the leek until tender. Remove from the heat.

Rub the turbot fillet with the remaining oil and the lemon juice. Arrange the fillet on top of the leek and place the pan in the oven. Roast until the turbot flakes easily with a fork, about 8 minutes.

Serve at once with the caramelized onions.

VARIATIONS: Other firm-fleshed fish can be substituted, such as red snapper, salmon, or any member of the bass family.

- Three boneless chicken breasts may be used instead of fish. Split the breasts in half and pound until they are thin. Then proceed as above, except increase the baking time to 10 minutes.

ROCK CORNISH GAME HEN EN COCOTTE

Cocotte is a French endearment used to describe a close, cozy relationship. It is also the word for dutch oven—particularly appropriate since meat cooked in a dutch oven should fit snugly inside the pot. The close fit allows steam to form, cooking the bird nicely in its own juices without braising. A familiar and comforting sight in Maman's kitchen was our dutch oven, gently simmering to the side of the fireplace. I could never resist taking a peek inside, even though this usually earned me a gentle rap on the knuckles for letting the steam escape.

6 SERVINGS

Three 12-ounce Cornish hens
3 tablespoons olive oil
1 small onion, peeled and coarsely
    chopped
6 whole shallots, peeled
4 garlic cloves, peeled and crushed
2 small carrots, ends trimmed, cut
    into ½-inch pieces

4 sprigs fresh thyme
½ pound mushroom caps
½ cup white wine
2 cups chicken stock (see Basics,
    page 375)
Salt and pepper

Rinse the Cornish hens under cold running water and pat dry. Salt and pepper inside and out.

Heat the oil in a heavy dutch oven with a close-fitting lid. Brown the hens on all sides. Add the onion, shallots, garlic, and carrots. Place the sprigs of thyme on top of the hens and cover tightly. Turn down the heat to very low and cook for 30 minutes.

Turn the hens over. Add the mushroom caps, cover, and continue cooking for 15 minutes, or until the meat from the thigh bone comes off easily.

Remove everything from the pan, cover with aluminum foil, and keep warm in the oven set at lowest temperature. Turn the heat under the dutch oven on high for a few minutes so that the fat separates from the juices. Pour off the fat, add the wine to the juices, and reduce the sauce by half, about 2 minutes. Add the chicken stock and all of the vegetables. Simmer for 10 minutes.

To serve, split the Cornish hens in half. Place on a deep serving platter and ladle the sauce and vegetables over the hens.

VARIATIONS: Use the recipe above to serve squab, chicken, and veal roast.

- Experiment by adding different spring vegetables and herbs to the pot. After browning the hens, place 2 sprigs each of thyme and tarragon on top. Cover tightly and simmer on low for 15 minutes. Turn the hens, then add 6 small knob onions, 12 fresh snow pea pods, 6 small new potatoes, and 6 morel mushrooms. Cover and simmer for 30 minutes more. Remove the hens and split. Toss the vegetables in the pan juices and cover for 5 minutes to finish steaming.

BREAST OF CHICKEN ON SWISS CHARD

I like to use a variety of crushed nuts to give the breading a different flavor each time I use this recipe. In the spring I especially like pine nuts, peanuts, pistachios, and cashews—nuts that are available in the market year-round and are not indigenous to my region. In the fall and winter I switch to walnuts and pecans, or other regionally grown nuts that give off a heavier, deeper note.

6 SERVINGS

Six 4-ounce chicken breast halves, skinned, boned, and flattened to ¼ inch
2 eggs
2 tablespoons water
1 cup toasted bread crumbs
½ cup toasted pine nuts, crushed

4 tablespoons olive oil, 1 tablespoon reserved
2 pounds Swiss chard, chopped
3 small onions, peeled and sliced
1 cup chicken stock (see Basics, page 375)
Salt and pepper

Preheat the oven to 375°F. Season chicken breasts with salt and pepper.

Beat the eggs and water with a fork. In a separate bowl, mix together the bread crumbs and pine nuts. Heat 1 tablespoon of the oil in an ovenproof sauté pan over high heat until hot but not smoking. Lightly dip 2 breast pieces in the egg coating, then roll in the bread crumbs. Sauté for 1 minute on each side. Set aside. Repeat with the remaining breasts, adding oil as necessary to evenly brown. Return all the breasts to the pan, placing it inside the oven for 5 minutes to finish the cooking process.

Meanwhile, sauté the Swiss chard and onions together with the reserved tablespoon of oil in a hot pan. Cook for approximately 3 minutes, or until the chard is wilted. Remove from the pan, add the chicken stock, and simmer for approximately 5 minutes. Return the chard to the pan and simmer gently until soft, about 2 minutes.

Remove the breasts from the oven. Divide the Swiss chard among 6 plates. Arrange 1 chicken breast half on top. Serve immediately.

VARIATIONS: Turkey breast, veal chops, or pork chops can be used.

Swiss chard is a member of the beet family, although it does not produce a tuber. The leaves are beautiful and distinctive to look at. Ruby-red stalks and veins trace the glossy, dark green leaves. Swiss chard can be steamed, baked, stir-fried, sautéed, or its leaves can be tossed in a salad.

Papa in his World War I uniform, age 19.

PAN-BROILED LAMB MEDALLIONS WITH CHIVES

Tender, rosy-red lamb raised in Colorado is one of the finest meats available to us. Medallions are round cuts of leg, about one inch thick. This simple, classic, and quick preparation of lamb medallions is one of the best ways I know to enhance their delicate springtime taste.

6 SERVINGS

1 cup chopped fresh chives
3 tablespoons unsalted butter
Six 4-ounce lamb medallions, ½ inch thick
3 tablespoons vegetable oil
2 tablespoons cracked black peppercorns

In a food processor, combine the chives with the butter. Process until blended.

Heat a heavy pan (I prefer cast iron) on very high heat. Rub each side of the medallions with oil. Press a little of the **cracked peppercorns** on both sides of the lamb, using more or less peppercorns according to taste.

When the pan is hot, set 3 of the medallions at a time to cook. After 1 minute, look for the first pearl of red juice to appear on the surface of the lamb, then turn and continue cooking for 2 minutes more for medium-rare.

As the medallions finish, place on a warm serving platter and top with about ½ teaspoon of butter and chives. The heat from the lamb will melt the butter and release the fresh aroma of chives. Serve at once.

VARIATIONS: Steak and boneless breast of chicken may be prepared this way, as can tuna, swordfish, halibut, or any firm-fleshed fish.

♥ *Monique's Touch:*

I use **cracked peppercorns** instead of freshly ground pepper because ground pepper releases too much spicy heat for the delicate medallions. To crack peppercorns, wrap whole peppercorns in a towel and pound with a heavy object, like the bottom of a pan. I prefer not to use a rolling pin because the peppercorns mark the wood, making it difficult to roll dough out smoothly.

FLANK STEAK WITH CHERVIL

Chervil is a delicate, lacy herb that is one of the first to appear in the garden. Maman always planted it next to her tomato plants so the broad tomato leaves would provide the chervil with some protection from the sun while the plants were young. That the tomatoes would nurture the chervil is not surprising—tomato slices sprinkled with chervil is a classic summer combination. In classical French cooking, chervil is used in fines herbes and bouquet garnis. It is also a must for a good béarnaise sauce, and the snow drop–like blossom makes a pretty garnish. But using it simply, as in the marinade below, is my favorite way to enjoy chervil's aromatic licorice flavor.

6 SERVINGS

1 flank steak, about 1½ pounds,
    trimmed, bias-cut against the
    grain into thin ⅛-inch strips
½ cup chopped shallots
1 tablespoon fresh cracked black
    peppercorns

1 cup chopped fresh chervil
3 tablespoons olive oil
1½ pounds fettuccine, cooked
    according to package directions

Bring 3 quarts of water to a boil. Reduce to a simmer.

Place the steak, shallots, peppercorns, chervil, and olive oil in a bowl and mix to coat the meat well.

Heat a heavy pan until very hot. Working in 3 batches, quickly sear the steak, stirring constantly until brown. Set each batch aside before adding the next. When finished, return the steak to the pan and keep warm over low heat.

To finish, drop the fettuccine into the simmering water for 1 minute to reheat. Drain, then set the pasta on a serving platter. Arrange the flank steak on top and serve.

VARIATIONS: Any meat or poultry may be used for this recipe. The secret is to cut it into thin strips against the grain of the meat. This ensures quick cooking and tenderness.

- Change the flavor of the dish by mixing in different herbs, depending on what is available and in season.

GNOCCHI WITH SPRING GREEN SAUCE

Every culture has its own version of the dumpling, whether it's known as a Chinese wonton or a Yiddish matzo ball. Gnocchi comes to us originally from Italy, but it was served often in our home. In the winter, gnocchi was a great way to extend a meal or to use yesterday's gravy and vegetables to make tonight's supper. Come spring, greens from the garden were the basis for a good sauce that turned gnocchi into a main meal.

6 SERVINGS

2 cups water	3 cups mixed chopped chives,
2 tablespoons unsalted butter	spinach, arugula
⅛ teaspoon nutmeg	2 cups cream
2 cups flour	1 cup grated Gruyère cheese
2 eggs	Salt and pepper

Preheat the oven to 375°F.

To make the **gnocchi paste,** bring the water, butter, and nutmeg to a boil in a saucepan. Add the flour, mixing constantly until it forms a thick paste. Beat in the eggs and mix well. Add 1 cup of the greens and season lightly with salt and pepper.

Bring a pot of water to a boil. Drop teaspoonfuls of gnocchi paste into the water until a third of the paste has been added. Simmer for 3 minutes, then lift out of the water with a slotted spoon. Place in a buttered baking dish. Repeat until all the gnocchi paste is cooked.

Blend the remaining greens with the cream and pour the mixture over the gnocchi. Sprinkle the top with the grated cheese. Bake for 15 minutes and serve.

VARIATIONS: Store-bought ravioli may be substituted for the gnocchi.

- Tomato sauce instead of cream makes a zesty change. Because of the acidic taste of tomatoes, decrease the amount of arugula according to taste.

- Any fresh greens found at your local farmers' market or grocery can be used. When picking combinations, think about balancing flavor intensity and texture.

♥ *Monique's Touch:*

I use a variety of ways to shape the **gnocchi paste,** the spoon-drop method being one. Another way is to fill a pastry bag fitted with a ½-inch tip with paste. Pipe the paste over the simmering water, cutting it with scissors into 1-inch lengths as the paste spools out. A third method is to roll the dough 1 inch thick onto parchment paper lightly brushed with vegetable oil. Cut it into small squares, diamonds, or triangles. Peel the shapes off the parchment paper and drop into boiling water.

WARM NEW POTATOES WITH CAMEMBERT

Memories often serve me as inspiration for recipes that become family favorites. When I was young and attended boarding school at a nearby convent, the punishment for talking during class was kitchen cleanup. A particular nun in the kitchen always took pity on the culprits and secretly prepared for us hot potatoes rolled in cheese, which she served on any greens that were left from the noon meal. I don't believe it was a coincidence that a high number of girls felt the need to talk incessantly when they knew Sister was cooking that day!

6 SERVINGS

2 dozen new potatoes, red, white, or mixed
6 cups mesclun spring greens
8 ounces Camembert cheese, cut into small dice

3 tablespoons olive oil
6 tablespoons cider vinegar
Freshly ground pepper

Peel a strip of skin around the center of each potato, leaving the ends unpeeled. Place the potatoes in a pot with enough lightly salted, cold water to cover. Bring to a boil, partially cover the pot, and cook until the potatoes can be pierced easily with a fork but do not come apart.

Meanwhile, wash and dry the mesclun and arrange on a large serving platter. Place the Camembert pieces in a large mixing bowl.

When the potatoes are finished cooking, drain and return to the hot pot to briefly heat the potatoes until all moisture is evaporated. Add the potatoes to the cheese, and toss until the cheese begins to melt and the potatoes are evenly coated. Season with pepper.

Sprinkle the greens with the olive oil and vinegar. Arrange the warm potatoes in the center of the mesclun and serve at once.

VARIATION: To give a nice texture and hint of smoke, sprinkle 3 tablespoons of smoked bacon bits over the potatoes before serving.

SIDENOTE:

Mesclun is a mixture of baby lettuces and herbs harvested before they are fully grown. It often includes varieties not found in the market as mature produce. A good mesclun mix will likely include arugula, chervil, valerian, Bibb lettuce, curly endive, baby romaine, and mustard greens. To grow in your home garden, plant a mixture of lettuce and herb seeds of your choice. Let the plants sprout and grow until they reach 3–5 inches. Cut the tender leaves for salad. Frequent cutting will encourage new growth from spring through summer.

Outdoor kitchen set up for a large festival.

MOTHER'S DAY CAKE

This cake recipe is the one Maman used to begin teaching my sisters and me how to make desserts. It contains all the basic skills necessary to not only make a simple cake but also to make praline and Chantilly cream, which are often used in other recipes. In turn, I used the same recipe to teach my own sons how to separate eggs, measure ingredients, use a candy thermometer, and whip cream. Besides being skills learned early that have served them well as they moved on in their own lives, we have a store of good memories of when we all worked in the kitchen together.

8 SERVINGS

CAKE:
4 egg yolks
1 cup sugar
2 tablespoons cornstarch
3 tablespoons flour
1 teaspoon vanilla extract
4 egg whites

PRALINE:
1 cup sugar
¼ cup water
½ cup slivered almonds, lightly
   toasted

CHANTILLY CREAM:
2 cups heavy cream for whipping,
   chilled
2 teaspoons sugar
2 teaspoons vanilla extract
2 cups sliced fresh strawberries

Preheat the oven to 350°F. Butter and flour a 9-inch cake pan, then line the bottom with parchment paper.

To make the cake, combine the egg yolks and sugar using the bowl of an electric mixer. Beat together until the batter is light and creamy. Sift together the cornstarch and flour, then add to the beaten yolks. Mix until the flour is just blended. Add the vanilla and mix gently.

In a separate bowl, beat the egg whites until stiff. Gently fold the whites into the yolk batter.

Pour the batter in the pan and bake for 15 minutes. Turn the oven up to 400°F and bake for an additional 5 minutes. When finished, remove the cake and turn upside down on a cake rack. Let cool for 5 minutes.

Meanwhile, to make the praline, lightly oil a jelly-roll pan. In a saucepan, stir together the sugar and water. Cook until the syrup is light caramel in color or a candy thermometer reaches 320°F, about 20 minutes. Do not stir during cooking. Remove from the heat and stir in the almonds all at once. Pour the praline onto the jelly-roll pan. Cool.

Lift the praline off the pan and crack into small pieces. In a food processor, process the praline into a fine powder. Or place the praline pieces between 2 layers of heavy towels and beat with a heavy pan until the praline powders.

To make the Chantilly cream and before assembling, beat the cream in a cold bowl until it starts foaming. Slowly add the sugar and keep beating until stiff. Beat in the vanilla.

Cut the cake into 2 thin layers. Spread half the Chantilly cream on top of 1 layer and sprinkle the cream with praline powder. Place the other half of the cake on top and spread the rest of the Chantilly cream. Arrange the sliced strawberries on top in a pretty pattern.

Refrigerate until serving time.

VARIATIONS: Strawberries in May dress up the cake as a special Mother's Day dessert, but any berry may be used to make this a seasonal favorite during spring or summer.

- In the winter, when fresh berries are not available, substitute more praline on the top layer instead of the berries.

- At Christmastime, sprinkle the Chantilly cream with a layer of crushed peppermint candy instead of praline.

STRAWBERRY TARTLETS

Besides the strawberries grown in Maman's garden, tiny wild Alpine strawberries grew along the hedgerows on our farm. They were bright red and the size of the tip of a pinkie finger. To keep occupied while the adults were busy harvesting the hay, we children would pick Alpine strawberries and string them on a dry hay straw so we could carry them more easily. We picked as many as we could find before running to my grandmother in the kitchen. After admiring our tiny treasures, she skimmed the very top layer of cream off of yesterday's milk. It was thick, like cream cheese, and she whipped it with sugar into big snowy mountains to spoon over our strawberries. Depending on the weather, strawberries come into season at the end of May to the beginning of June. I use the freshest, earliest strawberries available for the recipe below. Adding the whipping cream to the pastry cream lightens the filling, reminding me of the wonderful strawberries and cream from my grandmother's kitchen.

8 TARTLETS

1½ recipes sweet short pastry dough, blind-baked in eight 3-inch tartlet shells (see Basics, page 384)

2 cups cream

½ cup sugar

2 cups custard cream (see Basics, page 388)

2 cups fresh strawberries, hulled and sliced

½ cup apricot preserves

2 tablespoons water

Whip the cream until it begins to foam, then slowly add the sugar. Whip until soft peaks form. Fold in the custard cream. Spoon the cream into the tartlet shells. Overlap the strawberries on top to cover the cream.

Thin the apricot preserves with the water over low heat. When heated through, pass through a fine strainer. Discard the pulp. With a pastry brush, lightly brush the tops of the strawberries with the glaze. Refrigerate until serving time.

SIDENOTE:

For centuries strawberries throughout the world were most commonly found in the wild. Strawberries were notoriously difficult to cultivate, so the few varieties that were became prized in wealthy circles. Strawberries were not available in the marketplace to the general public. In 1713 a Breton naval officer named Frézier brought native strawberry plants from Chile to the town of Plougastel, in Brittany, where he successfully cross-cultivated them with the Alpine strawberry.

That began large-scale growing and exporting of strawberries from Brittany. Most strawberries found on the market today are direct ancestors of the plants introduced by Frézier.

STRAWBERRY-RHUBARB COMPOTE

I grew up with compotes instead of jams. Compotes rely on the natural perfume of the fruit and the flavor of the vanilla bean instead of more heavily sugared jams. They may be served as a dessert or as a topping for toast, cake, pancakes, crêpes, or ice cream. This particular compote takes advantage of rhubarb, which is very tart and crunchy when eaten by itself. Mixed with strawberries, it has a sweet taste and a pleasing, soft texture.

6 SERVINGS

1 pound strawberries, hulled and halved
¾ pound rhubarb, peeled and cut into
    2-inch pieces
1½ cups sugar
2 vanilla beans, split in half lengthwise,
    or 2 tablespoons vanilla extract

Set the strawberries in a large stainless steel or ceramic saucepan. Add the rhubarb, sugar, and **vanilla beans** or extract to the strawberries. Stir constantly as the sugar melts. Bring to a boil. Lower the heat to a simmer for 20 minutes. The rhubarb should begin to fall apart slightly. Occasionally skim the foam from the top. Serve warm or cold.

VARIATIONS: Strain the strawberry-rhubarb pulp and use it as filling for a 9-inch pie. Return the syrup to the sauce and bring to a boil. Reduce the syrup by half, then glaze the pie with the syrup just after it comes out of the oven. Serve warm.

- Make the above compote using the same amount of rhubarb along with ½ pound of raspberries mixed with ½ pound of strawberries.

♥ *Monique's Touch:*

Vanilla beans can be reused many times. Rinse and dry the bean after using, then store buried in a container of sugar. The sugar will take on a wonderful vanilla flavor and can be used as is for sweetening.

JUNE

A typical Breton wedding feast
for 1,800 friends and relatives held in
our village during the 1930s.

June gives us a wonderful sense of the summer season to come. It is a hybrid month—part spring, part summer. By the first week of June spring is over, but in its place the faithful promise of a new harvest creates a delightful feeling of anticipation. Come the warmth of June, there is a lush burst of vibrant green reaching up as plants start to climb toward the sun. Nature moves aboveground, and at last we get our first actual look at the food we will eat during the year. Young squash, carrot fingers, small peas, new potatoes—all make their appearance and activate our appetites to crave the full flavors of later summer. Baby animals, birds, and game leave the nest and start growing in earnest. All over the countryside a cascade of pale blossoms leave behind fruits and berries, reminding us that by the end of the month, it will be time to begin putting up jars of wild plums, red currants, fat strawberries, or inky blueberries. June rolls in off of spring and glides into deep summer. It is a transitional link in the culinary year, giving us the opportunity to look for signs of what's in store for us.

Looking to the past to provide for the future was a constant theme reflected in most parts of country life. It could be seen in the hayfields when the harvest began in June. At the beginning of the month came the sprouts of pale green as the new hay started coming up. Soon the bright green mature hay stood ready to cut. Family and neighbors moved from farm to farm, helping each other cut, stack, and store the hay while the weather held. Behind the clackety old harvesters, the cut stalks began to wilt away even as we tramped over the fields throwing out seed, beginning the whole process again. June was harvesting hay, growing it back, and harvesting more so we could replenish last year's stores and get ready for the coming seasons. With the entire village pitching in, several crops a summer could be raised this way.

I like to think that because June is full of beginnings, it was the traditional month for weddings in Brittany. In truth, it was the perfect time of year because the barns were empty and clean, waiting for the harvested hay to be stored. Just like the harvest we were experiencing all around us, a wedding was another faithful promise and was eagerly anticipated by all.

The weddings in our part of Brittany were very large. A wedding may be a union of two people, but it was shared by everyone the bridal families knew. Far-flung cousins from several generations came, as well as all the neighbors and their relatives. It was not unusual to have between three hundred and twelve hundred guests on hand to celebrate. With such a large group, preparations naturally began days before. After the old barn was swept out, big bouquets of field flowers, greens, and ferns were hung inside to make it festive. Large kegs of cider were rolled in to be enjoyed during the dancing that would come later. Huge trenches were dug, then boards held up by empty barrels were set up inside them. After the ceremony, people sat on the trench edges with their feet dangling belowground, using the board as a table for the wedding feast. Long tables were needed not only for seating but also so food could be passed easily as we enjoyed bagpipe and fiddle music reminiscent of our Gaelic ancestors.

The food at weddings was plentiful but simple. Always a savory stew of pork, lamb, or perhaps rabbit was served from a huge bubbling caldron hanging over an open fire. Andouille sausages that had cured in the winter chimney were brought down, wrapped in freshly cut hay, and then boiled. Bowls of new potatoes and baby vegetables arrived at the table within hours of leaving the ground, simply dressed with seasonal herbs. Huge rounds of crusty bread with newly made goat and farmer cheeses were washed down with gallons of cider or Calvados, an apple brandy produced in Brittany. Our desserts were plain sponge cakes, flans with prunes soaked in rum, crêpes, and *gâteau manqué*—the traditional wedding cake. Everything was shared, from one-pot stews to the loaves of bread to the cake. The wedding was a chance to see friends, reminisce about past gatherings, and celebrate the future.

You can devise our own ways of connecting what came before with what is to come next. When you begin visiting the farmers' markets in June, talk with the farmers and ask them what their spring was like. Check to see what kind of harvest they will have, what crops did well, and what didn't. Spring is finished, so now you ask Mother Nature, "What did you give us?" Anywhere you live, ask your farmer so you can make a checklist of what foods will be coming to market in the weeks ahead. In June in the Midwest I'm already looking forward to Michigan white peaches because the farmer has told me a good crop is on the way. I'm thinking of eating fresh warm peaches out of hand on lazy afternoons, planning peach tarts for summer desserts, dreaming of peach chutneys that will be put up to enjoy with a smoked turkey in the fall. Every month is linked one into another and can't be separated. One month's bloom is the next month's food.

JUNE RECIPES

Potage of Fresh Peas with Mint

Spinach Chowder

Talapia Florentine

Crab Cakes with Oregano Mustard Sauce

Pheasant Ragout with Morels and Chives

Chicken with Stuffed Lettuce Hearts

Veal Blanquette

Seared Pork Tenderloin Oriental

Potato Cakes with Ham and Ricotta

Risole New Potatoes

New Potato Salad with Lovage

Lime Fava Beans

Classic Green Beans

Confit of Fresh Onions

Braised Baby Vegetables

June Bridal Salad

Meringue Nests

Gâteau Manqué

Chocolate Brownies with Almonds

BRIDAL DINNER

Crab Cakes with Oregano Mustard Sauce

Chablis

Potage of Fresh Peas with Mint

Chicken with Stuffed Lettuce Hearts

Risole New Potatoes

Pinot Noir

June Bridal Salad

Variety of Cheeses

Merlot

Gateau Manqué with Fresh Berries

Champagne Brut

POTAGE OF FRESH PEAS
WITH MINT

As children, we had the task of shelling the peas. We were always amazed at Maman's ability to judge whether or not we had shelled enough peas for dinner, even though she was in the kitchen and we were outside where she couldn't see us. Later she confessed to her grown children that she listened to the ping of peas hitting the metal bowl as we talked. She knew exactly how long it should take to fill the bowl. If the chatter outdistanced the pinging, we had more work to do!

6 SERVINGS

2 tablespoons unsalted butter
1 head Boston lettuce, cored and
  coarsely chopped
3 scallions, wilted stems and roots
  trimmed, coarsely chopped
2 pounds fresh peas, shelled
1 small potato, peeled and diced
2 tablespoons chopped fresh mint

3 cups chicken stock (see Basics,
  page 375)
¼ cup lemon juice
6 tablespoons crème fraîche (see
  Basics, page 379) (optional)
6 sprigs mint, for garnish
Salt and pepper
Freshly ground nutmeg

In a large soup pot, melt the butter and slowly sauté the lettuce, scallions, peas, potato, and mint until the scallions and lettuce are tender but not brown.

Add the chicken stock and bring to a boil. Simmer over medium heat until the potatoes are tender, about 15 minutes.

Strain the vegetables, separating them from the stock. Purée the vegetables in a food processor, then stir the purée back into the stock. Pass the soup through a strainer to remove any coarse fiber. Return to the pot and add the lemon juice, then add freshly ground nutmeg and salt and pepper to taste. Heat through.

Divide into serving bowls. Dollop a tablespoon of crème fraîche on top of each serving, if desired, and garnish with a sprig of mint.

SPINACH CHOWDER

The word "chowder" descends from the French word chaudière, *a term for the large cooking caldron common to most Breton kitchens. Maman's caldron was at least two feet across, and it was often filled with chowder throughout the year. A chowder's basic ingredients are simply onion, milk, and potatoes, but it is a meal that moves with the seasons. Add to it whatever is fresh and available when you visit the farmers' market each week.*

4 SERVINGS

2 tablespoons unsalted butter
1 small onion, peeled and diced
1 small brown potato, diced
4 cups chicken stock (see Basics, page 375)

1 bunch spinach, cleaned and shredded
1 cup cream
Salt and pepper
Freshly ground nutmeg

Melt the butter in a 4-quart saucepan over low heat. Add the onion and slowly sauté until translucent but not brown. Add the potato and cook until all the butter is absorbed.

Add the chicken stock and bring to a boil. Lower the heat until the soup is simmering. To prevent evaporation, place a lid over but not quite covering the soup. Simmer for approximately 15 minutes, or until the potatoes are cooked but still firm to the fork. Add the spinach and stir gently. Simmer until the spinach is cooked through and soft. Leave the lid off during this last simmering, as the spinach will lose its green color if covered.

Slowly add the cream, stirring constantly. Season with salt and pepper. After ladling the soup into serving bowls, finish with nutmeg on top.

VARIATIONS: Substituting a turnip for the potato and adding ¼ cup chopped fresh basil with the spinach will give the chowder a sharper taste.

- Other leafy greens, like arugula, watercress, beets, mustard, and kale, or any combination of greens, can be used in this basic recipe. Experiment with the intensity of flavors, mixing in available fresh herbs according to taste.

TALAPIA FLORENTINE

To me, food and friends are inseparable. I try to show my love for the pleasures of the table with people I care about by serving meals that are appropriate to the moment and the season. This is an elegant meal to serve guests during early summer, when the soft June weather has brought spinach to its fullest flavor.

6 SERVINGS

1½ cups cooked spinach, finely chopped
1½ cups milk
3 tablespoons unsalted butter

Six 5-ounce pieces talapia
1 cup grated Parmesan cheese
½ cup soft bread crumbs
Salt and pepper

Preheat the oven to 350°F.

Squeeze the excess water from the spinach. In a bowl, mix the spinach with the milk and half the butter. Spread the spinach mixture on the bottom of an ovenproof au gratin dish or other shallow ovenproof pan. Arrange the talapia on top of the spinach. Sprinkle evenly with the Parmesan cheese, bread crumbs, and remaining butter. Salt and pepper lightly.

Bake in the upper third of the oven for 10 minutes, or until the cheese and bread crumbs are browned. Serve immediately.

VARIATIONS: Any firm white fish may be used in the recipe.

• Swiss or Romano cheeses are a good alternative to Parmesan.

SIDENOTE:

Talapia was brought to the United States from Africa, where it is still found wild in Kenya. It is a fish that adapts easily to both fresh and salt water, and was first used to control algae growth in Florida. Very easy to raise, talapia resembles a sunfish and is farmed in the United States, Central America, and Indonesia. Each fish weighs around 1 pound, and the meat is mild-tasting and sweet. Talapia is lean and tender and adaptable to most fish recipes. It's easy to cook and available year-round. Talapia is usually sold as a fillet. Look for flesh that is slightly pink, not gray.

CRAB CAKES WITH OREGANO MUSTARD SAUCE

Crab is an exquisite though costly delicacy. This recipe makes an elegant dinner entrée for four, or a delicious appetizer for eight. Shaped into bite-size morsels, these crab cakes make perfect hors d'oeuvres for a wedding reception.

4 SERVINGS

CRAB CAKES:

1 tablespoon unsalted butter
2 tablespoons chopped red onion
2 garlic cloves, peeled and minced
3 tablespoons flour
½ cup cream
4 tablespoons chopped fresh oregano

1 tablespoon balsamic vinegar
½ cup bread crumbs
2 eggs
1½ pounds crabmeat
Salt and pepper

SAUCE:

1 cup white wine
2 tablespoons cider vinegar
3 tablespoons chopped shallots

1 cup cream
2 tablespoons chopped fresh oregano
2 tablespoons Dijon-style mustard

BREADING:

2 eggs
1 cup milk
1 cup bread crumbs

1 cup flour
2 cups vegetable oil, for frying
Sprigs fresh oregano, for garnish

For the crab mixture, melt the butter in a large skillet, then sauté the onion and garlic for 1 minute. Add the flour and stir to make a smooth paste. Do not brown.

Remove from the heat and slowly stir in the cream. Place over medium heat until thickened. Transfer the mixture to a mixing bowl and cool.

Add the oregano, vinegar, bread crumbs, eggs, and crab. Season with salt and pepper. Cover and refrigerate for 2 hours. If time is short, chill over a bowl of ice until cold.

Meanwhile, prepare the sauce. In a saucepan, bring the wine, vinegar, and shallots to a boil. Simmer over high heat for 3 minutes to reduce the liquid to 2 tablespoons. Slowly whisk in the cream and simmer until thick. Add the oregano and mustard.

To finish the crab cakes, prepare the breading. Beat the eggs and milk together in a small bowl. Mix the bread crumbs and flour together, and place on a sheet of waxed paper. Shape the chilled crab into 4 large or 8 small cakes. Heat the oil in a large skillet over high heat, being careful not to let the oil smoke. Dip the cakes, one at a time, into the egg mixture, then roll in the bread crumbs. Place the cakes in the skillet and cook on both sides until golden brown. Drain the excess oil on a paper towel.

Spread a spoonful of sauce on each plate. Serve the cakes on the sauce, garnished with a sprig of fresh oregano. Pass the remaining sauce.

VARIATIONS: This recipe will make 16 small crab cakes for hors d'oeuvres. Shape the crab cakes into bite-size pieces instead of large patties and use the sauce for dipping. The recipe can be easily doubled, and extra crab cakes can be frozen for future use.

- For a cold appetizer, chill the crab cakes after finishing. Instead of a wine sauce, mix 2 tablespoons of capers with 1 cup of mayonnaise and serve.

- Eliminate the step for breading and frying, and instead heat the crab mixture and use it as a dip for raw vegetables.

SIDENOTE:
There are several types of crab available in the market.

Dungeness:
Caught fresh on the Northwest coast. Best time for sweet and delicate flavor is during the winter and spring.

King or Snow:
Located in the Arctic waters off the coast of Alaska and Russia. Also sweet and delicate, they are usually sold frozen.

Blue:
Very rich and sweetly flavored, the blue crab sheds its shell during the spring season. Found on the Atlantic coast.

Stone:
Found in Florida waters, fishermen remove the claws and return the whole crab back to the water. This flavorful crab will regenerate its claws, providing a continuing delicacy.

PHEASANT RAGOUT WITH MORELS AND CHIVES

We tend to think of game birds as a staple of smoky autumn meals, but of course, they are available in the spring as well. Spring game birds come out of the long winter less meaty than in the fall. The birds depend on a sparse winter diet for survival, so the flavor that the lean meat retains is mild. Today most game birds are farm-raised on a steady diet designed to give them a uniformity of flavor and weight, then frozen for mass transport. If possible, locate a wild-game supplier in your area that offers fresh game. Experiment with the different flavors the game has during the seasons, using the basic cooking technique I've described here but substituting ingredients found in your area appropriate to the time of year.

4 SERVINGS

2 tablespoons unsalted butter
Two 2-pound pheasants, quartered
8 shallots, peeled and quartered
½ cup flour
2 garlic cloves, peeled and minced
1 cup dry white wine

16 medium morel mushrooms
½ cup chopped fresh chives
3 cups chicken stock (see Basics, page 375)
1 cup cream
Salt and pepper

In a dutch oven, melt the butter, then brown each pheasant piece on all sides.

Add the shallots. Sprinkle evenly with the flour and toss gently to ensure the even coating of the meat. Add the garlic.

Stir in the wine, carefully scraping loose the brown bits at the bottom of the pan. Simmer about 3 minutes to reduce the liquid by half. Add the morels, chives, and enough chicken stock to cover the pheasant pieces. Gently stir, trying not to disturb the birds. Lightly season with salt and pepper.

Bring to a boil, then lower the heat to a simmer. Cover and cook gently for about 45 minutes. The meat should be tender and come off the bone easily with a fork. Remove the pheasant pieces and keep warm.

Simmer for 5 minutes to reduce the liquid by one fourth, then add the cream and simmer for 15 minutes more. Adjust the seasoning.

Arrange the pheasant on a serving platter and cover with the sauce before serving.

CHICKEN WITH STUFFED LETTUCE HEARTS

By the middle of June the lettuce in our garden was bolting fast. We always shared or traded much of it with other families, since throwing food away because there was an overabundance was out of the question. Maman always found ways to make use of everything we had. One of her favorite recipes for using lettuce hearts is below. I return to this delicious dish again and again. Not only does it make use of the part of the lettuce usually discarded after the outer leaves have gone into a salad, it calls for the whole chicken to be used. Nothing goes to waste, and its versatility makes it impossible for even the most particular appetite to resist.

4 SERVINGS

One 3-pound chicken, quartered, plus chicken giblets
3 tablespoons olive oil
½ cup dry sherry
4 heads Boston lettuce
½ pound mushrooms
3 shallots, peeled and minced
2 garlic cloves, peeled and minced
2 tablespoons mixed fresh chervil, tarragon, and Italian parsley, finely chopped
½ cup chicken stock (see Basics, page 375)
Salt and pepper

Preheat the oven to 400°F. Rinse the chicken and pat dry. Reserving 1 tablespoon, lightly brush the quarters with the remaining oil. Season with salt and pepper.

Place the chicken in a roasting pan, skin side up. Roast, uncovered, in the oven for 15 minutes. Add the sherry to the pan and baste. Continue cooking for another 25 minutes.

Remove the outer leaves of each head of lettuce down to the firm heart. Reserve the leaves for use in a salad. Bring a pot of lightly salted water to a boil. Place the hearts in the water and blanch until the water returns to a boil. Remove and place in cold water to stop the cooking. Drain.

Sauté the mushrooms in the reserved tablespoon of oil on high heat to evaporate the moisture. Combine the uncooked giblets, mushrooms, shallots, garlic, and herbs in a food processor. Process until the mixture is chopped fine but not puréed.

Take each lettuce heart and, with a spoon, stuff the giblet mixture between the leaves. Secure the stuffing by tying each heart around the middle with kitchen twine. Twenty minutes before the end of the roasting time, place the stuffed lettuce hearts around the chicken.

After removing the pan from the oven, set aside the chicken and lettuce hearts. Place the roasting pan on high heat. Add the chicken stock to the pan juices, scraping up the brown bits and swirling to mix. Simmer for 3 minutes to thicken.

To serve, divide the chicken among serving plates and add the sauce on the side.

VARIATIONS: Add ½ cup of cream with the chicken stock to give the sauce a smoother texture.

- Chives, basil, and cilantro will give this dish an interesting flavor.

- Adding 4 tablespoons of goat cheese to the giblet mixture will add zest to the stuffed lettuce hearts.

VEAL BLANQUETTE

Veal blanquette, a dish served in most Breton homes for special occasions, was often served at weddings, as it is simple and inexpensive to prepare. Always tasty because it is slow-cooked until the meat falls apart, veal blanquette had the advantage of feeding lots of people quickly because it could be served out of a caldron and passed down the long wedding tables with ease. My recipe of veal blanquette can be doubled for larger groups and freezes well.

6 SERVINGS

1 quart chicken stock (see Basics, page 375)
1 cup white wine
2 sprigs fresh thyme
2 pounds veal shoulder, trimmed and cut into 1-inch cubes
3 tablespoons unsalted butter
1 cup sliced mushrooms
1 medium white onion, peeled and sliced

3 tablespoons flour
1 teaspoon dry mustard
1 pound fresh peas, shelled
1 egg yolk
1 cup cream
6 cups cooked rice
Salt and pepper
Freshly ground nutmeg

In a large saucepan, bring the stock, wine, and thyme to a boil. Lower to a simmer for 20 minutes.

Add the veal and simmer for another 10 minutes, occasionally skimming the surface. Remove the veal and set aside. Reserve the stock.

In the same pan, melt the butter and sauté the mushrooms and onion until soft. Stir in the flour and cook over low heat until pale blond in color. Do not burn.

Slowly pour in the stock, whisking constantly. Mix well. Add the veal and lightly season with mustard, salt and pepper, and nutmeg. Slowly simmer over low heat for 20 minutes, or until the meat is tender. Add the peas and cook for another 10 minutes.

Blend together the egg yolk and cream. Right before serving, remove the blanquette from the heat and whisk in the egg-and-cream mixture. Do not return to a boil, as this will curdle the egg. Serve immediately over rice.

SEARED PORK TENDERLOIN ORIENTAL

Many foods not native to Brittany found their way into traditional dishes I grew up with. Throughout history, seafaring trade routes began and ended on the Breton coast, providing access to a number of delicious delicacies from far-off countries. Some, like rum, prunes, vanilla, and tropical fruits, became staples of my heritage. France's colonization of foreign territory, particularly in Africa and Indochina, also had a lasting influence on the flavors and spices I enjoy using as we learned how to season our foods with exotic taste combinations.

6 SERVINGS

2 tablespoons sesame oil
1 tablespoon sesame seeds, crushed
1 tablespoon soy sauce
2 garlic cloves, peeled and minced
1 tablespoon Dijon-style mustard

3 tablespoons chopped fresh cilantro
or 1 teaspoon coriander seeds,
crushed
Two ¾-pound pork tenderloins,
trimmed

Preheat the oven to 425°F.

In a mixing bowl, blend the oil, sesame seeds, soy sauce, garlic, mustard, and cilantro or coriander seeds into a paste. Rub the tenderloins all over with the marinating paste. Tightly wrap in plastic wrap and marinate at room temperature for 30 minutes, or refrigerate overnight. The tenderloins may also be frozen at this point for later use.

In a heavy, lightly oiled skillet, sear both sides of the tenderloins until well browned but not burned. Place on a baking sheet and bake for 15 minutes. Slice and serve.

VARIATIONS: Beef tenderloin, boneless chicken breasts, or a turkey breast may be substituted.

- Rubbing curry paste purchased from an Indian grocer all over the meat before marinating will give an East Indian twist of heat that is good for winter meals.

SIDENOTE:
Cilantro, a member of the parsley family, comes to us originally from the Orient. The seeds of cilantro become what we know as coriander. The ancient Chinese believed coriander seeds conferred immortality on those who consumed them. It

is an important herb in many ethnic traditions, particularly Indian, Egyptian, and Peruvian. It is often used in German sausages, and the Greeks favor the seeds to flavor bread, cakes, puddings, and chocolate, as well as meat and vegetable dishes.

My brother Albert (left), *and my brother-in-law, Michel* (right), *picking green beans from the potager.*

POTATO CAKES WITH HAM AND RICOTTA

Between lunch and dinner (which is not served until at least eight o'clock in the evening in France) is a delightful little meal called casse-croute. *"Casse-croute" means "to break the crust," and so it is customary to serve some form of bread along with a simple dish or two. For us restless children at the end of a school day, the nuns passed around* petits pains *with chunks of chocolate baked in the middle. On the farm casse-croute was the meal the farmhands ate after coming back from the fields and before going on to their evening chores. The potato cake, along with crusty sourdough bread and cups of steaming coffee, made a simple but hardy snack that sustained the men until dinner. Add a fresh green salad and today's family can enjoy a complete supper.*

4 SERVINGS

2 tablespoons olive oil
12 slices smoked ham, thinly sliced
12 medium new potatoes, cut into
⅛-inch slices, covered with cold
water

½ cup ricotta or farmer cheese
4 tablespoons crème fraîche (see
Basics, page 379)
6 tablespoons chopped fresh chives
Freshly ground pepper

Preheat the oven to 425°F.

Brush a large ovenproof baking dish with the oil. Line the dish with ham, leaving the ends overhanging the sides. Season with pepper.

Pat the **potatoes** dry. Arrange half the potatoes on top of the ham, overlapping the slices. Spread the cheese to within ½-inch around the edge of the potatoes. Layer the remaining potatoes on top. Fold the edges of the ham back onto the potatoes. Season again with pepper.

Cover with parchment paper or aluminum foil and bake for 20 minutes. Remove the cover and continue cooking for approximately 30 additional minutes, until the potatoes are soft and golden brown.

To serve, turn over onto a serving platter and cut into 4 serving pieces. Mix together the crème fraîche and chives, and top each potato cake with 1 tablespoon.

♥ *Monique's Touch:*

When exposed to air, **potatoes** will darken to an unappetizing gray color. To prevent this, keep whole peeled potatoes in cold water until ready to use. It is important not to slice the potatoes in this recipe until they are ready to use, because the starch found on the potato slices is what seals the cheese in the casserole.

RISOLE NEW POTATOES

In the first few days of June we always watched very carefully for the blossom to appear on the potato plant because it meant the potato tubers were forming underground. By then we were anxious to leave behind the very last of the winter store of mature, starchy potatoes for the nutty-flavored potatoes of summer. Today I know the new potato crop is just around the corner when, at the earliest farmers' markets, I find caneles, tiny potatoes about the size of a dime. Sure enough, within a week or two, the walnut-size new potatoes are available. New potatoes need little preparation, as their natural flavors complement almost any meal. Because of their small size and thin, delicate skins, cooking time is minimal.

6 SERVINGS

1 tablespoon unsalted butter
1 tablespoon olive oil
1½ pounds red or white new potatoes,
    scrubbed
Salt and pepper

In a heavy pan, melt the butter with the oil on high heat and add the potatoes. Brown on one side, turn, cover, and lower the heat. Cook for 5 minutes. Turn the potatoes once again, cover, and cook for 5 minutes more. Salt and pepper to taste and serve immediately.

VARIATIONS: Add 1 tablespoon of soy sauce or mustard during the last 5 minutes of cooking.

NEW POTATO SALAD
WITH LOVAGE

By mid-June I am looking for the dirtiest potatoes I can find at the farmers' market. Dirt on a potato means it's just come out of the ground, probably within the previous twenty-four hours. New potatoes found in supermarkets are shipped and stored for weeks before being sold, causing most of the fresh flavor to dissipate. As we did on the farm, I clean and peel new potatoes in one step by soaking them briefly in cold water, then rubbing them firmly between my fingers. Much of the thin skin slips off with the soil, and what doesn't remains to give an extra nutty flavor to my dish.

6 SERVINGS

2 pounds new potatoes, unpeeled and covered in cold water	2 tablespoons Dijon-style mustard
1 cup diced red onions	¾ cup vegetable oil
¼ cup cider vinegar	2 tablespoons chopped fresh parsley
	4 tablespoons chopped fresh lovage

Rub the potatoes to remove any dirt clinging to the skins. Bring a pot of lightly salted water to boil. Cook potatoes until tender, about 15 minutes. Drain and cool until warm to the touch.

Meanwhile, in a mixing bowl, whisk together the vinegar and mustard until creamy. Continue beating as the oil is added in a slow stream. Mix in the onions and herbs.

Cut the potatoes into ¼-inch slices and mix gently with the dressing. Serve warm or cold.

VARIATIONS: White or red new potatoes are used for the recipe above, as these types hold their shape better. In the winter, when tastes turn to comforting textures, use starchy, mature potatoes such as baking potatoes and serve the dish hot for a creamy German-style potato salad. Cook the potatoes with the skins on to retain as much flavor as possible, then peel before combining the salad. Substitute dillseeds for the lovage.

SIDENOTE:
Ancient herbal lore holds that lovage added to food makes the cook more attractive to the opposite sex. Today lovage is often overlooked in cooking, even

though it can be added to soups, stews, and salads just like any other herb. The large, spiky, dark green leaves have a strong, almost yeasty scent that is particularly complementary to potatoes. The hollow-channeled stem can be blanched and eaten like celery.

LIME FAVA BEANS

Fava beans have recently become popular on the American culinary scene, but they have been known and cultivated throughout Europe since the Middle Ages. Look for them quickly at the farmers' market, since they are not in season long, usually only from mid-June to July. The pods contain beans of mixed sizes, between a quarter inch to three quarters of an inch long. The larger beans have a more buttery taste. In Europe the beans would be separated, and the smaller ones would go into a soup and the large ones would be used in vegetable dishes where their taste is more prominent. Here we don't go to the trouble of separating the beans. Instead, we cook them all together. I prefer fava beans with the skins on, but some people prefer the beans skinned for appearance.

6 SERVINGS

3 pounds fresh fava beans, shelled
½ pound ripe tomatoes, peeled,
   seeded, and coarsely chopped
1 teaspoon sugar

2 tablespoons unsalted butter
Zest of 1 lime, grated
Salt and pepper

Preheat the oven to 200°F.

Bring a large pot of water to boil. Add the beans and blanch until soft, about 10 minutes. Drain and rinse under cold running water. Slip the skin off each bean, if desired. Keep warm.

Meanwhile, spread the tomatoes on a baking sheet and sprinkle with sugar. Place in the oven for 15 minutes. Melt the butter in a saucepan and stir in the lime.

To serve, drizzle the lime butter over the fava beans and toss with the tomatoes.

VARIATIONS: Lima beans, fresh peas, and green beans are a good choice for this recipe.

SIDENOTE:
To quickly skin tomatoes or peaches, bring a pot of water to boil. Puncture the skin of the fruit two or three times with a fork. Drop the fruit into the boiling water for 30 seconds. Remove and cool under cold running water. The skins will slip off easily.

CLASSIC GREEN BEANS

Green beans are just about the most versatile vegetable in the garden. They can be harvested when they are not much thicker than yarn or left on the vine to mature into sturdy pods snapping with flavor. In all of the variations below, the beans can be served warm or prepared several hours ahead and served at room temperature. Chilled green beans make a wonderful summer salad.

4 SERVINGS

4 quarts lightly salted water
2 pounds fresh green beans, ends and
 strings removed
1 tablespoon unsalted butter
Salt and pepper

In a large pot, bring 4 quarts of lightly salted water to boil.

Drop the beans into the boiling water. Cover and bring back to a boil. As soon as the water reaches the boiling point, remove the cover and cook up to 5 minutes, or until the beans turn bright green and are tender but still crunchy. Drain and rinse once more under cold running water.

Just before serving, melt the butter in a pan and toss the beans until warm. Add salt and pepper to taste.

VARIATIONS: Add 2 tablespoons of fresh snipped herbs of your choice while the beans are warm.

- Mince 2 garlic cloves with 2 tablespoons of fresh parsley and add while the beans are warm.

- After melting the butter in the pan, add ½ cup of blanched almonds and sauté until golden. Add the beans and toss gently.

- Replace the melted butter with 1 tablespoon of sesame oil. Add the beans, then sprinkle with 1 tablespoon of sesame seeds and toss. Chill before serving.

- After warming the beans, toss with 1 coarsely chopped tomato. Serve at room temperature.

CONFIT OF FRESH ONIONS

A dish is not finished until it is garnished. A garnish is meant to add a final note of visual interest to a dish and can be as simple as an herb stem placed jauntily on the plate rim. It can also be edible, like this confit, which adds a rich caramel color and teases the palate with a little sweetness.

6 SERVINGS

1 pound pearl onions, loose skin removed
¼ cup brown sugar
Juice of 1 lime

½ cup dry white wine
½ cup cider vinegar
Zest of 1 lime, grated
Salt and pepper

In a saucepan, place the onions, brown sugar, and lime juice. Over medium heat, melt the sugar, stirring to blend with the juice. Cook slowly for approximately 35 minutes, stirring occasionally, until the mixture caramelizes and the juice and sugar form a thick, dark brown syrup that coats the onions.

In a saucepan, combine the wine and vinegar, and simmer for approximately 5 minutes, or until the mixture is reduced to ¼ cup. Add this along with the lime zest to the onions. Season with salt and pepper to taste. Cook over low heat until all the liquid has evaporated, about 10 minutes. Serve hot or cold as a garnish.

SIDENOTE:
Onions come in hundreds of varieties, but these are staples for most recipes.

Scallions:
Also known simply as green onions, they are picked when young and tender, before the bulb has a chance to form. Use the scallion stems as well as the bulb for chopping, sautéing, stir-frying, grilling, or serve as is.

Pearl:
Onions that have matured beyond the scallion stage to about the size of cherries. They are picked, then left on the ground so the stems will dry and wither before being cut off. Remove the dry, loose skin, but do not peel. Pearl onions should be chopped or boiled. Larger pearl onions may be grilled.

Knob:

Knob onions have become more popular in the last few years. The pure-white onion bulb is about the size of a golf ball and can be round or oval in shape. They are sold fresh, with the green stems attached. Use as you would the scallion, but be aware that knob onions have a stronger taste.

Mature:

Left in the ground long enough, onions mature to sizes between a plum and a grapefruit. This is true for all varieties and colors. Mature onions are harvested just like pearl onions. Some varieties, like Vidalia onions, are seasonal and should be enjoyed when they become available.

BRAISED BABY VEGETABLES

Recently baby vegetables have gained popularity as a staple of nouvelle cuisine, making appearances in fine restaurants around the world. But baby vegetables are not new to cooking, and have the most humble of origins in country gardens everywhere. After planting our garden in early spring, every couple of weeks Maman sent us to thin out the young seedlings and make growing room for the vegetables. Instead of throwing away the immature roots, we always braised and enjoyed them as another treat from nature's calendar of seasonal delights.

6 SERVINGS

5 outer leaves baby Boston lettuce or
 any young seasonal lettuce available
1 cup whole baby carrots
6 baby turnips, halved
3 baby fennel bulbs, halved
6 whole pearl onions or 1 medium
 onion, peeled and sliced
¼ cup chicken stock (see Basics, page
 375)

2 tablespoons unsalted butter
1 cup fresh peas, shelled
3 tablespoons fresh dill
2 tablespoons chopped fresh chervil
 or 1 tablespoon chopped fresh
 parsley
Salt and pepper

In a saucepan, place the lettuce leaves and on top arrange the carrots, turnips, fennel, and pearl onions or sliced onion. Add the chicken stock and butter. Salt and pepper to taste. Cover and cook gently on low heat for 10 minutes.

Add the peas, dill, and chervil or parsley, tossing gently. Cover and cook on low heat for 5 minutes. Remove from heat and keep covered for 10 minutes.

Adjust the seasoning and serve.

SIDENOTE:

As consumers, it is important that we know that not all carrots sold as baby carrots truly are young carrots harvested early. Since the popularity of baby carrots has grown, processors are now packaging the tips of mature carrots that have been machine-cut to look like baby carrots. This often explains why "baby" carrots are tough, fibrous, or tasteless.

JUNE BRIDAL SALAD

Creativity was important in our kitchen. At times Maman liked to make food look pretty or unusual for the moment. It was not for everyday, but she knew that sometimes small touches like mixing in flower petals to dress up a salad made even the simplest meal seem special. To me, entertaining, whether planned ahead of time or spur of the moment, should not be difficult or complicated. Entertaining is taking something simple and using your creativity to present it differently.

6 SERVINGS

DRESSING:
1 cup raspberries
3 tablespoons cider vinegar
1 tablespoon lemon juice
1 garlic clove, peeled and minced
1 teaspoon Dijon-style mustard
⅔ cup olive oil
1 tablespoon chopped fresh parsley
Freshly ground pepper

SALAD:
1 bunch each of Boston, oak leaf, and baby romaine lettuce, torn into bite-size pieces
12 nasturtium flowers
1 dozen chive blossoms
1 dozen sprigs chive

To make the dressing, purée ¼ cup of the raspberries and strain through a piece of cheesecloth or through a fine strainer. Discard the seeds.

In a bowl, combine the strained raspberry juice, vinegar, lemon juice, garlic, and mustard. Slowly whisk in the olive oil in a steady stream to emulsify the ingredients. Add the parsley and pepper to taste.

To make the salad, toss the lettuce, nasturtium flowers, and chive blossoms with the dressing. Garnish with the remaining raspberries and chive sprigs on top of the salad before serving.

SIDENOTE:
Edible flowers are pretty to look at and can add a hint of flavor to salads or soups. Many flowers from the garden can be used, provided they are pesticide-free. Cut the blossoms often to keep the plant blooming. Don't be afraid to experiment with color and flavor. Nasturtiums are a favorite, but spicy carnations, sweet violets, and yeasty marigolds are also delightful. Other suggestions are rose petals, pansies, geraniums, and any blossom from flowering herbs.

MERINGUE NESTS

Meringues were always a part of our family celebrations because they could be made into wonderfully fanciful desserts. Heart-shaped meringues sprinkled with sugar were for Valentine's Day, while the Christmas Yule-log cake usually sprouted several meringue mushrooms. In the summer, baby christenings were marked with a meringue bird's nest filled with fresh fruit and whipped cream. Use your leftover egg whites to create alphabet letters and kisses for little hands helping in the kitchen.

6 SERVINGS

6 egg whites
Pinch of salt or cream of tartar
1 cup superfine sugar
1 teaspoon vanilla extract
3 cups fresh seasonal berries, for garnish

Preheat the oven to 200°F. Line a baking sheet with parchment paper. Using a small bowl as a guide, draw six 4-inch circles on the paper.

In a large mixing bowl, beat the **egg whites** and salt or cream of tartar until foamy. Gradually beat in the sugar, beating until the egg whites are glossy. Beat in the vanilla until just blended.

Place the meringue mixture in a pastry bag fitted with a ½-inch decorative tip. Pipe around the outline of the parchment circles, then fill the circles in completely. On top of the meringue circles, pipe around the edge, creating sides for the "nest."

Place in the oven and bake for 1 hour and 20 minutes, or until the meringue is dry. Turn off the oven and leave overnight to allow the meringues to dry completely.

To serve, fill with your choice of ice cream, fresh fruit and berries, chocolate mousse, sorbet, etc. (Ice cream–filled meringues can be prepared ahead and kept in the freezer until serving time.) Garnish with fresh berries.

To store empty meringues for later use, place in a paper bag and keep at room temperature.

VARIATIONS: To make meringue mushrooms, fill a pastry bag with a ¼-inch-round tip with meringue. Pressing the tip to the pan, pipe out several meringue buttons on the parchment paper, allowing the meringue to spread slightly before lifting the tip. These will serve as mushroom caps. To make the stems, squeeze out several ¾-inch-high cone shapes. Bake about 1 hour, or until the meringue is dry. To assemble, with a small knife pierce a hole in the bottom of the mushroom cap. Spread a dab of frosting in the hole and insert the pointed end of the stem.

- To make chocolate meringue, add 3 tablespoons of cocoa powder to the sugar mixture.

- For a nutty flavor, gently add 3 teaspoons of ground roasted hazelnuts after the sugar.

♥ *Monique's Touch:*

Egg whites will not beat into peaks if fat is present. It is important that not even a small amount of egg yolk, which contains fat, remains after separating. Make sure the bowl and beaters are free of fat by cleaning them first with a paper towel moistened in vinegar.

GÂTEAU MANQUÉ

For simple country weddings, gâteau manqué was usually served for the wedding cake. Legend has it the gâteau manqué, which means "missed cake," was invented when an apprentice pastry chef mistakenly overbeat the egg whites intended for a lighter, fluffier cake. Knowing he dare not discard the batter containing costly ingredients, he added some extra butter and baked the cake anyway. The result was this denser, richer cake. The young baker may have missed the mark on his first cake, but gâteau manqué soon became a perennial favorite. If you make a mistake on a recipe, don't be afraid to experiment. Cooking is an act of discovery and creation!

12 SERVINGS

8 egg yolks
1¼ cups sugar
Pinch of salt
1 teaspoon vanilla extract

½ cup unsalted butter, melted
1¾ cups flour
8 egg whites

Preheat the oven to 375°F. Prepare a 9-inch springform pan by lightly buttering the inside and lining the bottom with parchment paper.

In a mixing bowl, cream together the egg yolks, sugar, salt, and vanilla until foamy and pale yellow in color.

Add the melted butter to the egg mixture slowly, beating well to incorporate. Sift the flour a little at a time into the mixture, beating well to blend.

In a separate bowl, beat the egg whites until stiff. Using a spatula, gently fold the egg whites into the batter.

Pour the batter into the prepared pan. Place on the middle rack of the oven for 45 minutes. When done, the center will be dry to the touch. Turn upside down on a cake rack to cool.

CHOCOLATE BROWNIES WITH ALMONDS

Chocolate was not only a treat for all seasons, but for me it was a window to the world. Inside every chocolate bar produced by the Menier chocolate company was a tiny picture of a foreign country. We children would collect and trade the cards, much like baseball cards are traded today. Then we pasted them in a geography book provided by Menier that taught us a little something about each country. I'm sure my love of travel was sparked by many daydreams spun over my little geography book as I enjoyed brownies made from Menier chocolate!

18 BROWNIES

½ pound unsalted butter
4 ounces unsweetened chocolate, chopped
1½ cups sugar
4 eggs

1 cup flour
½ teaspoon baking powder
1 tablespoon vanilla extract
1 cup toasted almonds, chopped

Preheat the oven to 350°F. Butter and flour a 12 × 9-inch cake pan.

Place the butter and chocolate in a saucepan over low heat until both are melted. Set aside to cool.

In a mixing bowl, combine the remaining ingredients and mix well. Blend in the chocolate mixture.

Pour the batter into the pan and place on the middle rack of the oven for 30 minutes. A toothpick inserted in the middle should come out clean.

Remove from the oven and set on a rack to cool. When completely cool, cut into 18 squares. Wrap in plastic wrap to keep moist.

VARIATIONS: For the ultimate chocolate version of brownies, add up to 1 cup of chocolate chips along with the unsweetened chocolate.

• All types of nuts are suitable in brownies.

JULY

A pardon *picnic in July.*

Compared to the giddy hesitation of early summer in June, July is a brash month loudly announcing itself as the center stage of the season. The hours spin out in golden abandon. Freedom, buoyant with a sense of exhilaration, propels the days. Everywhere we look there are enticements to live life outdoors. The weather is fine, school is out, and it's time to enjoy a respite from the hard work of a long winter and busy spring. We find the rhythm of our lives moving us further away from the house, which suddenly feels too restrictive and bothersome. We have a need to get out, explore our surroundings, and socialize with our friends.

Even the plants in the garden are breaking out. Vegetables stretch their tangled vines and sturdy stems, climbing through the heat toward the sun, to offer up the first rush of summer's bounty. It's almost as if they find the ground too confining, so they free themselves from the earth and explode into a celebration of color and superlative flavor. The farmers at the market are displaying a wide selection of bright green beans, full heads of lettuce, the first small tomatoes, fist-size potatoes, crunchy cucumbers, small but robust eggplants, summer squashes the color of the sun, and all varieties of greens and herbs. Apricots and raspberries also make their first appearance of the year, but it is the cherry that is the queen of midsummer. The little red cherries hanging from the trees look like firecrackers bursting over our heads, reminding us that July is a time to give ourselves up to celebrating the gift of summer.

By the beginning of the month, throughout the countryside in Brittany, the hay was completely cut and the wheat in the fields swayed green, its coming of age still a month away. July hung suspended between harvests, tantalizing in its promise of ease. We took advantage of this time by attending the many festivals and fairs that are a weekly part of Breton life in July. Beginning in July until the end of summer, Brittany is alive with celebrations inspired by its Celtic culture and religious heritage. Sometimes the pardons, or festivals, honor the patron saint of the town, or sometimes it is a festival honoring a more ancient pagan ritual, usually having to do with ensuring a good harvest. For us, the festivals were a thread in the fabric of our community and a reason to gather with family and friends.

On Sunday mornings we children ran down to the river to bathe before dressing in our best clothes. After church we went immediately to the festival, which often started with a procession through the fields and streets by local people carrying banners and relics, dressed in traditional costume and singing songs in the Breton language. The afternoon was spent playing games and joining races, with a prize of perhaps a live rabbit or a few bottles of cider going to the winner. Stalls lined the streets selling crêpes and cider. At the end of the day there was always folk dancing to the sound of the accordion and bagpipes. Pardons have been a part of Breton life for centuries, with some people celebrating their sixteenth-century rituals annually. Each year that we went, we took part in a tradition, carrying it forward in time.

The highlight of the festival season was and always will be Bastille Day, on July 14. Similar to the Fourth of July, Bastille Day has been celebrated nationally as a day of independence for France since 1792. Every town across the country has a celebration. In years gone by, a huge bonfire was built in the center of each town. Thousands of people poured into the streets to celebrate around the bonfire. Today there are still some bonfires, but most towns offer fireworks displays instead, a tradition borrowed from the United States. It doesn't matter which it is, for the next twenty-four hours France is given over to wild dancing, singing, and, of course, eating.

The food at Bastille Day and at the pardons of my childhood had the same sense of easy celebration that drives the month of July. Everything was fresh and simple to bring along, giving the celebrations the feel of a great picnic. Perhaps a whole suckling pig might be roasted if it were a particularly important pardon, but mostly there were summer salads of grated carrots or celery root *rémoulade,* the first young cavaillon melons, sliced cucumbers, pâtés, hams of different kinds, good salamis, or baguette sandwiches of ham and cheese, with cake and flan for dessert. Bastille Day always included paper cones filled with *pommes frites,* french fries cooked in peanut oil and served piping hot. Vendors wandered the streets selling baskets of cherries picked fresh that morning. Tables were set up under tents, and people came and went throughout the day, taking breaks to nibble or to just sit and celebrate moving from the heat into the shade. Best of all, there was ample time to visit with friends during the festivals, a luxury not always found during the rest of the summer, when the pace of the harvest would quicken.

Even though we don't have pardons in the United States, I spend the month of July with the same spirit today as I did forty years ago in Brittany. When we look around us, there are celebrations and a joy of independence everywhere. People are hiking in the country, going to the beach, and having backyard barbecues. The parks are full of people holding company picnics and family reunions. Neighborhoods and towns surrounding large cities are holding fairs and festivals that are easy to get to. Many celebrate local food specialties, like the wonderful cheeses and bratwurst found in Wisconsin, or the juicy blackberries found in the Oregon countryside, or the spectacular seafood of the Northeast. Make a habit of keeping a blanket in the trunk of the car so if you're driving and see a farm stand, you can purchase an on-the-spot picnic. Independence Day always kicks off the summer season, but we don't really need a holiday for our natural exuberance during this time of year to come out in celebration. Just being outdoors and enjoying the height of the summer season with simple food and friends is a festival all on its own.

JULY RECIPES

Steamed Clams with Muscadet and Shallots

Aromatic Shrimp

Cold Salmon Mousse

Monkfish with Roasted Red Pepper Sauce

Grilled Tuna Salad Sandwich

Grilled Butterflied Quail with Gooseberries

Marinated Grilled Chicken Tenders

Pasta Salad with Roasted Garlic–Basil Chicken

Roast Beef and Pesto Sour Cream Sandwich

Purée of Grilled Eggplant

Bastille Day "Pommes Frites" French Fries

Baked Zucchini Fan

Summer Bounty Vegetable Salad

Three Cabbage Summer Slaw

Grated Carrot Salad

Fourth of July Cherry Pie

Apricot Tart

FOURTH OF JULY PICNIC

Cold Salmon Mousse

Roast Beef and Pesto Sour Cream Sandwich

Ale Beer

Three Cabbage Summer Slaw

Summer Bounty Vegetable Salad

Oven-Roasted Potato Chips

Fourth of July Cherry Pie

Ice Tea

STEAMED CLAMS WITH MUSCADET AND SHALLOTS

The waters off the Brittany coast are quite cold, so many afternoons, instead of swimming, we passed the time by digging for clams. All sorts of other shellfish washed in as the tide went down, exposing themselves along the beach and trapped among the rocks. It made gathering them easy and fun. This is my version of the classic moules marinières.

6 SERVINGS

6 dozen littleneck clams, scrubbed
3 cups water
1 cup chopped shallots
4 garlic cloves, peeled and minced

2 tablespoons chopped fresh parsley
6 cups Muscadet or other dry white wine
Freshly ground pepper

Place the clams in a pot and add enough water to cover. Bring to a boil and let simmer until all the clams have opened, about 5 minutes. Drain and set aside in a covered bowl to keep warm.

In the same pot, mix the shallots, garlic, parsley, and Muscadet or other white wine. Bring to a boil, lower the heat, and simmer for 10 minutes, or until reduced by one third. Strain the broth through a fine sieve or a triple layer of cheesecloth so as not to let any sand from the clams pass through. Reduce the broth by one third again and season with pepper to taste.

To serve, arrange a dozen clams in the bottom of a shallow bowl. Ladle the broth over and serve hot.

VARIATIONS: Mussels can be prepared in the same proportion as the clams.

- While it is traditional to serve clams and mussels in their shells, if preferred, they can be removed from the shells after steaming and added to the broth before serving. Do not add the shellfish to the broth as it's reducing, or they will become tough and rubbery.

- Fresh diced tomatoes can also be added for flavor and color.

AROMATIC SHRIMP

For those who love fresh seafood, a plateau de fruits de mer, *or seafood platter, is one of the highlights of Breton cuisine. Huge platters, sometimes several feet long, are piled with many kinds of steamed oysters, crabs, langoustines, shrimp, clams, and periwinkles. The platter is set in the middle of the table and served with melted butter, mustard, capers, and hot or cold mayonnaise with chopped onions. Whenever I go home to Brittany, I look forward to sitting down with family and friends around a plateau de fruits de mer, catching up with everybody as we shuck, peel, and crack our way through dinner. At home, when I serve a seafood platter, it always includes aromatic shrimp with ravigote sauce, a highly seasoned white sauce.*

6 SERVINGS

2 garlic cloves, peeled and crushed

1 tablespoon each fresh thyme, rosemary, oregano, and parsley

1 dozen whole black peppercorns

1 bay leaf, crushed

1 cup white wine

1 cup white wine vinegar

1 cup water

2 stalks celery heart, with leaves, chopped

2 pounds 18–24-count shrimp, rinsed and unpeeled

RAVIGOTE SAUCE:

1 cup Monique's Mayonnaise (see Basics, page 380)

1 garlic clove, peeled and pressed

1 tablespoon cider vinegar

1 tablespoon Dijon-style mustard

1 tablespoon chopped fresh parsley

Combine the garlic, herbs, peppercorns, and bay leaf. Wrap in a 4 × 4-inch-square piece of cheesecloth, securing it with kitchen twine to make an herb bag.

To make the marinade, combine the wine, vinegar, and water in a saucepan. Add the celery and the herb bag. Bring to a boil, then immediately lower the heat and simmer for 20 minutes. Add water, if necessary, to maintain the liquid level.

Add the shrimp to the marinade and bring to a boil. Lower the heat to medium and simmer for 2 minutes. The shells are left on to retain the flavor of the shrimp during cooking.

Transfer the shrimp and marinade to a plastic or glass bowl and let come to room temperature. Refrigerate until cold, about 2 hours. Can be done ahead to this point and refrigerated overnight.

Meanwhile, combine all the ingredients for the sauce and refrigerate until ready to use. To serve, remove the shrimp from the marinade and peel and eat with the ravigotte sauce on the side for dipping.

VARIATIONS:

- A batch of aromatic shrimp in the refrigerator during the summer is a versatile item to have on hand. Besides serving as an appetizer with sauce, aromatic shrimp can be peeled and tossed in a green salad, or added to pasta and grilled vegetables for an elegant supper.

- For a spicier shrimp, add a teaspoon of Tabasco or hot pepper sauce to the marinade, along with the other liquids.

SIDENOTE:

Shrimp are sold by count (pieces) per pound. The more shrimp pieces in a pound, the smaller the shrimp will be, so this should be a consideration when estimating portion size. A good rule of thumb for a main course is 6 shrimp per person of 18-count shrimp, or 1 pound of 18-count shrimp for 3 people.

COLD SALMON MOUSSE

The art of aspic, or the use of gelatin in cooking, is rarely practiced in culinary traditions of the United States. Here gelatin is used mainly to mold fruit and vegetable salads. In France aspic has long been used as a way to preserve meats and other cold food for a lovely presentation. This classic salmon-mousse aspic is a perfect picnic choice because it travels well and can withstand the summer heat without spoiling.

6 SERVINGS

½ cup coarsely chopped green
   onions
1 package unflavored gelatin
½ cup hot water
½ cup cream cheese, softened
1 cup crème fraîche (see Basics, page
   379)

12 ounces cooked salmon
2 tablespoons lemon juice
3 tablespoons chopped fresh fennel
1 teaspoon paprika
Pinch of cayenne pepper

In a food processor, combine the onions and gelatin. Pulse the machine to blend. Add the hot water and process for 30 seconds. Add the cream cheese, ½ cup of the crème fraîche, salmon, lemon juice, fennel, paprika, and cayenne pepper. Process for 45 seconds, or until the mixture is well blended. Adjust the seasoning, if necessary, and add the rest of the crème fraîche. Pulse until the crème fraîche is just mixed.

Fill a large ceramic or metal mold, or 4 individual ramekins, with the salmon mousse. Cover with plastic wrap and refrigerate. The flavors will mingle better the longer the mousse is refrigerated, so refrigerate overnight if time permits, or for at least 2 hours.

To unmold, dip the bottom and sides of the mold quickly in hot water and then turn it upside down onto a serving plate.

VARIATIONS: Instead of molding the mousse, use a pastry bag fitted with a decorative tip to pipe the mousse into hollowed-out cherry tomatoes or onto individual Belgian endive leaves as an appetizer.

- Peel a cucumber and cut in half crosswise. Hollow-out the seeds from the center. Stuff the mousse down the center of the cucumber and chill until the mousse is firm. Cut the cucumber into ¼-inch slices and serve.

- Other fish and herbs will also make a nice mousse. This is a good way to use up any small pieces of cooked fish or small amounts of herbs that are on hand.

Fennel is available as a vegetable bulb or as an herb plant. The vegetable has bright green, feathery leaves topping a thick, celerylike bulb. The leaves can be used on their own, and the bulb can be prepared as would any rib vegetable. The herb fennel is grown and cultivated in most areas around the United States. It has a delicate anise flavor and for centuries has been a popular culinary and medicinal herb. It has a purple tip and looks similar to dill. Fennel herb grows much taller than the bulb, and its yellow flower has a heavier licorice flavor. Fennel seeds come from the herb.

MONKFISH WITH ROASTED RED PEPPER SAUCE

Monkfish is a very popular fish in Brittany, as it is abundant around our coastal area. It is often called the "poor man's lobster" because of its sweet and firm flesh. Monkfish has a large, oversized head and a tail. The tail is gaining popularity in the United States because it is very well suited for kebobs, stews, and soups.

6 SERVINGS

2 roasted red peppers, peeled, seeded, and cut into 1-inch pieces

4 tablespoons olive oil

2 garlic cloves, peeled and minced

2 tablespoons chopped fresh basil

2 pounds monkfish, cut into 1-inch pieces

6 small onions, peeled and quartered

½ cup fish stock (see Basics, page 377)

Purée the **roasted** peppers in a food processor, along with the olive oil, garlic, and basil. Toss the monkfish in the pepper purée until coated on all sides. Refrigerate for 1 hour.

Soak 6 wooden skewers in water for 10 minutes. On 1 skewer thread 4 pieces of monkfish, alternating with 4 quarters of onion. Prepare the other 5 skewers in the same manner. Place the skewers on a very hot grill and cook for 5 minutes. Turn and continue cooking for 3 minutes.

Meanwhile, combine the pepper purée with the fish stock in a saucepan and heat. Reduce for 2 to 3 minutes, or until the sauce coats the back of a spoon.

To serve, spread a spoonful of sauce on a plate and arrange a skewer of monkfish and onions on top. Pass additional sauce, if desired.

VARIATIONS: Scallops, shrimp, swordfish, or tuna can be grilled in this manner.

- The red pepper sauce lets the strong natural flavor of peppers come clearly through. For a more subtle pepper taste, whisk ½ cup of cream into the sauce before reducing it.

- This can also be prepared by eliminating the skewers and sautéeing on top of the stove.

♥ *Monique's Touch:*

I like to **roast** green or red peppers directly on top of a gas-stove burner. That way I can watch and smell them continuously as they roast. To roast any pepper, either place it directly onto a burner or hot grill (or turn on the broiler at 475°F and place the peppers on a baking sheet 6 inches below the heat). Turn the pepper every few minutes while it scorches. The skin will blister and turn from its original color to black and finally to white ash when it is done. After roasting, immediately put the pepper in a plastic or paper bag. Close the bag tightly and allow the pepper to sweat until cool enough to handle. The skin will rub off easily under cold running water. I like to do several at once and keep extras in my refrigerator or freezer.

GRILLED TUNA SALAD SANDWICH

Many times the farm women of Brittany intermarry with fishermen from the coast. It was through such a marriage that we had a fisherman in our family. My father's cousin Etienne was a deep-sea fisherman who fascinated me as a child with his stories of trawling off coastal waters as far away as Ireland. One day he brought more than stories. Riding behind him on his motorcycle was strapped a huge whole fresh tuna. Tuna was on the menu for several days after that, prepared as a main dish baked in wine with tomatoes or served simply as a salad or sandwich. I have never lost my love of tuna and take great pleasure in cooking it with ingredients I have become acquainted with from other cultures.

6 SERVINGS

3 tablespoons chopped fresh cilantro

3 tablespoons chopped fresh garlic
   chives

6 tablespoons olive oil

2 tablespoons lemon juice

2 tablespoons rice vinegar

1 tablespoon sesame oil

One 1½-pound fresh tuna steak,
   ¾–1 inch thick

1 cucumber, peeled, seeded, and
   diced

½ cup crushed cashew nuts

12 red lettuce leaves

1½ cups alfalfa sprouts

6 pieces pita bread, halved

In a small bowl, mix together the cilantro, garlic chives, olive oil, lemon juice, vinegar, and sesame oil. Cover the tuna with the marinade and set aside for 15 minutes while heating the grill. When the grill is hot, shake the excess marinade off the tuna and grill for 3 minutes. Turn and continue grilling for 4 minutes more. Cool.

Cut tuna into small pieces before crushing it with a fork. Add the cucumber and cashews, mixing well. Heat the marinade until it simmers, then whisk vigorously to thicken. Toss the tuna with the marinade **dressing.**

Fill each of the pita halves with the lettuce leaves and half the alfalfa sprouts. Divide the tuna among the 12 portions, top with the remaining sprouts, and serve.

VARIATIONS: For a cold lunch, serve the tuna salad without the pita bread in the center of a plate lined with cucumber slices.

- Other cooking methods include broiling on the middle rack, searing the tuna in a hot pan on top of the stove, or placing the tuna in a 450°–475°F oven. Each method requires approximately 3 to 5 minutes cooking time per side.

♥ *Monique's Touch:*

Often after marinating foods, I use the marinade as a sauce or **dressing** to accompany the cooked food. Marinades used to flavor vegetables can be served cold without further preparation. However, marinades from meat, fish, or poultry must be heated first to ensure any bacteria from the animal is destroyed. Heat the marinade until boiling, then simmer for 10 minutes before serving.

GRILLED BUTTERFLIED QUAIL WITH GOOSEBERRIES

Gooseberries are grown in every garden in Brittany. Because they are so delicious, I grow them in my garden here, and I am pleased to see gooseberries becoming more popular each year at the farmers' market. Gooseberries have a tartness that is somewhat reminiscent of cranberries. Like cranberries, gooseberries jell well when cooked and cooled. The green or wine-colored berries are about the size of a grape and grow wild on prickly bushes through-out the cooler northern regions of the United States.

6 SERVINGS

12 quails, semiboneless, with the backbone and breastbone removed

6 garlic cloves, peeled and minced

½ cup fresh rosemary needles stripped from stems and stems reserved

2 tablespoons fresh lavender, stems reserved

3 tablespoons chopped fresh thyme, stems reserved

1 tablespoon paprika

½ teaspoon salt

¼ teaspoon pepper

½ cup olive oil

3 dozen plump gooseberries

Butterfly each quail by slitting it with kitchen shears three quarters of the way down the middle of the back so the quail will lie flat.

In a large stainless steel pan or bowl, blend together the garlic, rosemary, lavender, thyme, paprika, salt, pepper, and olive oil. Coat each quail with the marinade and let rest in the pan, refrigerated overnight, or for at least 30 minutes.

Before grilling, soak the herb stems in water for several minutes. Place 2 quails each on 6 long metal skewers. Place on a very hot grill, skin side down, and cook for 5 minutes. Turn and cook for 10 minutes more. Add the soaked herb stems to the coals for the last 5 minutes of cooking to give the quail a smoky flavor.

Thread 6 **gooseberries** each on 6 small metal skewers or on wooden skewers that have been soaked in water for 10 minutes. Grill for about 5 minutes until tender. Serve at once with the quail.

VARIATIONS: Cornish hens, rack of lamb, pork tenderloin, and boneless breast of chicken can be done this way.

- Grilled gooseberries are a good garnish for a green salad or grilled mixed vegetables.

- Roast the quail by placing them in a preheated 400°F oven for 25 to 30 minutes. Add the gooseberries during the last 10 minutes of cooking.

♥ *Monique's Touch:*

Because of the ability of **gooseberries** to jell so well when cooked, I will add a handful to jam if the fruit I'm making the jam with is slightly overripe and soft. Gooseberries firm the jam up, as well as add a nice flavor to other summer berries.

MARINATED GRILLED CHICKEN TENDERS

The tender is the choice morsel of the turkey or chicken breast. Its texture is velvety and its petite size makes the tender perfect for salads, sandwiches, appetizers, or soups. Butchers have taken note of the popularity of tenders and often sell them at needlessly high prices, but you can collect them yourself from breasts prepared for other uses.

6 SERVINGS

¾ cup olive oil
¼ cup lemon juice
4 garlic cloves, peeled and minced
1 tablespoon each chopped fresh
    rosemary, thyme, oregano, fennel
1½ pounds chicken tenders, about
    30 pieces, flattened to ⅛ inch

2 roasted red peppers, seeded,
    peeled, and cut into ½-inch strips
    (see Monique's Touch, page 109)
2 pounds fresh spinach, washed,
    dried, and torn into bite-size
    pieces
1 cup crumbled goat cheese
¼ cup chopped shallots

Mix together the olive oil, lemon juice, garlic, and herbs. Pour the marinade over the chicken **tenders** and let stand for 10 minutes. Drain off the marinade into a saucepan and reserve.

Grill the tenders on a very hot grill for 2 minutes. Meanwhile, heat the marinade to a simmer.

Toss the peppers with the spinach. Place the spinach on a serving platter. Sprinkle the goat cheese and shallots over the greens. Arrange the chicken tenders on top, then drizzle the hot marinade over all and serve.

VARIATIONS: Substitute with turkey tenders, peeled shrimp, or scallops.

- Instead of grilling, chicken tenders may be sautéed on top of the stove in a very hot pan for 5 minutes.

♥ *Monique's Touch:*

I collect breast **tenders** in a zip-lock bag and freeze them until needed. The tender sits along the breastbone underneath the top meat of the breast. If the breast is boned, the tender hangs on the underside of the breast. It can be separated easily by running your finger around the tender and lifting it from the bone.

PASTA SALAD WITH ROASTED GARLIC–BASIL CHICKEN

The roast chicken that is the basis for this pasta salad is wonderful on its own. I often roast two at once and then take one chicken with us on a picnic. With the other I prepare this pasta salad the next day. The carcasses are made into a flavorful chicken stock for soup.

8 SERVINGS

1 head garlic, roasted, pulp reserved (see Sidenote, page 24)

1 cup chopped holly basil or sweet basil

One 3-pound chicken

2 tablespoons olive oil

1 pound rotini pasta, cooked according to package directions

2 cups cooked lima beans

1 cup shredded radicchio

4 scallions, wilted stems and roots trimmed, finely chopped

1 red pepper, diced

1 small yellow summer squash, halved lengthwise and cut into ¼-inch slices

1 small zucchini, halved lengthwise and cut into ¼-inch slices

DRESSING:

⅓ cup balsamic vinegar

⅔ cup olive oil

1 teaspoon Dijon-style mustard

Preheat the oven to 400°F.

Blend the garlic and basil well. Using your fingertips, separate the skin of the chicken from the meat. Spread the garlic basil under the skin, coating as much of the meat as possible. Brush the olive oil on the chicken skin. Place the chicken on a rack in a roasting pan and roast for 45 minutes, or until the **skin** is crisp and the meat has absorbed the flavor of the garlic. Remove from the oven and cool. Remove the skin from the chicken and set aside for soup another day.

Meanwhile, combine the pasta, lima beans, radicchio, scallions, red pepper, squash, and zucchini. Cut the meat from the bone and dice into bite-size pieces. Add the chicken to the pasta salad.

Combine the vinegar, olive oil, and mustard, blending well. Toss the salad with the dressing and serve.

VARIATIONS: To serve hot, combine the diced chicken, beans, radicchio, scallions, red pepper, squash, and zucchini in a sauté pan and cook over medium heat until warm. Combine with the cooked pasta and serve immediately.

- Plain slices of fresh tomato and cucumber are a nice accompaniment when this is served as a main dish.

- Sprinkle with freshly grated Parmesan cheese or crumble feta or goat cheese on top before serving.

♥ *Monique's Touch:*

I like to add the roasted **skin** of chicken or turkey to soup. The fat has already been removed during the roasting process, so the roasted skin adds only good flavor and color to the soup base.

SIDENOTE:
Basil, which is part of the mint family, originated in India and the Middle East, but today it is cultivated in almost every part of the world. Common basil's heady scent and strong flavor are the very essence of summer cooking. Today basil comes in many varieties, giving off entrancing aromas and inviting adventurous palates to explore. Lemon basil, sweet basil, purple basil, and anise basil are just a few of the kinds available all over the country. A favorite of mine, holly basil, is fairly recent. Its unusual flavor is similar to spicy licorice.

ROAST BEEF AND PESTO SOUR CREAM SANDWICH

Pesto is best made in the summer when herbs have a high oil content. Basil pesto is well known, but I also like pesto made with arugula, cilantro, and other leafy herbs. It is a good way to take advantage of the abundant summer harvest of herbs in the garden.

8 SERVINGS

2 pounds beef tenderloin or boneless
   rib roast
3 tablespoons Dijon-style mustard
1 tablespoon crushed black
   peppercorns
1 tablespoon chopped fresh thyme
½ cup pesto

2 cups sour cream or crème fraîche
   (see Basics, page 379)
½ cup cream cheese
2 baguettes, halved lengthwise, each
   half quartered
16 Boston lettuce leaves
16 tomato slices

Preheat the oven to 475°F.

Rub the meat on all sides with the mustard, then sprinkle with the peppercorns and thyme. Place in the preheated oven for 10 minutes, then turn the heat down to 375°F. Continue roasting until preferred doneness: 10 minutes for rare or 20 minutes for medium-rare. Let stand at room temperature until cool before slicing, or refrigerate overnight to make slicing easier.

Whisk together the **pesto,** sour cream or crème fraîche, and cream cheese until light and creamy. Spread each baguette section with pesto sour cream. Layer 8 bread halves as follows: 1 lettuce leaf, 3 to 4 ounces of beef, 2 slices of tomato, another lettuce leaf topped by the remaining baguette half. Serve cold or at room temperature.

♥ *Monique's Touch:*

I make **pesto** in large batches and then freeze it in ice-cube trays. During the cold winter I use the melted cubes on top of hot pasta to boost our spirits when summer seems so far away. To make pesto, combine in a food processor or blender, 1 pound any type fresh leafy herb or combination of herbs, ¼ pound Parmesan cheese, ¼ pound pine nuts or walnuts, 10 garlic cloves, 1 cup olive oil, and 1 teaspoon pepper. Purée until smooth.

PURÉE OF GRILLED EGGPLANT

The species of eggplant I grew up with in Brittany was large, moist, and bitter, reflecting the wet climate we had. Consequently, this recipe came about because our eggplant was often seasoned and puréed to make it more appealing to us as children. Even though the eggplants I use in this country are of a sweeter variety, I still return to this favorite side dish as a different way to serve a summer favorite.

6 SERVINGS

¼ cup salt
4 medium eggplants cut into 1-inch slices
½ cup olive oil

4 garlic cloves, peeled and minced
¼ cup chopped fresh parsley
1 cup toasted bread crumbs
Salt and pepper

Salt the eggplant slices lightly on both sides and set in a strainer to drain for 30 minutes. The salt draws out extra water from the eggplant and keeps the slices from falling apart during cooking. Rinse quickly under cold running water, then pat dry with a towel.

Rub each eggplant slice with olive oil and set on a very hot grill for 1 minute on each side. When cool to the touch, peel off the skins and discard. In a food processor, combine the eggplant with the garlic, parsley, and bread crumbs. Process until the eggplant reaches a smooth spreading consistency. Adjust the seasoning with salt and pepper.

VARIATIONS: Add sesame paste or garbanzo beans for a more Mediterranean flavor.

- Add 1 tablespoon of chopped fresh basil or 1 teaspoon of chopped fresh cilantro.

- Cut the eggplant in half, salt, then drain, cut side down, for 30 minutes. Instead of grilling, roast on a baking sheet in a preheated 450°F oven for 15 minutes.

BASTILLE DAY "POMMES FRITES" FRENCH FRIES

On Bastille Day I could always be found near the booth where vendors hawked the pommes frites, or french fries. By mid-July the first starchy mature potatoes were available from the garden, and it was those knobby, flavorful spuds that produced oddly shaped fries crispy on the outside and creamy on the inside. The french-fry maker sat to the side of the deep-fryer, quickly peeling the potatoes as needed. The pommes frites were made to order and served up hot and salty in cones shaped from yesterday's newspapers.

6 SERVINGS

1 quart peanut oil
8 large baking potatoes
Kosher salt, for seasoning

Heat the peanut oil in a deep 4-quart pan.

Peel the potatoes and cut into ¼-inch slices lengthwise. Stack the slices on top of each other and cut them into ¼-inch sticks. Cover in cold water until ready to use.

Dry one third of the potatoes, leaving the rest in the cold water. Check the heat of the oil by dropping a dried potato into the pan. If the oil sizzles around the edges of the potato, it is hot enough.

Drop the potatoes in the oil and let cook for about 5 minutes. Do not let the potatoes brown.

Lift the potatoes out of the oil and drain in a strainer over a plate. Repeat twice with the remaining potatoes.

When ready to serve, reheat the oil until hot. Cook once more in 3 batches, but this time cook until browned to taste.

Shake well as the potatoes are lifted from the oil. Season with kosher salt and serve immediately.

VARIATIONS: Adapt this recipe to make homemade potato chips. Slice the potatoes crosswise into round ⅛-inch or thinner slices. Wash in a cold-water bath as above and pat dry. Toss the potato slices with 2 tablespoons of peanut oil. Place in a preheated 350°F oven until browned to taste. To serve, put in a brown paper bag, sprinkle with salt, and shake.

BAKED ZUCCHINI FAN

Zucchini was not a vegetable I grew up with, but I fell in love with this versatile summer squash when I worked in a restaurant in the south of France. Upon my arrival in New York in 1965, I went straightaway to visit my first American supermarket. I stared in amazement at the largest zucchini I had ever seen—as long as my arm, as big around as a baseball bat, and available in November! I vowed then and there to someday teach people how to cook foods at the peak of their maturity within their natural growing season.

6 SERVINGS

6 zucchini, about 6 inches long and
   1 inch in diameter
3 medium tomatoes, cut into 12
   slices
2 medium white onions, peeled and
   cut into 12 thin slices

½ cup olive oil
2 tablespoons each chopped basil,
   oregano, and thyme
3 garlic cloves, peeled and minced
Salt and pepper

Holding each zucchini firmly by the stem end, cut lengthwise into thirds starting ½ inch from the stem. Fan the 3 sections, being careful not to break the stem. Place each one on a separate piece of 6 × 9-inch aluminum foil. Keeping the fan shape, insert 2 slices each of tomato and onion between the sections of each zucchini.

In a small mixing bowl, combine the olive oil, herbs, and garlic. Brush the fans with the mixture. Season with salt and pepper. Wrap each zucchini fan tightly and place on the side of a hot grill for 10 minutes.

VARIATIONS: Yellow summer squash can be prepared in the same way.

- Instead of grilling, place the wrapped zucchini on a baking sheet and bake for 10 minutes in a preheated 400°F oven.

- After grilling or baking, crumble feta or goat cheese on top of the fans before serving.

SIDENOTE:
Zucchini, as well as eggplant and other summer squash, absorb a lot of moisture and will swell, depending on the amount of rain or watering they receive on the vine. Smaller squashes render less juice, so are more suitable for baking or grilling.

Large squash are great for adding to soups and stews. Some vine vegetables like cucumber, eggplant, and tomato can be salted to draw out the excess moisture and drained prior to cooking.

A leisurely Sunday at the beach.
Seated, my sisters Danielle (left) *and*
Madeleine (right) *and brother Albert.*
I stand with Maman and Papa.

SUMMER BOUNTY
VEGETABLE SALAD

This is a salad that is truly planned by nature. The vegetables listed are merely suggestions. Take a basket into the garden or to the farmers' market and pick vegetables according to what is seasonally available. Choose a mixture that complements each other in taste, color, and texture.

10 SERVINGS

3 cups water
1 cup each, uncooked:
broccoli florets
green beans, ends trimmed
snow peas, ends and strings removed
carrots, cut into ¼-inch slices
celery, cut into ¼-inch slices
zucchini, cut into ¼-inch slices
yellow squash, cut into ¼-inch slices
cucumber, cut into ¼-inch slices
green onion, cut into ¼-inch slices

red pepper, seeded and cut into
   ¼-inch strips
6 cherry tomatoes

DRESSING:

⅓ cup red wine vinegar
¼ cup chopped fresh parsley
1 tablespoon Dijon-style mustard
2 tablespoons honey
½ cup olive oil
½ cup Gorgonzola cheese

Bring the water to a boil. Drop the broccoli, green beans, and snow peas into the water for 1 minute. Remove with a slotted spoon and plunge immediately into cold running water. Drain. Repeat with the carrots.

Place the cooked **vegetables** and the celery, zucchini, squash, cucumber, green onion, red pepper, and tomatoes into a large salad bowl.

To make the dressing, combine the vinegar, parsley, mustard, and honey in a small mixing bowl. Whisk in the olive oil until all the ingredients are well blended. Drizzle the dressing over the vegetables and crumble the cheese on top. Toss the salad gently and let rest for 30 minutes so the flavors blend.

VARIATIONS: To turn today's vegetable salad into tomorrow's supper, toss any salad that is left with cooked rotini or mostaccioli pasta. Serve at room temperature accompanied by a loaf of crusty French bread.

♥ *Monique's Touch:*

Before cutting **vegetables,** I consider the purpose the vegetables have in the dish I'm preparing. If the vegetables are to be used for seasoning and will be discarded later, I coarsely chop them to expose as much of their insides as possible so all the flavor will leach into the liquid quickly and easily. When the vegetables will be served in soup, stuffing, or sauces, I cut them small and evenly so they will give flavor, cook quickly, and look attractive. When the vegetables are to be served as a main dish or side dish, even cooking time and appearance are important, so I slice them evenly on the diagonal, straight or into small, medium, or large dice.

THREE CABBAGE SUMMER SLAW

Cabbage slaw was a salad served at every Sunday lunch on the farm from mid-July through September. Each week it tasted slightly different, as the taste of the cabbage intensified during the progression of the summer heat. Slaw made with cabbage picked in mid-July has a mild flavor that blends well with honey dressing. By September the taste of the cabbage spoke for itself, so a subtle creamy dressing was often used.

8 SERVINGS

3 cups shredded red cabbage
3 cups shredded green cabbage
3 cups shredded Napa cabbage
3 scallions, wilted stems and roots
  trimmed, chopped
1 cup shredded carrots
½ cup chopped fresh lovage or celery
  leaves

DRESSING:
¼ cup red wine vinegar
2 tablespoons Dijon-style mustard
1 cup honey
½ cup poppy seeds
Freshly ground pepper

In a large mixing bowl, combine the cabbage, scallions, carrots, and lovage or celery leaves.

To make the dressing, blend together the vinegar, mustard, and honey in a small mixing bowl. Season with pepper to taste. Toss the dressing with the cabbage and sprinkle with poppy seeds.

VARIATIONS: To make a creamy dressing for fall cabbage slaw, reduce the amount of honey in the dressing to ¼ cup and replace it with ¾ cup mayonnaise or sour cream.

- The French prefer cabbage slaw that is crisp and dressed at the last moment before serving. For a softer, American-style slaw, mix the dressing with the cabbage 1 or more hours ahead so the cabbage will wilt before serving.

GRATED CARROT SALAD

The French eat carrot salad the same way Americans eat carrot sticks, so a picnic or summer lunch would not be the same without it. Charcuteries throughout France offer several varieties of grated carrot salad during the summer season. Summer carrots are so bright in color and have such a purity of flavor that the salad needs only a simple mustard vinaigrette to keep the carrots tender and to heighten their sweetness.

6 SERVINGS

1 tablespoon Dijon-style mustard
3 tablespoons red or white wine
    vinegar
3 tablespoons finely chopped shallots
⅓ cup peanut oil

6 medium carrots, trimmed, peeled,
    and coarsely grated
½ cup chopped fresh celery leaves
Salt and pepper

In a large serving bowl, whisk together the mustard, vinegar, and shallots. Slowly add the peanut oil while whisking, making sure all the ingredients blend together. Season with salt and pepper.

Add the **grated** carrots and celery leaves to the dressing. Grated carrots have a tendency to become compact, so toss gently to keep the carrots loose, allowing the dressing to distribute evenly. Chill before serving.

VARIATIONS: Add raisins and nuts to taste before tossing with the dressing.

- Grated broccoli stems used in place of carrots is a good use of peeled broccoli stems.

♥ *Monique's Touch:*

Vegetables should be cut for flavor and texture as well as appearance. Carrot salad has more flavor if the carrots are **grated** rather than sliced, because more of the inner carrot is exposed for deeper flavor.

FOURTH OF JULY CHERRY PIE

Cherries are a true food link between my childhood and now. The first thing my grandfather Jamet did after purchasing our farm in the late 1800s was to plant young cherry saplings. By the time I came along, the trees were very tall and irresistible to children for climbing. July brought ripe cherries, which we picked and often made into a dessert tart. Today I celebrate the birthday of my adopted home by making a traditional American pie filled with this favorite fruit from my family home.

Double recipe short pastry dough
(see Basics, page 382)
2 cups pitted cherries, juice reserved
½ cup sugar

3 tablespoons cornstarch
2 teaspoons vanilla extract
1 egg
1 tablespoon milk

Preheat the oven to 400°F.

Divide the short pastry dough in half. Wrap half in plastic and refrigerate until needed. On a lightly floured work surface, roll out one half of the dough 2 inches wider all around than a 9-inch pie tin. Line the tin with dough, trim the edges, and chill for 20 minutes.

In a bowl, combine the cherries, cherry juice, sugar, and cornstarch. Pour the filling into the prepared pie shell. Using a finger, moisten the edge of the piecrust with water.

Roll out the other half of the dough as above and place it on top of the pie. Gently tuck the surplus dough under itself. Crimp tight by pressing the tip of a fork all around the edges, sealing the pie completely. With a sharp knife, cut a cross in the center of the pie to allow the steam to escape during baking.

Beat the egg with the milk. Brush the top of the pie with the egg wash. Bake in the oven for approximately 50 minutes, or until the pie is golden brown. Turn the heat down if the crust begins to brown too quickly. Let cool to room temperature before slicing. Serve with whipped cream or ice cream.

APRICOT TART

Apricots have a short season in Brittany, appearing after Bastille Day and disappearing by the first of August, which makes them all the more desirable. During that time we picked apricots off the tree in the morning and spent the afternoon making jams, preserves, and candied apricots. Many of the apricots were dried for use during the winter months. But at least once during apricot season, Maman would choose the prettiest of the fruit to make into an apricot tart. As she prepared the apricots, we children sat in the courtyard cracking open the pits between two rocks to get at the almond centers. These she added to the tart to give it a nutty texture and to enhance the flavor of the apricots.

8 SERVINGS

½ pound fresh apricots, halved and
    pitted, pits reserved
½ cup sugar
3 tablespoons water
1 tablespoon vanilla extract

Zest of 1 lemon, grated
Juice of 1 lemon
3 eggs
1 recipe sweet short pastry dough,
    blind-baked (see Basics, page 384)

With a nutcracker, crack the apricot pits and remove the centers, discarding the pit shell. Break the centers, called almonds, into small pieces. Toast in a pan over medium heat. Grind the apricot almonds in a food processor and reserve.

Place the apricot halves in a saucepan with the sugar and water. Cover and cook over low heat for about 5 minutes, or until the apricots become slightly soft. Reserve half the apricots in a bowl and cook the rest until very soft, about 10 minutes more.

Purée the very soft apricots and blend with the ground nuts, vanilla, lemon zest, lemon juice, and eggs. Set over medium heat for 5 minutes until thick. Do not boil.

Pour the apricot purée into the tart shell and arrange the reserved apricot halves on top. Refrigerate until ready to serve.

VARIATIONS: Apricot filling can be used as a sauce served over ice cream.

- Instead of thickening the filling with eggs, 1 tablespoon of cornstarch may be substituted by diluting it in the lemon juice, then adding the mixture to the apricot purée.

AUGUST

*Neighbors and family gather on our farm
to help bring in the August harvest.*

August is the crescendo in the symphony that is the culinary year. After months of anticipation the foods of August burst over the peak and over-whelm us with brilliant color, big tastes, and wild abundance. What started out as a trickle in June, with baby carrots, new potatoes, and young leafy greens, has built up into a tumbling profusion of full-flavored variety. There are dozens of choices of tomatoes, zucchini, summer squash, star-shaped pattypan, shiny purple eggplant, flat-leaf spinach, romaine lettuce, Boston lettuce, summer cabbage, torrid red or flashy golden peppers, beans of every type, beets the size of baseballs, and carrots so sweet their only rival is the corn that becomes an American passion toward the end of the month. The air is redolent with flourishing basil, oregano, tarragon, and rosemary. Juicy watermelon, cantaloupe, fat blueberries, muskmelon, sunny nectarines, and silky peaches—nature pro-duces so much, the challenge to find ways to cook it all pales against the challenge of con-suming it all.

The pace on the farm accelerated to near frantic speed during August. Besides the ex-plosion taking place in the garden, the wheat fields stood golden and ready to harvest. A feeling of urgency to get the crop in was triggered when we heard the dry rustle of the stalks in the wind, reminding us that should the rains come before our task was complete, winter would be hard. Papa set up a schedule among the neighbors to work each farm in turn. As always with farm life we were already moving ahead to the next season, de-pending on each other to make the journey smooth.

A big horse-drawn cutter felled the wheat with a razorlike motion. Afterward the wheat was gathered up and tied into bundles, then stacked one against the other in groups of five or six. There it stayed until the entire crop was cut and stacked. As quickly as possible a wagon jolted through the fields to gather the bundles and brought them to the courtyard of the farm. The thresher began the work of separating the grain from the chaff, and the whole courtyard became dusty from all the hay and straw being thrown about. Nothing was wasted, so the children began gathering up the straw that would be used in the fall to press the cider and in the winter to line our wooden shoes to keep us warm, or to lay over the winter vegetables to protect them from frost. The hay was saved for feeding the animals. The chaff of grain made mattresses and pillows. The grain was stored in the attic above the barn, eventually to be sold for flour and sent to the mill. Instead of money, Maman received coupons in exchange for grain from the baker, which we used later on to get bread.

During August the women in the village had to prepare meals to feed the dozens of men who worked the harvest. Between meals they also began the task of putting up the summer vegetables, making the pickles, jams, and chutneys that would be eaten later in the winter. Because Maman didn't want to spend any more time in the kitchen than was necessary and time was fairly short, the preparation of meals changed during late summer. She relied on the beautiful full flavors of the fruits and vegetables to speak for themselves. Summer fish, full grown and heavy with flavor, were caught in the morning, lightly poached with a sprig or two of tarragon, and served without sauces. Summer meats were generally an assortment of cold cuts from the beautiful hams smoked the previous fall or pâtés put up during the winter. They were delicious garnished only with sliced tomato sprinkled with chopped basil. Salads of grated carrot or celery root were simply dressed with vinegar and oil because the sweetness of the roots needed no additional help to satisfy the appetite. Maman fed twenty-four workers a day from the big courtyard table throughout the month of August, but she spent less time in the kitchen than at any other time of the year.

Today we may not feed dozens of farmhands, but we have our own need to understand how to cook for large numbers quickly. Summer is a time when many weekends are spent entertaining large groups of friends in our backyards. August cooking, more than any other time of year, dispenses with rules and relies on the generosity of the harvest to provide just the right meals. My criteria for whether or not a dish is on the summer menu correlates closely with my mother's. It's warm, the weather is fine, so who wants to be in the kitchen? Is it fast, easy, and will it satisfy the appetites of my guests? By using the seasonal flavors of foods and serving them as close to fresh as possible, I find all my demands are met. The grill is a fabulous tool to help us do this. Fish, vegetables, poultry, and most meats take grilling well, and it's so easy to throw extra vegetables on the grill one evening to use later in the week for sandwiches or perhaps a summer soup. Cold grilled meats can be cut up and served later with fresh greens to make a meal out of a salad. All that's necessary is a little planning, which can be done with the help of the producers at your local farmers' market.

The farmers' market is where I go today to recapture the sense of community and sharing that came naturally during the August hay harvest. Just as the farmers of our village liked to admire and compare each other's harvests, every grower I meet is proud to talk about how he or she grows an unusual lettuce, how the spring weather affected this year's crop of beans, or about the process used to make his or her own handmade cheeses. The producers are eager to share the joy of a good harvest. Take advantage of their expertise by asking questions about how to choose fruits and vegetables to get the maximum flavor and enjoyment from the meals you serve to family and friends. At the farmers' market, ask them to let you touch, taste, and smell their product. They will teach you to look not only at the size but also at the color and feel of an eggplant to help make a decision as to whether it's too ripe with moisture for the grill but perfect for a saucy ratatouille. The producers will teach you how to tell the difference between a melon ripe for eating today and one that will be ready when you want to serve it later in the week with a pasta salad made from grilled vegetables cooked that evening. If you take the time to ask questions, soon you will be able to visit the market and plan a week's worth of menus on the spot, depending on what's fresh and available at the moment. Experiment with the unfamiliar. Farmers' markets are often the only place to find specialty sausages, fresh herbs and edible flowers, wild game, indigenous mushrooms, homemade jams and jellies, or fruits and vegetables found only in your area. August is the month to try them all.

While you are asking questions, the farmers will be learning from you as well. They want to know what you think of what is being grown and what tastes good to you. Most farmers live on their farms year-round, so coming into the city once a week teaches them what urban shoppers are interested in. Perhaps the grower you go to for potatoes will try a new species next year if you let him know you are curious to have it. Often the farmers at the market live for the rest of the year on what they can sell during the summer. They want to please you as much as you want to learn from them. The farmers' market is a community exchange. We benefit from each farmer's expertise, and he benefits from our opinion so he'll know what to grow in the coming season. It is all a matter of understanding the progression from field to table while always looking forward.

AUGUST RECIPES

Grilled Vegetables and Goat Cheese Soup

Sweet Corn Soup with Dill

Cold Summer Tomato Bisque

Baked Lobster à la Bretonne

Cotriade Stew

Sautéed Cod and Shrimp with Flageolets

Herb Ravioli with Shrimp and Fennel

Lamb and Vegetable Brochette

Pork Tenderloin with Tomato Relish

Cider Sausage

Cheese-Stuffed Tomatoes on the Grill

Celery Root Rémoulade

Creamy Summer Spinach and Peaches

Couscous-Stuffed Vegetables

Tomato Fondant with Macaroni

Mediterranean Ratatouille

Classic Summer Corn on the Cob

Blackberry Cobbler

Peach Compote

Glazed Fresh Figs

Breton Pudding

SUPPER UNDER THE STARS

Sweet Corn Soup with Dill

Baked Lobster à la Bretonne

Couscous-Stuffed Vegetables

Muscadet

Creamy Summer Spinach and Peaches

Cheese and Summer Fruit Tray

Blackberry Cobbler

Pinot Grigio

GRILLED VEGETABLES AND GOAT CHEESE SOUP

This is a summer soup recipe that came about because I grilled too many vegetables one afternoon when I was entertaining. Now, whenever I have the grill hot, I throw on extra vegetables so I can make this soup the next day. It is versatile because all vegetables work well in it, and I like it because it is so quick to make.

6 SERVINGS

1 teaspoon freshly ground pepper
¼ cup olive oil
1 red pepper, halved
2 zucchini, halved
1 large tomato, halved
3 scallions, wilted stems and roots
   trimmed

1 tablespoon chopped fresh thyme
2 cups chicken stock (see Basics,
   page 375)
1 cup crumbled goat cheese
1 lemon, cut into 6 wedges

Heat the grill until very hot. Combine the pepper and olive oil in a pan.

Brush the vegetables with the oil, coating all sides well. Place on the grill about 3 minutes and turn. Grill until soft, about another 2 minutes. Watch carefully, as the time will vary by vegetable, with the red pepper taking the longest, followed by the zucchini, tomato, and scallions.

Place the vegetables and thyme in a food processor along with the chicken stock, and purée until the vegetables are bite-size. Transfer to a saucepan and heat the soup until bubbling. Add the goat cheese, stirring until melted. Adjust the seasoning, if necessary, and serve at once with the lemon wedges.

VARIATIONS: Any summer vegetable available can be added to the soup. This is a good way to use up vegetables that will otherwise overripen or to use grilled vegetables left from a previous meal.

- Swiss or feta cheese melts easily and gives a nice flavor to grilled vegetable purée.

- The vegetables may be broiled on the middle rack of the oven for the same amount of time.

- To give the soup a smooth texture, completely purée the vegetables, then pass through a fine strainer before heating.

SIDENOTE:

The goat cheese available year-round in the dairy section of the market is often imported French goat cheese, which is different from fresh goat cheese made here. French goat cheese is aged, giving it a strong, musty flavor that Americans sometimes find overpowering. Fresh goat cheese is made locally and sold at farmers' markets throughout the season. Its taste is sweeter than its French cousin. Fresh goat cheese can give a creamy texture to dishes without competing with the strong summer flavors vegetables naturally have. When buying French goat cheese, the shape of the package indicates the strength of the cheese. Cheeses sold in pyramid-shape boxes have a strong taste and aroma, while logs of goat cheese indicate a sweeter taste and creamier texture.

SWEET CORN SOUP WITH DILL

Big swishy bunches of dill and beautiful summer corn arrive at about the same time at the farmers' market, so the flavors of this soup seem to me a natural combination. Take time to stroll through the farmers' market to see what is available concurrently, then devise your own taste combinations to make creative summer soups.

6 SERVINGS

4 ears fresh corn on the cob, husk
   and silk removed
1 tablespoon safflower oil
1 white onion, peeled and diced
3 garlic cloves, peeled and minced
1 teaspoon dillseeds
1 large tomato, peeled, seeded, and
   coarsely chopped

3 cups chicken stock (see Basics,
   page 375)
2 scallions, wilted ends and roots
   trimmed, chopped
2 tablespoons chopped fresh dill
Salt and pepper

With a sharp knife, remove the corn kernels from the cob.

Heat the oil in a saucepan and sauté the onion until translucent. Add the garlic and dillseeds, stirring until the dill aroma is released. Add the corn, tomato, and chicken stock, then bring to a boil. Lower the heat to a simmer for 5 minutes. Add the scallions and dill. Adjust the seasoning with salt and pepper. Serve at once.

VARIATIONS: Use leftover grilled corn and substitute cilantro and hot pepper flakes for the fresh dill and dillseeds for a southwestern flavor.

- Purée half of the vegetables and then mix them back into the soup to give it a chowder texture.

COLD SUMMER TOMATO BISQUE

Originally a bisque referred to a hot soup made from the liquor of shellfish in a thick cream base. Today we extend our definition of what a bisque is to include any number of ingredients that are rich in flavor. Whether using fruit or vegetables, today's bisques achieve their traditional velvety texture by balancing the amount of pulp, juice, and yogurt in a recipe. This gives a satisfying consistency without using cream.

6 SERVINGS

1 small onion, peeled and diced
2 stalks celery heart, with leaves, diced
4 tablespoons chopped fresh cilantro
1 cup yogurt

6 large tomatoes
Zest of 2 lemons, grated
Juice of 2 lemons
½ cup chopped celery leaves
Salt and pepper

In a food processor, purée the onion, celery stalks, and cilantro. Add the yogurt and process until mixed. Pass the mixture through a fine strainer, pressing as much pulp and juice through as possible. Discard the remaining fibers. Transfer to a bowl.

Purée the tomatoes and strain, discarding the tomato fiber. Add to the onion, celery stalks, and cilantro. Add the lemon zest, lemon juice, celery leaves, and salt and pepper to taste. Blend together until smooth. Add more yogurt, if desired, to thicken the soup. Cover and refrigerate for at least 4 hours. Mix well before serving.

VARIATIONS: Cucumber dill bisque can be made the same way. Omit the tomatoes and cilantro, replacing them with 2 cucumbers and the same amount of dillweed.

- Replace the celery stalks and cilantro with equal amounts of fennel and fennel weed.

- A half teaspoon of curry powder will warm the tomato bisque in the mouth, while a pinch of cayenne pepper will make it spicy.

BAKED LOBSTER À LA BRETONNE

Breton lobster was always a favorite treat served on special occasions in our home, and I am delighted to have wonderful Maine lobsters available to continue this tradition with my family here. I have always been attracted to Maine because it reminds me so much of Brittany. The rocky terrain, the rough simplicity of the local food, and the tough independence of the people of Maine always seem to me a balancing counterpart to the Bretons who live almost directly across the Atlantic. I like this recipe because it reflects the cultural food link shared by both people.

6 SERVINGS

3 live Maine lobsters, approximately
   1½–2 pounds each
1 medium onion, peeled and
   coarsely chopped
1 garlic clove, peeled and halved

1 tablespoon chopped fresh thyme
1 cup heavy cream
¼ cup applejack
½ teaspoon freshly ground pepper

Preheat the oven to 450°F.

Split the lobsters in half lengthwise. Remove the fingertip-size sandbag located near the eye and discard. The thick gray-green substance also found in the body is the liver, called tomalley. Spoon out the tomalley and place in the bowl of a food processor.

Add the onion, garlic, and thyme to the tomalley and process until well blended. Continue processing while slowly adding the cream, applejack, and pepper.

Brush the lobster meat with the tomalley sauce. Place the lobsters, split side up, on a baking sheet and set in the oven for 12 minutes, or until the tops are golden and the tomalley sauce has turned pink.

SIDENOTE:
Lobsters are expensive, so it is helpful to know their differences.

Maine lobster:
Sporting huge, delicious claws, the Maine lobster is actually caught in waters from Maine to the Carolinas. Found inside the female where the tail and body meet is the roe, also called coral. The roe reddens during cooking, adding sweetness and flavor. One- to two-pound lobsters have the best flavor.

Spiny lobster:

Also called rock lobster, it is found in warm waters of the Pacific, near Asia, and off the coast of Florida. Spiny lobster has extra long antennae but no claws. Since most of its meat is in the tail, it is the lobster used for lobster tail dishes. Because it can be tough, the spiny lobster usually comes to us frozen.

My youngest brother, Albert, watching the wheat harvest.

COTRIADE STEW

Cotriade is a fish stew from Britanny that uses whatever fresh fish is at hand to give it an endless variation of flavors. On the farm we would often add freshwater river eel to the pot, along with the fish and shellfish caught off the coast that morning. The same recipe can be modified to reflect the fish available in local areas.

6 SERVINGS

1 large onion, peeled and cut into 6 wedges

3 leeks, tough ends trimmed, halved lengthwise

2 tablespoons olive oil

1 pound small potatoes, peeled and quartered

1 sachet (see Basics, page 374)

2 quarts court bouillon (see Basics, page 378)

1 pound strong fish, such as mackerel, eel, or tuna, cut into 1-inch pieces

1 pound mild fish, such as monkfish, cod, or bass, cut into 1-inch pieces

12 clams, rinsed

4 tablespoons unsalted butter

6 slices country bread

3 garlic cloves, peeled and crushed

2 tablespoons chopped fresh parsley

In a large pot, sauté the onion and leeks about 1 minute, until soft but not brown. Add the potatoes, sachet, and court bouillon. Bring to a boil and simmer for about 10 minutes, or until the potatoes can be pierced with a fork but remain firm.

Add the stronger-flavored fish to the pot. Add the milder fish after 3 minutes and continue to simmer for 5 minutes more. Add the clams and cook until they open, about 5 minutes. Discard any unopened clams. Remove the fish and clams, and divide among 6 serving bowls. Continue to simmer the broth for 10 minutes, reducing it by one third.

Meanwhile, melt the butter in a pan. Brown both sides of the bread until golden. Rub the toasted bread slices with the crushed garlic. Place a slice of bread in each of the serving bowls. Ladle the broth over the bread and fish, sprinkle with parsley, and serve.

VARIATIONS: A popular variation of cotriade is to add crushed tomatoes along with the fish.

- Cut the fish and vegetables into spoon-size pieces. Finish with 1 cup of cream whisked into the broth before serving. This gives cotriade a consistency more like New England clam chowder and is a filling cold-weather variation.

SAUTÉED COD AND SHRIMP
WITH FLAGEOLETS

By August fresh green beans had disappeared off the Sunday lunch table, replaced by fresh kidney beans, known as flageolets in France. Flageolets have been difficult to find in the United States until recently. In the last few years home gardeners began cultivating them for their delicate flavor. They are beginning to be seen more often at the farmers' market, but if you can't find them, try this recipe with regular kidney beans, fava beans, or lima beans.

6 SERVINGS

1 quart water	Six 5-ounce cod fillets
3 cups fresh flageolet beans, shelled	¼ pound small shrimp, peeled
4 slices day-old sourdough bread	Juice of 2 lemons
3 tablespoons peanut oil	1 cup Muscadet or dry white wine
4 tablespoons unsalted butter	3 tablespoons chopped fresh chives

Bring the water to a boil and add the beans. Lower to a simmer for 15 minutes, or until the beans are tender. Drain and return to the pot to keep warm.

In a sauté pan, brown the bread in the peanut oil until golden. Process the bread into crumbs with a food processor. Toss the beans with the **bread crumbs** and arrange on a serving platter.

In the same pan, melt the butter and sauté the cod for 2 minutes on each side. Arrange the fillets on top of the beans. Quickly sauté the shrimp until they turn pink and transfer to the top of the fillets.

Add the lemon juice, Muscadet or dry white wine, and chives to the pan, swirling for 2 minutes. Drizzle over the cod, shrimp, and beans, and serve.

VARIATIONS: An assortment of fish, such as trout, bass, catfish, and scrod, can be prepared as above.

♥ *Monique's Touch:*

Most people think of **bread crumbs** as a breading or an au gratin–style topping. However, I often use bread crumbs as a thickener for sauce. Bread is made up of flour and water, and flour is one of the basic thickeners used by all cooks. Mixing fresh bread with the natural juices of meat, fish, poultry, or vegetables helps to absorb the juice, dampening the bread, so it releases the flour that slightly thickens the dish.

HERB RAVIOLI WITH SHRIMP AND FENNEL

Maman knew how to pair whatever ingredients she had on hand to extend small amounts of ordinary everyday fare into a spectacular-tasting meal. One way she did this was by balancing two foods with strong flavors with a starch, as I'm doing with the shrimp, fennel, and ravioli in this recipe. Not only does the ravioli tame the strong tastes of the shrimp and fennel, it is also an inexpensive way to make less serve more.

6 SERVINGS

2 fennel bulbs, thinly sliced
4 shallots, peeled and thinly sliced
2 tablespoons olive oil
½ pound shrimp, cleaned and peeled
2 cups mixed fresh oregano, basil, thyme, and tarragon, stems removed
3 garlic cloves, peeled and minced

½ teaspoon fennel seeds, crushed
2 pounds cheese ravioli, cooked according to package directions, drained, and kept warm
2 tablespoons unsalted butter
½ cup bread crumbs
Salt and pepper

In a large pan, sauté the fennel and shallots in the oil until tender but not brown. Remove from the pan.

Add the shrimp, herbs, garlic, and fennel seeds to the pan. Cook for 5 minutes, or until the shrimp turn pink. Add back the fennel and shallots along with the ravioli. Toss well together until warmed through. Season to taste with salt and pepper before transferring to a serving platter.

In a separate pan, melt the butter and add the bread crumbs, tossing until they are toasted. Sprinkle over the top of the ravioli and serve.

VARIATIONS: Instead of ravioli, use red or white waxy potatoes with the shrimp. Peel and dice 6 medium potatoes and boil in water about 15 minutes until soft. Proceed as directed.

- Either variation can be served cold with a green salad for a complete lunch or light supper.

LAMB AND VEGETABLE BROCHETTE

Even though we all spent a great deal of time outdoors in the summer, grilling was not a cooking method we used frequently in Brittany. Today life there is quite different, and grilling is enjoyed by people with a more leisurely lifestyle. Still, a taste for dishes that in the past were slow-stewed is strong. I often take old recipes for stews and adapt them for grilling. The cubed meat and vegetables that went into the stews now go on the kebob skewers, and the other ingredients go into marinades that bring out a similar purity of flavors and freshness found in slow-cooking stews.

6 SERVINGS

6 garlic cloves, peeled and minced
1 cup olive oil
1 tablespoon freshly ground black
    pepper
¼ cup chopped fresh oregano
½ cup chopped fresh mint leaves

2 pounds boneless leg of lamb, cut
    into 1-inch cubes
12 cherry tomatoes
2 small zucchini, each cut into 6
    pieces
6 small onions, peeled and quartered

Mix the garlic, olive oil, pepper, oregano, and mint in a shallow pan. Add the lamb and stir to coat the pieces. Refrigerate for at least 1 hour. For the best mingling of flavors, **marinate** in the refrigerator overnight.

Using wooden skewers soaked in water for 10 minutes, skewer 3 pieces of lamb, alternating with each of the vegetables until 6 brochettes are prepared. Place on a very hot grill for 3 minutes. Turn, grill for 3 minutes more. Serve from the grill.

VARIATIONS: This is an all-purpose marinade that complements pork, beef, fish, shellfish, and chicken.

- Brochettes can be broiled 4 inches from the heat source for the same
  amount of time.

♥ *Monique's Touch:*

I rarely **marinate** vegetables in the same pan as meat. I like to keep the true flavors of the vegetables separate from the meat, especially in the summer, when they are at the peak of the season and their tastes don't need enhancing.

PORK TENDERLOIN WITH TOMATO RELISH

August was always one of my favorite months on the farm because of the variety of vegetables we had for the table. But it is also a very insistent month. Along with the variety of produce August offers, it also brings abundance. Something had to be done with the large amount of fruits and vegetables that were picked nearly every day. It was during August that the women in my family put up relishes, chutneys, and pickles. But we didn't spend a lot of time processing jars over a hot stove in August heat. The easiest way to put up condiments is to pickle them by mixing the ingredients in an acidic liquid like lemon juice or vinegar. They keep for weeks in the refrigerator and are a nice accompaniment to roasted meat.

6 SERVINGS

RELISH:

1 cup diced tomato
½ cup diced red pepper
½ cup diced green pepper
½ cup diced cucumber
1 tablespoon chopped jalapeño
   pepper
¼ cup minced fresh cilantro

½ cup minced scallions
2 tablespoons cider vinegar
2 tablespoons fresh lime juice
2 teaspoons grated lime zest

TENDERLOIN:

3 tablespoons olive oil
3 pork tenderloins, ¾ pound each

Combine all the ingredients for the relish in a bowl and chill, covered, for 1 hour, or make the relish ahead of time and refrigerate for up to 2 weeks. The longer it is kept, the more fully the flavors develop and blend.

Brush the tenderloins with olive oil on both sides and cook over a hot grill for 4 minutes. Give a quarter turn and grill for 4 minutes more. Repeat until each tenderloin has been grilled all around and is slightly pink inside.

Spoon some of the relish on the bottom of a serving platter. Slice the tenderloins 1 inch thick and place on top of the relish. Serve, passing more of the relish.

VARIATIONS: The relish can be used as a marinade for the tenderloin. Purée part of the relish and rub it over the meat before refrigerating overnight.

- One-inch-thick tuna steak, grilled until the middle is pink and the outside scored, is an excellent choice for a fish variation.

- Pork tenderloin may be seared on all sides in a hot pan on top of the stove and then finished in preheated 450°F oven for 15 minutes.

A neighbor distributes bread from his wagon during a wedding feast.

CIDER SAUSAGE

During the grain harvest the big table outside was often set with this particular dish because it was substantial enough to satisfy the large appetites of the field-workers. In the summer, cider sausages were usually served with a selection of steamed garden vegetables, a green salad, a variety of cheeses, and a bottle of good red table wine. In the winter, they were always served next to a mound of mashed potatoes. Maman would make a well in the center of the potatoes and fill it with the sauce for us to dip the sausages in. I still serve it this way to my grown sons. For my family, cider sausages are the ultimate comfort food that can be enjoyed year-round.

6 SERVINGS

2 quarts water, lightly salted
12 fresh garlic sausages
2 medium onions, peeled and quartered
4 garlic cloves, peeled
4 tablespoons unsalted butter
1 quart apple cider

Bring the water to a boil, then lower the **sausages** into the pot. Simmer for 5 minutes. Drain.

Purée the onions and garlic cloves in a food processor.

Melt the butter in a pan and sauté the sausages until brown on all sides. Remove from the pan and keep warm. Discard the excess fat and add the onions and garlic, stirring for 1 minute, just until the onions begin to give up their moisture. Add the cider and simmer for 10 minutes to reduce by half. Add the sausages back to the pan and heat for 5 minutes more.

VARIATIONS: A variation of this recipe substitutes dark bock beer for the cider. Serve the sausages with braised cabbage.

♥ *Monique's Touch:*

I always buy my **sausages** fresh from a butcher rather than using commercial brands sold in the market. Butchers take great pride in their sausage recipes, and each one usually has several unique varieties made with pure meats and different flavorings, like garlic or fennel. I stop by the butcher about once every three months and buy several pounds of sausages or other meats I need at the same time. I then freeze everything in amounts large enough for a meal and use them as needed.

Fireplace in the kitchen of the manoir. As a newlywed
Maman used it for cooking before she moved to a cottage
with a similar fireplace on the family property.

CHEESE-STUFFED TOMATOES ON THE GRILL

I learned this technique for stuffing tomatoes as a young woman when I interned at a restaurant in the French Alps. They are easy to prepare in advance and always make a lovely presentation next to grilled fish or meat. It is a good way to use very ripe or odd-shaped tomatoes.

6 SERVINGS

6 large whole tomatoes, peeled (see
   Sidenote, page 86)
2 tablespoons chopped fresh parsley
1 scallion, wilted stems and roots
   trimmed, minced

½ cup bread crumbs
1½ cups crumbled blue cheese
3 tablespoons olive oil
Salt and pepper

For each tomato, cut a slice from the bottom large enough to expose the seeds inside. With your hands, gently squeeze the seeds out and discard.

Combine the parsley, scallion, bread crumbs, cheese, and oil. Salt and pepper to taste. Fill each hollow tomato with the cheese mixture.

Place the tomatoes, one at a time, top down, on a clean towel. Twist the towel until it is tight around the tomato. Squeeze it gently to extract the juice and shape the tomato into a round ball. This will enclose the stuffing without crushing the tomato. Wrap all the tomatoes together in one piece of aluminum foil, sealing the edges tightly to trap heat and steam inside. Place on the grill for 10 minutes.

VARIATIONS: Other cheeses that can be substituted for blue cheese are goat, feta, ricotta, or a mixture of all three.

- Vary the stuffing texture and taste by mixing in walnuts, pine nuts, or pesto, or by adding in a tablespoon of herbs.

- After wrapping the tomatoes in foil, they may be placed in a baking dish, uncovered, in a preheated 450°F oven for 10 minutes.

CELERY ROOT RÉMOULADE

When it was too warm for hot foods, Maman invited everyone for a cold lunch. She made a variety of salads, along with a selection of cold pâtés and meats. The shady courtyard of our house provided a pleasant setting for passing the afternoon over a casual meal. Celery root rémoulade was always on the table and continues to be a favorite with my family today.

6 SERVINGS

3 whole celery roots
1 lemon, halved
½ cup crème fraîche (see Basics, page 379)

2 tablespoons Dijon-style mustard
¼ cup cider vinegar
1 cup Monique's Mayonnaise (see Basics, page 380)

Peel the celery roots and immediately rub with the lemon to prevent darkening. Cut the lemon halves into thin slices.

Grate the celery root with the coarse side of a grater and cover it, along with the lemon slices, with cold water for 20 minutes. Drain well, discard the lemon, and pat the celery root dry.

Mix the crème fraîche, mustard, vinegar, and mayonnaise in a bowl. Add all the celery root at once. Mix well and refrigerate until ready to serve.

SIDENOTE:

The celery root is in the same family as celery, but it forms a tuber at the bottom, which common celery does not. Along with parsley root and parsnip, it is the earliest of root vegetables to make an appearance in late August. It is available fresh through the end of September and stores well for the winter.

CREAMY SUMMER SPINACH AND PEACHES

Even with modern transportation and refrigeration, some local culinary items do not travel well and become specialties in the area where they are grown. Here in the Midwest, peach lovers look forward all summer long to silky sweet white peaches from Michigan. The anticipation reaches a crescendo by the middle of August as we wait each week to see if the weather has been fine enough for the farmers to harvest this wonderful treat. The peaches make an appearance at the farmers' markets and grocery stores for a week or two, during which time we eat as many as we can hold; then they are gone. Like the summer that brings them, the white peach season is never long enough. Here peaches are combined with the unusual choice of summer spinach. The tastes complement each other because the mild flavor of the spinach brings out the sweetness of the peaches.

6 SERVINGS

2 pounds fresh summer spinach, cleaned, stemmed, and covered in cold water

4 ripe peaches, peeled (see Sidenote, page 86), pitted, and coarsely chopped

Juice of 1 lemon
Salt and pepper
Freshly ground nutmeg

Heat a large pan until very hot. Taking a handful of spinach at a time out of the water, shake well, then add to the pan. Quickly repeat with the rest of the spinach, letting it steam as it hits the pan.

As soon as the leaves are wilted, transfer to a clean kitchen towel and squeeze out as much moisture as possible. When cool, coarsely chop the spinach.

Over medium heat, combine the peaches and spinach, and gently toss until heated through. Season with the lemon juice, salt and pepper, and nutmeg to taste. Serve at once.

VARIATIONS: The word "creamy" in the title refers to the texture the peaches give the spinach when heated together. A true cream spinach can be made by adding ¼ cup of cream to the peaches and spinach while heating.

- For an elegant soup, take the recipe above one step further. After combining the peaches and spinach, add 3 cups chicken stock. Heat through and serve.

SIDENOTE:

Summer spinach is harvested mid- to late summer. It has a flat leaf and mild flavor that contrasts with the strong-tasting, curly leaf spring crop. To stem both types of spinach, fold each leaf in half with the underside facing out. Pull down gently on the stem.

COUSCOUS-STUFFED VEGETABLES

August vegetables are beautiful to look at, so I like to present them in ways to show off their natural shapes and colors. Stuffed vegetables allow me to do that. Not only do they look nice on the table, but since little cutting or sautéeing is involved in the preparation, I don't have to spend long hours in the kitchen.

6 SERVINGS

3 medium green peppers
6 medium tomatoes
3 medium yellow squash
3 cups chicken stock (see Basics, page 375)
2 cups couscous
Zest of 2 lemons, grated
Juice of 2 lemons
¼ cup olive oil

6 tablespoons chopped fresh basil
2 tablespoons chopped fresh parsley
½ cup raisins
½ cup toasted pine nuts
6 garlic cloves, minced
4 scallions, chopped
½ cup white wine
Salt

Preheat the oven to 375°F, then prepare the vegetables.

Peppers: Cut ½ inch off the stem end and finely chop that piece. Scoop the seeds and white membrane out of the peppers and discard.

Tomatoes: Cut ½ inch off the top of each tomato and set aside. Scoop out the pulp and seeds. Strain, reserving the juice but discarding the pulp and seeds. Salt the inside of the tomatoes and turn upside down on a plate to drain. This will help the tomatoes hold their shape during baking. Chop the tomato tops and drain.

Squash: Cut each in half lengthwise and scoop out the center pulp and reserve.

Bring 2 cups chicken stock to boil. Stir in the couscous, immediately remove from the heat, and cover. Let stand until all the liquid is absorbed, about 5 minutes.

In a large bowl, mix together the reserved pepper and tomato tops, squash pulp, and tomato juice. Add the lemon zest, lemon juice, olive oil, basil, parsley, raisins, pine nuts, garlic, and scallions. With a fork, mix in the couscous.

Stuff the tomato shells, peppers, and squash two thirds full and place in a baking dish. Pour the remaining cup of chicken stock and the wine in the bottom of the dish, cover tightly with aluminum foil, and bake for 20 minutes.

To serve, cut the peppers in half and arrange with the other vegetables on a large platter. Can be served hot, at room temperature, or cold.

VARIATIONS: Other vegetables suitable for stuffing are zucchini, eggplant, red peppers, or the first late summer cabbages. For a beautiful presentation, mix vegetables together, keeping color balance in mind.

- Diced bread or rice can be used as stuffing instead of couscous.

Carrying home spring trout strung on a willow branch after a morning of fishing on our river.

TOMATO FONDANT
WITH MACARONI

Because August tomatoes are so intense in flavor, this is a quick sauce that takes little fussing over in the kitchen. Fondant means "melt" in French, and that is what is done to this sauce. It is not completely cooked, but heated just enough to evaporate the moisture from the tomatoes and make it spoonable, melting all the elements together. Tomato fondant depends on using tomatoes that have come into full flavor, so it is perfect for overripe tomatoes that won't slice without falling apart.

6 SERVINGS

6 shallots, peeled and chopped
2 tablespoons olive oil
6 large tomatoes, peeled, seeded, and chopped (see Sidenote, page 86)
4 garlic cloves, peeled and minced

½ cup chopped fresh parsley
1½ pounds elbow macaroni, cooked according to package directions
Salt and pepper

In a large pan, sauté the shallots in the olive oil until translucent but not brown. Add the tomatoes and garlic, stirring gently. Lower the heat and simmer, uncovered, for 15 minutes, or until the moisture evaporates and the tomatoes are dry but soft. Add the parsley and season with salt and pepper to taste.

Serve over the hot macaroni.

VARIATIONS: Tomato fondant can be served over great northern white beans or boiled potatoes.

MEDITERRANEAN RATATOUILLE

Ratatouille is a dish that has traveled many places from its original home in the south of France. You can find similar dishes all over the world created by cooks using vegetables that are indigenous to their particular area. The summer here allows us to do the same, using whatever vegetables appeal to us as we shop during the week. The secret to good ratatouille is to balance the flavors and amounts so that no one vegetable takes over the dish. Each bite should be a concert of taste and texture, allowing the vegetables to blend equally.

6 SERVINGS

3 tablespoons olive oil
1 medium onion, peeled and diced
1 red pepper, sliced
1 green pepper, sliced
3 small zucchini, cut into ½-inch slices
1 medium eggplant, cut in ½-inch slices

3 garlic cloves, peeled and minced
8 plum tomatoes, halved
1 tablespoon chopped fresh thyme
2 tablespoons chopped fresh oregano
¼ cup chopped fresh parsley
Salt and pepper

In a large pot, heat the oil, then sauté the diced onions until they give up their moisture. Do not brown. Add the sliced peppers and toss gently. Cover and cook on low heat for 3 minutes.

Add the zucchini, eggplant, and garlic to the onions and peppers, tossing gently. Cover and cook for 10 minutes over low heat. Stir in the tomatoes and herbs, and season with salt and pepper to taste. Cover once again and cook until the tomatoes are softened, about 10 minutes. Toss gently and serve immediately.

VARIATIONS: Yesterday's ratatouille can be turned into many suppers. Drain the liquid from the ratatouille to make a soup broth or to add to another broth needing tomato flavor.

- Once drained, the vegetables are a delicious omelet filling.

- Spread the vegetables over a pizza crust, top with mozzarella cheese, and bake in a preheated 350°F oven until bubbly.

- Purée the ratatouille to make a summer soup, adding chicken stock if necessary.

- If stovetop space is scarce, combine all the ratatouille ingredients in a dutch oven. Cover and bake at 325°F for 20 to 30 minutes.

SIDENOTE:

True ratatouille recipes do not add extra liquids. They allow the vegetables to achieve flavor from their own juices. It is a dish that can best be done at the end of summer, when the vegetables have grown their largest. Large eggplant, zucchini, squash, tomatoes, etc., are heavy with water, making them perfect for ratatouille. Heat and cook the vegetables slowly over a low flame to allow the vegetables time to sweat their own juices.

CLASSIC SUMMER CORN ON THE COB

Corn was not a crop I was familiar with in Brittany, so I felt I discovered a whole new world when I encountered it fresh on the cob in the United States. Faced with cooking it for the first time, I assumed corn should be treated like other starches, so I boiled it for twenty-five minutes, just as I would a potato. The result was more like corn chowder on the cob! Since then I have come to love corn on the cob as one of the summer's most anticipated seasonal treats. Here are some of the ways I have learned to cook the pick of the season. Keep in mind that corn will mature during the summer months from white, young, and sweet to a larger yellow size with fuller flavor. I have found the following recipes to work well with both.

Basic Grilled Corn:
Soak whole ears of corn with the husk and silk on in water for a couple of hours. Place directly on a hot grill for 5 minutes. This combination of steaming and smoking will allow the corn to steam within its own husk while giving it a smoky flavor as the outside husks burn. To serve, let cool slightly, then peel down the husk and silk and serve with butter.

Corn Wrap:
Pull down the husk of the corn, but do not remove. Remove the corn silk off the cob and then rub with seasoned butter or oil. Pull the husk back over the corn, wrap in aluminum foil, and place the corn on the grill or in a preheated 450°F oven for 10 minutes.

Marinated Corn:

½ cup mixed chopped fresh herbs
1 cup apple juice
¼ cup honey
¼ cup tomato purée

Husk the ears of corn, remove the silk, then cut in halves or thirds, depending on the size. Combine the herbs, apple juice, honey, and tomato purée, then cover the corn with the marinade. Let rest for 15 minutes. Skewer the corn, along with other vegetables like tomato wedges, onions, and zucchini, then place on the grill for 5 minutes. Turn as it grills for even cooking.

Corn Salad:

> 6 ears of corn, cooked
> 1 cup chopped tomato
> 4 tablespoons chopped fresh cilantro
> ½ cup olive oil
> ½ cup lime juice

Strip the corn kernels from the cob with a sharp knife. Combine with the rest of the ingredients and serve.

Corn-on-the-Cob Herb Butter:

> 6 tablespoons unsalted butter, softened
> 3 garlic cloves, peeled and minced
> 4 tablespoons chopped fresh dill
> Salt and pepper

Combine all the ingredients, and salt and pepper to taste. Rub on the corn before grilling or serving. Any summer herb may be used.

Corn-on-the-Cob Seasoned Oil:

> 4 tablespoons olive oil
> 3 tablespoons chopped fresh basil
> 1 tablespoon balsamic vinegar
> Juice of 1 lemon
> ½ cup freshly grated Parmesan cheese
> 1 teaspoon freshly ground pepper

Combine all the ingredients. Rub on the corn before grilling or serving.

BLACKBERRY COBBLER

The hedgerows on our farm were covered with wild blackberries, and one of my biggest pleasures from those days was berry picking in August. We always knew which section would provide the biggest blackberry harvest because in June we watched for the light pink blossoms on the bushes to show us where the clusters would be thickest. With our baskets lined with chestnut leaves, we set off in the morning and didn't come home until the basket was full. Today my anticipation of blackberries at the farmers' market is still keen, and the sight of them there momentarily transports me home.

6 SERVINGS

5 cups very ripe blackberries
1 cup sugar
1 vanilla bean, cut in half lengthwise,
   or 1 tablespoon vanilla extract

1 recipe sweet short pastry dough
   (see Basics, page 384)
5 tablespoons unsalted butter

Preheat the oven to 400°F. Butter a baking sheet.

In a large saucepan, combine the berries, sugar, and vanilla bean or extract. Cook over medium heat until the berries are soft but not falling apart, about 10 minutes. The time will depend on the ripeness of the berries. Remove the vanilla bean.

Crumble the short pastry dough into pieces the size of oatmeal and spread them over the baking sheet. Bake in the oven until crusty and light golden, about 5 minutes.

Fill an ovenproof dish one third of the way with berries, then sprinkle with half of the crust. Dot with half the butter, repeat with the rest of the berries and the crust. Top with the remaining butter.

Bake in the oven for 15 to 20 minutes. Serve warm or at room temperature with whipped cream or ice cream.

VARIATIONS: Mix equal parts of peaches and summer raspberries with the blackberries to make a berry medley cobbler.

PEACH COMPOTE

In the summer I favor compotes made with honey rather than sugar because more of the natural fruit flavor, which is so strong in late summer fruit, is allowed to come through. I also like the texture of the bits and pieces of fruit found in compotes. Each time I make a compote in August, I make extra to freeze and put away for winter days to come.

6 SERVINGS

2 pounds ripe peaches, peeled (see
　　Sidenote, page 86), pitted, and
　　coarsely chopped

¼ cup honey
1 vanilla bean or 1 tablespoon vanilla
　　extract

Place the peaches in a saucepan with the honey and vanilla bean or extract. Stew over medium heat for about 10 to 20 minutes, or until the peaches soften. The timing will depend on the ripeness of the fruit. Transfer to a serving bowl and cool. Serve at room temperature or refrigerate and serve cold.

GLAZED FRESH FIGS

Figs are a sensuous fruit synonymous with warm climates, so it is surprising to visitors that figs have found their way into traditional Breton cooking. Maman would often mash figs with white turnips to give the turnip a creamier texture and add a pleasing golden color to the dish. However, I find figs to be a fine end to a summer meal when a sweet finish is wanted but a heavy dessert is too much.

6 SERVINGS

1 cup sugar
1 vanilla bean, split in half
   lengthwise
1 cup water

2 cups red wine
1 pound fresh figs, halved
1 cup black currants or ¼ cup cassis
   syrup

In a large saucepan, combine the sugar, vanilla bean, water, and red wine. Bring to a boil and cook for 5 minutes. Lower to a simmer, add the figs, and poach for 5 minutes. Let the figs cool to room temperature in the syrup.

Lift out the figs and set aside. Stir the currants or cassis into the poaching liquid and bring to a boil, then simmer for about 10 minutes to reduce by half. If currants are used, pass the mixture through a fine strainer and discard the pulp.

Spoon a small amount of the syrup on each plate. Arrange 4 fig halves on top of the glaze and serve.

VARIATIONS: Figs glazed in this manner can be used as tart filling. Fill a baked tart shell with figs. Reduce the currant syrup to 1 cup. Brush the figs with the syrup before serving.

- This recipe can be done using apricots instead of figs.

- Replace the black currants and cassis with the same amount of red currants and fruity white wine.

BRETON PUDDING

Grand religious processions (pardons) are held in villages throughout Brittany beginning in June, peaking in August, and continuing through the end of September. During the festivities scores of townspeople in traditional dress—the women in lace caps called coiffes, the men in heavily embroidered trousers and coats—parade through the streets and around the countryside carrying religious banners honoring the patron saints of the area. While the history of the pardon is religious, any reason for celebration brings out the best of Breton cuisine. Breton pudding, known as Far Breton, *is always part of the outdoor summer festival season.*

6 SERVINGS

1¼ cups prunes or ¾ cup raisins	3 eggs
3 tablespoons rum	1 cup flour
1 cup sugar	1¼ cups whole milk

Preheat the oven to 350°F. Butter a 2-quart baking dish. Soak the fruit in rum for 5 minutes until soft.

In a mixing bowl, cream together the sugar and eggs. Drain the rum from the fruit into the sugar and eggs. Add the flour, mixing well to prevent lumps. Slowly add the milk, mixing constantly, to make a smooth batter.

Arrange the fruit at the bottom of the baking dish. Carefully pour the batter over the fruit. Do not stir. Set the baking dish in the oven and bake until the custard is set, about 1 hour and 20 minutes. It is ready when a knife in the center comes out clean.

Serve warm or at room temperature.

VARIATIONS: The Far Breton is traditionally made with prunes, raisins, or apples. But pitted cherries or apricot halves are a nice variation. Use fruit that softens but will hold its shape during baking.

SEPTEMBER

*My father, Louis Jamet, and I with my sons
Dan* (right), *and P. K.* (left), *setting out
to gather wild hazlenuts in September.*

September is a glint of time between two seasons when the fierce heat of a summer day breaks against the gentle chill of an autumn evening. The breeze, so recently perfumed with the sweet odors of summer melons, moves across our nostrils carrying a tantalizing mixture of smoky burning leaves and the sharp tang of fall apples. Some afternoons a purple haze hangs in the air where only that morning sunshine washed down. Gradually over the month we notice a change within ourselves as we begin to feel the exhilaration of summer freedom seep away, replaced with a desire for comfort, familiarity, and security. As for the garden, it becomes a bittersweet mélange as all the summer herbs and vegetables complete their growth and begin a dance between ripeness and decay. The strong herbs of July and August have gone to seed, leaving behind only sage and dill, whose flavors seem to blend perfectly with our autumn taste for mellower fare. By the end of September we feel the dashing romance we enjoyed with the summer tomato give way to a lingering affection, as the tomato itself grows from a firm and pretty maiden into a bloated matron, much of her flavorful charm intact but less noticeable to the eye. It is so with all summer vegetables as one by one their tall vines begin to wither and make way for earth-bound vines snaking through the garden, heavy with winter squash.

On the farm we couldn't let the last of the summer bounty lay fallow. Winter was coming, so our efforts moved from growing to gathering to prepare for the cold months ahead. The remainder of the summer harvest came into the kitchen loaded in willow baskets and left the kitchen dried or canned. Onions and garlic lay drying in the fields before their soft stems were braided together, and the bundles hung in the barn to be used to flavor savory stews and roasts that would appear on the table in the coming months. Fat potatoes were dug and sorted into winter bins designating piles to be sold, saved, or fed to the animals. My sisters, brothers, and I spent hours in the woods racing against the squirrels to find fresh hazelnuts for storage. All of the canning and storing we did now would come back to us in deep winter, a welcome reminder of the fullness of the previous summer's crops. But more than jeweled cherries winking at us from inside a glass jar, which we knew would make our mouths water in February for a taste of summer, the September apple pressing most clearly represented the goodness of putting food by.

In a country celebrated for wine, Brittany produces no wine of its own, since the climate is inhospitable to grape growing. However, the Bretons have managed to make an art of distilling the juice of their magnificent apples. Just like wine vintners, who pass on the secrets of their family trade through the generations, each Breton family has a secret blend of apples used to make their own recipes for cider and strong apple brandy. No two ciders ever taste alike in Brittany, even within a family. Competitions are held every year for the best cider, and the pride taken for winning is strong. Papa, who was among the best of the cider makers in our town, took his cider very seriously.

Beginning in September, when the cider apples began dropping from the trees, we children spent a part of each day gathering apples and piling them up behind the barn. Toward the end of the month, Papa and Maman began sorting the crop, choosing the best to go into that year's cider. While they sorted, Papa decided exactly which mix of apples would be used, whether or not to add some pears this year, and how long the cider would ferment in the oak casks before being bottled in early winter. During all of September, talk among friends at the market and after church revolved around the best way to make cider, as everyone tried to tease the secrets of success from their neighbors. Papa kept his recipe and how he arrived at it to himself—probably a good idea in a family with ten chattering children.

The morning to press the apples finally arrived. We went to my grandfather's farm, where the family press was kept. My family took turns with my aunts and uncles using the press on different days, since mixing the apples or divulging each other's recipe would be unthinkable. The press was seven feet high and four feet long on each side, set inside a shallow wooden tub. A sieve drained the juice into a collecting bucket placed by the tub's side. To begin, we laid a thick bed of fresh straw, saved from the summer wheat harvest, on the bottom of the press to act as a filter. Next came a layer of apples. Another layer of hay covered the apples, then a wooden slat cut to fit inside the press weighted it all down. This layering of straw, apples, and slats was repeated until the press was full. After the apples were in place, my father tightened down a heavy weight on top so the apples would be crushed. The first burst of apples saturated the barn air with the sweet, heady scent of apples and hay.

Periodically the weight would be tightened throughout the day to force the apples to give up more moisture. Eventually the bucket filled with foamy juice. It was then siphoned into oak casks and stored in the barn. The cider would ferment for several weeks before being bottled. It would be ready to drink a year later. It took days of hard work to make the cider, but the result was a year's worth of the taste of fall. Opening a bottle of cider in March always brought back to me the musty smell of an autumn afternoon.

For us cider making was more than a fascinating production. Cider was used almost every day as a refreshing drink, a flavoring agent, or as cooking liquid. For something that was so much a part of our life, my father would never have considered using inferior apples, nor would Maman have settled for using store-bought cider in her cooking. We need to take the same care with our families when thinking about nurturing them with good food throughout the winter. Home canning today is not necessary for our survival, but preserving food is a good habit to get into if our sense of the seasons is to survive. A tomato bought in January, grown out of season on a commercial farm two thousand miles away, does not have the flavor of a tomato grown locally and put by in August.

Modern food storage makes putting food up an easy alternative for even the busiest cook. Thanks to the freezer, gone are the days when it was necessary to spend long, hot hours over a steamy pot to can. Most foods today can be easily frozen in zip-lock bags and stored for months. Though the choices at the farmers' market can be overwhelming, be as particular about what you take time to put up as Papa was about his mixture of apples. Take note of what your family enjoys eating that year and only preserve what will be used. Also, in September most food sections of local newspapers run features about how to pickle produce. It's simple, doesn't take much time, and pickled vegetables make a wonderful accompaniment to winter stews. Buy extra tomatoes at the farmers' market to turn into tomato sauce. Freeze it for a cold February night to serve over pasta. Do the same with applesauce. Take advantage of the local apple crop in September to make your own special applesauce, mixing and matching types of apples to create a one-of-a-kind flavor for your family, just like Papa did with his cider. Fresh summer berries are very easy to freeze and have a far superior taste than commercially frozen berries. What a treat to have raspberry cobbler in front of a fire as snow lay on the ground!

September arrives with the heat of summer and ends with the chill of autumn in the air. It provides us with an opportunity to enjoy the last of the year's fresh harvest as we look forward to stews coddled for hours in a warm oven. Even today, when we don't need to plan our food to have enough during the winter months, we can still think about moving from growing to gathering. Take the best summer has to offer and put some away for winter. September is time to catch all of summer and put it in a jar.

SEPTEMBER RECIPES

Beef and Vegetable Soup

Wild Mushroom Fricassee

Roast Salmon with Cider-Apple Cream Sauce

Grilled Sea Scallops

Grouper with Fennel Greens

Turkey Scaloppine with Chanterelles

Braised Pork Roast with Carrots and Plums

Shepherd's Pie

Oven-Roasted Tomatoes Mylène

Roasted Beets

End-of-Summer Vegetable Medley

Dill Bread

Apple Tarte Hélène

Chocolate Walnut Cake

HARVEST DINNER

Wild Mushroom Fricassee

Dill Bread

Braised Pork Roast with Carrots and Plums

End-of-Summer Vegetable Medley

Apple Tarte Hélène

Apple Cider

BEEF AND VEGETABLE SOUP

Cooler nights in September naturally spark a hunger for the warmth of good soup without the heaviness of later-season stews. We ate a lot of vegetable soup on the farm during September because the harvest was coming in and provided an abundance of deeply flavored vegetables to add to the pot. The soup practically cooks itself without requiring very much attention.

6 SERVINGS

2 tablespoons unsalted butter
8 ounces top round beef, thinly
    sliced
1 leek, tough stem trimmed, finely
    chopped
1 celery stalk, diced
1 small carrot, trimmed and diced
3 plum tomatoes, coarsely chopped
6 cups brown stock (see Basics, page
    376)

1 sachet (see Basics, page 374)
½ cup each small-diced zucchini,
    yellow squash, and eggplant
2 garlic cloves, peeled and minced
2 tablespoons mixed chopped fresh
    herbs
1 tablespoon chopped fresh parsley
Salt and pepper

In a large soup pot, melt the butter, then add the beef and stir while browning. Set aside the meat, discarding the excess fat. Add the leek and celery to the pot and toss gently for 1 minute. Do the same with the carrot. Return the meat to the pot and stir in the tomatoes. Add the stock and sachet, and bring to a boil. Lower heat to a simmer, cover, and cook for 10 minutes.

Add the zucchini, squash, eggplant, garlic, and herbs. (The herbs can be a mix of whatever is at hand.) Season to taste with salt and pepper. Cook for another 10 minutes, or until the **vegetables** are tender. Sprinkle with parsley and serve.

♥ *Monique's Touch:*

Variations for vegetable soup are as abundant as the harvest. Work with combinations of vegetables that appeal to the eye and the palate. I find that whatever **vegetables** are used, fall vegetable soup needs a root of some kind. Root vegetables like carrot, parsnip, and turnip have deep flavors that hold well and give soup a good flavor base.

Regardless of the ingredients that make each soup unique, the basic steps for making soup remain the same: 1. Sauté the meats and remove from the pan. 2. Sauté the onion family vegetables next, then the ribbed vegetables like celery, followed by the root vegetables like carrots, and last, the potato. 3. Add the liquid, tomatoes, flavorings, and seasonings. 4. Return the meat to the pot. 5. Cover and cook until the vegetables begin to soften. 6. Uncover and add any vine vegetables, like zucchini, fresh beans, peas, etc. Choose vegetables for appearance, flavor, and texture. They should be cut thin to release their flavors into the broth and small enough to fit in the spoon. When making soup, always start with cold liquid, as the vegetables have more time to flavor the broth during the cooking process.

WILD MUSHROOM FRICASSEE

Wild mushrooms found in the countryside and forests have a musty flavor that is redolent of the fall season just beginning. Because they spring up in the nooks and crannies of tree trunks, wild mushrooms will sometimes faintly taste of the wood they grow in. Safe mushrooms can be hard to identify, so I don't recommend foraging for mushrooms without the guidance of a fungus expert. Every year the farmers' markets offer a wide variety of wild mushrooms, making it easy to buy from a safe and reliable source. The fricassee below takes advantage of the numerous wild mushrooms available. Any combination of Portobellos, cremini, shiitake, chanterelles, or oyster mushrooms, or even a single type of mushroom, makes a wonderful fricassee.

6 SERVINGS

2 pounds mixed wild mushrooms, coarsely chopped, or 3 cups dried mushrooms

1 tablespoon unsalted butter, melted

3 tablespoons chopped shallots

½ cup Madeira wine

1 cup brown stock (see Basics, page 376)

If using **dried mushrooms,** reconstitute by soaking in a pan with enough water to cover for 15 minutes. Remove the mushrooms and chop them coarsely. Bring the soaking liquid to a simmer and reduce to 3 tablespoons. Set aside.

Lightly coat the bottom of a large pan with butter, then sauté the shallots until tender. Brown slightly. Add the wild or reconstituted mushrooms and toss around the pan very gently. Add the wine and simmer for 1 minute. Add the stock and the 3 tablespoons of soaking liquid, if any. Reduce on high heat until all the liquid evaporates, about 10 minutes, being careful not to scorch the mushrooms.

VARIATIONS: Mushroom fricassee is a good omelet filling.

- Serve on baked potatoes or stuff the mushrooms between 2 layers of thinly sliced potatoes, then bake in a preheated 350°F oven until the potatoes are done.

- Add 3 cups of chicken or beef stock, then purée the mixture to make a beautiful soup.

♥ Monique's Touch:

Dried mushrooms are expensive, but drying them yourself for winter use is economical, quick, and easy. Wipe the mushrooms clean with a towel or soft brush. Do not wash, as mushrooms absorb water like a sponge. Lay the mushrooms on an elevated screen and store in a cool, dry place for 2 or 3 days. A fan can be used to encourage faster drying. Once dry, store the mushrooms in a paper bag in a cool, dry place.

ROAST SALMON WITH CIDER-APPLE CREAM SAUCE

When certain foods seem to belong together because of taste, color, or texture, often it's because they all originate from the same geographical region. For the ingredients in the recipe below I've used the most flavorful salmon available in the United States from the Pacific Northwest. That is also the region where some of the best apples and hazelnuts are grown. All these tastes complement each other, as well as look pleasing to the eye. Keeping geographic compatibility in mind, a variation on the same recipe might include mahi mahi, caught off the Hawaiian coast, combined with local pineapple and macadamia nuts. One of the easiest ways to become creative in cooking is to concentrate regionally when choosing ingredients.

6 SERVINGS

Six 4-ounce salmon fillets or one
    24-ounce salmon fillet
3 tablespoons olive oil
1 leek, tough end trimmed, white
    part minced, green part cut into
    2 × ¼-inch strips
1 cup apple cider
3 tablespoons unsalted butter
2 Granny Smith or Golden Delicious
    apples, peeled, cored, and coarsely
    chopped

2 cups fish stock or court bouillon
    (see Basics, page 377 or
    page 378)
2 tablespoons chopped shallots
1 cup hazelnuts, toasted and crushed
1 cup cream
Salt and pepper

Preheat the oven to 400°F. Butter an ovenproof pan large enough for all the fillets.

Rub the salmon on both sides with the olive oil, then season with salt and pepper. Line the ovenproof pan with green leek strips and place the fish on top. Sprinkle with ½ cup of the cider.

Melt 2 tablespoons of the butter to mix with half of the apples. Spread the apples on top of the salmon. Pour ½ cup of the fish stock or court bouillon around the fish before setting the pan in the oven. Bake for 10 to 15 minutes, or until the meat flakes easily with the touch of a fork.

Meanwhile, in a medium saucepan, melt the remaining tablespoon of butter and sauté the shallots and white leek pieces until tender but not brown. Add the remaining apples and cook until tender. Add the remaining cider, fish stock or court bouillon, and ½ cup of the hazelnuts, then reduce the sauce over medium heat for 10 minutes. Whisk in the cream and reduce at medium heat until the sauce coats the back of a spoon, about 4 minutes. Strain, then adjust the seasonings to taste.

Sprinkle the top of the salmon with the remaining hazelnuts. Serve, passing the sauce.

Our cousins and friends in Breton costume walking to a town festival.

GRILLED SEA SCALLOPS

Sea scallops have a long tradition in Brittany. The French call them coquilles Saint-Jacques, *after St. James of Compostella, who wore a necklace of scallop shells around his neck. Later, pilgrims visiting his shrine in northwest Spain ate the mollusks as a rather joyful penance, adopting as their symbol scallop shells pinned to their hats. Scallops are fished in deep Atlantic sea waters during the fall and winter. In Brittany they are sold fresh in the shells, so Bretons enjoy the coral of the scallop, which has a sweet taste. In the United States fresh scallops in their shell are found on the east and west coasts. The coral does not ship well, so Americans are most familiar with the abductor muscle, which is the white meat of the scallop.*

6 SERVINGS

1 red pepper, roasted, peeled, and seeded (see Monique's Touch, page 109)
2 shallots, peeled and halved
1 tablespoon chopped fresh dill
1 cup dry vermouth

3 dozen sea scallops
6 plum tomatoes, halved
1 cup cream
2 tablespoons chopped fresh parsley
Salt and pepper

In a food processor, place the red pepper, shallots, dill, and ¼ cup of the vermouth. Purée to a smooth paste. Transfer to a bowl and add the sea scallops. Toss gently to coat each scallop. Let stand for 30 minutes. Remove the scallops and transfer the marinade to a saucepan.

Heat a grill until very hot. Place the scallops on the grill and cook for 1 minute on each side. Also grill the tomatoes, cooking about 2 minutes on each side, long enough to make grill marks.

Stir the rest of the vermouth into the marinade. Bring to a simmer, reduce for 5 minutes, then gently stir in the cream. Season with salt and pepper to taste. Simmer for 2 minutes until the cream binds with the vermouth. Strain, then add the parsley.

To serve, place 2 grilled tomato halves on each plate. Ladle sauce over the tomatoes, then arrange 6 scallops on top.

VARIATIONS: Other firm-fleshed fish that are suitable include halibut, tuna, and monkfish.

- Boneless breast of chicken can be used.

- The scallops and tomatoes can be broiled for the same amount of time.

GROUPER WITH FENNEL GREENS

Grouper is what I always recommend to friends just being introduced to eating fish. It is lean, with a mild, sweet flavor that is not overpowering. It is also appealing because grouper fillets are boneless, making it an excellent fish to serve to children.

6 SERVINGS

6 grouper fillets, about ⅓ pound each

1 fresh fennel bulb, thinly sliced, greens cut off and reserved, stalk discarded

1 small onion, peeled and diced

1 pound plum tomatoes, sliced

½ cup reserved fennel greens, finely chopped

1 tablespoon fennel seeds, crushed

2 cups white wine

2 tablespoons unsalted butter

Salt and pepper

Preheat the oven to 375°F. Lightly oil the bottom of an ovenproof pan large enough for the grouper.

Season the fillets with salt and pepper. Arrange the fennel, onion, and tomatoes on the bottom of the pan. Place the fish on top and sprinkle with the fennel greens and crushed fennel seed. Pour the wine around the fillets. Cut a piece of parchment paper the size of the inside perimeter of the pan. Butter one side and lay it, butter side down, over the fish, tucking in the sides. Bake for 25 minutes, or until the fish flakes at the touch of a fork.

Arrange the grouper on a serving platter. Toss the fennel and tomatoes together with the broth, adjust the seasonings, and spoon over the fish. Serve at once.

VARIATIONS: Red snapper, any member of the bass family, or any lean fish can be prepared this way.

- Save the remainder of the fennel greens for another use, such as a flavoring for soups, to mix with butter and mayonnaise for a sandwich spread, or in sour cream as a dip.

TURKEY SCALOPPINE
WITH CHANTERELLES

I always looked forward to chanterelle mushrooms with the same anticipation I feel for spring morels. The sweet, musty flavor of chanterelles goes well with cream, as does that of morels, but the deeper flavor of the fall chanterelle speaks of burnt leaves in autumn. Maman usually made this dish with veal because it was readily available and we did not have turkey. Here I substitute turkey because it has a similar texture to veal but is more economical.

6 SERVINGS

1 teaspoon cider vinegar
½ pound fresh chanterelle
   mushrooms
2 tablespoons unsalted butter
2 tablespoons olive oil
1½ pounds turkey breast or turkey
   tender, cut into ¼-inch slices,
   flattened to ⅛ inch

2 tablespoons chopped shallots
1 tablespoon brandy
1 cup cream
3 tablespoons crème fraîche (see
   Basics, page 379)
2 tablespoons chopped fresh parsley
Salt and pepper

Mix the vinegar with enough water to cover the chanterelles, then soak for 3 minutes. Drain well, shaking in a towel to dry. Coarsely chop the mushrooms.

In a heavy skillet, melt the butter with the oil until hot. Brown the turkey on both sides, keeping the heat as high as possible without smoking. Pour off the excess fat, then add the shallots and mushrooms. Sauté until the mushrooms are dry. Add the turkey back to the pan. Heat through, then add the brandy and flambé. When the flame dies down, stir in the cream. Simmer for 5 minutes, then adjust the seasoning with salt and pepper. Finish by stirring in the crème fraîche and chopped parsley. Divide among 6 plates and serve.

VARIATIONS: Scaloppine can be made with veal, chicken, pork, or a fish fillet such as turbot, sole, and even scallops.

SIDENOTE:
Flambéing is a rather dramatic but very simple technique to master. Over a strong heat source make sure the food to be flambéed is very hot. From a ladle

or separate cup, pour the liquor into the pan. Never pour straight from the bottle, as flames can climb up the stream of alcohol and explode the bottle. Let bubble for a moment, then ignite with a flaming match or tilt the pan into the flame of a gas burner. Spoon the flaming liquid over the food until the flame dies out.

BRAISED PORK ROAST WITH CARROTS AND PLUMS

Maman rarely cooked by written recipe, but she intuitively created dishes that became family favorites and have been passed on to the next generation. This roast was always served when special company sat at our table. My siblings and I learned how to make it by watching and helping in the kitchen. Now it is the dish we serve when we are guests in each other's homes, and all our children have learned how to make it from us. It intertwines the generations and truly brings us home. I try to use Italian plums because they are particular to the fall. These small, olive-shaped purple plums are the type that are dried to become prunes, so if Italian plums are unavailable, use prunes.

6 SERVINGS

One 3-pound boneless pork loin
3 garlic cloves, peeled and quartered
2 tablespoons unsalted butter
2 tablespoons olive oil
3 carrots, trimmed and cut into ¼-inch slices

12 whole pearl onions or 2 medium onions, peeled and sliced
1 sachet (see Basics, page 374)
12 Italian plums
2 cups brown stock (see Basics, page 376)

Make 12 small cuts with the point of a sharp knife all over the roast. Insert the garlic in the incisions.

Melt the butter with the olive oil in a dutch oven, then brown the pork loin on all sides, including the ends. Cover and cook gently over very low heat for 25 minutes, turning the meat occasionally. Place the carrots and onions around the pork loin. Drop in the sachet. Cover and cook again for 25 minutes, or until the meat flakes easily with a fork.

Arrange the plums around the roast, cover, and cook for 10 minutes. Remove the pork loin from the pan and keep warm. Add the stock to the pan and let reduce by half for about 10 minutes. Discard the sachet. Reduce a bit more if a thicker sauce is desired.

To serve, place the vegetables and plums in the center of a platter. Slice the meat, arranging it around the vegetables. Pour the sauce over the meat before serving.

VARIATIONS: If plums are not available, replace them with 24 prunes. More prunes than plums are used to compensate for the sweetness of fresh plums.

- Quartered apples and shelled walnuts instead of plums also make a good fall variation.

SHEPHERD'S PIE

Shepherd's pie was always served for supper on a very busy harvest day when roast lamb or lamb stew had been on the menu the day before. Today I serve it when my schedule is full and I don't have much time to spend in the kitchen. Any type of meat works as a filling, and shepherd's pie freezes well, so I always make an extra one to serve on another hectic day.

6 SERVINGS

FILLING:

1 pound cooked lamb shoulder or uncooked lamb stew meat, cut into ¼-inch cubes
3 tablespoons olive oil
2 leeks, washed and tough ends trimmed, thinly sliced
1 cup chopped onions
4 garlic cloves, peeled and minced
1 tablespoon chopped fresh thyme
1 tablespoon paprika
½ teaspoon freshly ground pepper
2 cups brown stock (see Basics, page 376)
¼ cup tomato paste
1 cup bread crumbs

POTATO "CRUST":

2 pounds starchy brown potatoes, peeled and quartered
1 teaspoon salt
2 cups warm milk
2 eggs
4 tablespoons unsalted butter
Salt and pepper
Freshly ground nutmeg

Preheat the oven to 350°F. Butter a 4-quart ovenproof pan.

Sauté the lamb pieces in the oil until brown on all sides. Add the leeks, onions, and garlic. Sauté for 3 minutes. Blend in the thyme, paprika, and pepper.

Slowly add the stock and simmer for 10 minutes. Mix in the tomato paste and blend well. Mix in the bread crumbs.

Meanwhile, in a deep saucepan, place the potatoes and salt with enough cold water to cover. Bring to a boil, lower the heat, and simmer, covered, until tender, about 30 minutes. Drain well and return to the warm pot over medium heat for 20 seconds to dry. Add the milk, eggs, and 3 tablespoons of the butter. Crush together with a potato ricer, then beat until creamy. Season with nutmeg and salt and pepper to taste.

Spread half of the mashed potatoes in the bottom and up the sides of the pan. Spread the lamb mixture over the potatoes. Spread the remaining potatoes over the top of the lamb, making sure to seal the top and sides of the pie. Dot the top with the remaining 1 tablespoon of butter. Sprinkle with salt and pepper and nutmeg.

Bake in the oven for 40 minutes, or until the top is golden brown. Remove from the oven and let sit for 10 minutes before serving.

VARIATIONS: One pound of ground lamb may be used instead of cubed lamb leg or stew meat.

- Replace the meat filling with a combination of cooked vegetables such as eggplant, zucchini, carrots, turnips, celery, parsnips, and mushrooms for a meatless version of shepherd's pie.

OVEN-ROASTED
TOMATOES MYLÈNE

Like most people today my sister Mylène, who is a very successful career woman, doesn't have any use for old-fashioned canning techniques. With this recipe she showed me how easy it is to put up tomatoes for the winter to come, taking advantage of both the season and the freezer.

2 DOZEN

2 dozen Italian plum tomatoes, halved
1 cup mixed chopped fresh basil, oregano,
    marjoram, and thyme
Salt and pepper

Preheat the oven to 325°F.

In a mixing bowl, combine the **tomatoes** with the chopped herbs. Toss gently until evenly coated. Season with salt and pepper.

Place the tomatoes on a baking sheet in the middle of the oven for 1 to 1½ hours. The time will depend on how juicy the tomatoes are. They will be semidry to the touch when ready. If the tomatoes start browning, turn the oven down to 275°F. During the last 15 minutes of baking, turn the heat up once again so the natural sugar in the tomatoes caramelizes the top to a golden-brown color.

Serve warm or cold. Will keep for several days in the refrigerator.

VARIATIONS: Serve as an appetizer with a thin slice of proscuitto on top.

♥ *Monique's Touch:*

I make several pans of baked **tomatoes** at one time because they are so easy to do. After baking, cool, then put them in the freezer on the baking sheet until frozen. Transfer them to plastic zip-lock bags for freezer storage. During the winter, use the tomatoes in soups and stews, or thaw and toss them with hot pasta to remind you of warm summer breezes when a cold blast of winter wind is whipping outside.

ROASTED BEETS

Roasting root vegetables like sweet potatoes, yams, and beets is a good preparation technique during this time of year because the roots are fresh and have not lost any of their moisture. Caramelizing vegetables before turning down the heat to finish roasting them brings the natural sugars to the surface, making them crisp on the outside but still soft on the inside.

6 SERVINGS

> 3 medium beets, peeled and cut into
>   ½-inch slices
> ½ cup olive oil
> 1 tablespoon caraway seeds, crushed
> Salt and pepper

Preheat the oven to 450°F.

Wipe each beet slice with olive oil and place in a single layer on an oiled baking pan. Sprinkle with the caraway seeds and salt and pepper to taste.

Place the beets in the oven and immediately lower the oven heat to 375°F. Roast for 15 minutes, then turn the beets and continue cooking until brown and tender. Serve immediately.

END-OF-SUMMER VEGETABLE MEDLEY

By the first weeks of September, when the evening air can hint of a chill, the grill has lost some of its appeal. My thoughts start to turn back to the coziness of cooking in the oven. Yet I'm still enjoying the individual full-bodied tastes found in late summer vegetables, and I'm not quite ready for the melting together of flavors that happens to oven-braised vegetables. I developed the method below of cooking tomatoes and zucchini together in the oven without having them stew in their own juices. The onions layered at the bottom of the pan lift the tightly packed tomatoes and zucchini out of their juices. Instead of falling apart, the vegetables keep their shape while gently steaming.

6 SERVINGS

¼ cup olive oil
6 onions, peeled and chopped
4 tomatoes, cut into ½-inch slices
Three ½-pound zucchini, cut on the
    diagonal into ½-inch pieces

1 tablespoon chopped fresh thyme
2 tablespoons chopped fresh parsley
Grated Parmesan cheese

Preheat the oven to 425°F.

In a sauté pan, heat half the olive oil, then sauté the onions until translucent but not brown.

Sprinkle the onions on the bottom of an oblong baking dish. Standing the tomato and zucchini slices on their edges, alternate the tomatoes and zucchini, packing them tightly so the pan is filled from end to end. This will allow juices to pool on the bottom of the pan so the vegetables will bake without stewing or falling apart. Drizzle the rest of the olive oil on top. Place in the oven and bake for about 20 minutes, or until fork-tender. Sprinkle with parsley and Parmesan cheese.

VARIATIONS: To make a quick soup, add the cooked vegetables to a large pot with one quart of chicken stock, heat, and serve. For thick soup, purée before serving.

DILL BREAD

This is a version of farm bread Maman used to make in a cast-iron pan, tucked away to bake in a hot corner of the hearth. Whenever somebody passed by the hearth, the pan was given a quarter turn so it would brown evenly all the way around. At the time, we didn't use ricotta cheese, but instead flavored the bread with cream skimmed off the milk collected during the week. After three or four days the cream rose to the top of the milk bucket, ripening almost like cheese. It gave the bread a wonderful, mild flavor similar to the results you will find with ricotta cheese.

2 LOAVES

1 medium onion, finely chopped
1 tablespoon unsalted butter
¾ cup water
1-ounce yeast cake or 2 packets dry yeast
1 tablespoon sugar
5 cups bread flour

4 tablespoons dillweed
1 tablespoon dillseeds, crushed
1 cup ricotta cheese, drained
2 eggs
1 teaspoon salt
Coarse kosher salt
Chopped fresh dill

Preheat the oven to 375°F. Lightly oil two 1½-pound loaf pans.

Sauté the onion in the butter until soft but not brown. Heat the water to 90°F. Dissolve the yeast in the water with the sugar. Let stand until the yeast becomes active and a foamy head develops on the surface of the water.

In a large mixing bowl, combine the flour, dillweed, and dillseeds. Add the onion, ricotta cheese, eggs, salt, and yeast mixture. Mix all the ingredients until moistened.

Turn the dough onto a floured work surface. Knead the bread until smooth and elastic, about 5 minutes. Keep the work surface floured to prevent sticking. Continue kneading for another 5 minutes to develop the elasticity in the dough.

Place the dough in a large, lightly oiled mixing bowl and set aside in a warm (85–90°F), draft-free area. Let rise until double in size, about 1 hour or more, depending on the temperature.

Punch the dough down and divide into 2 equal pieces. Knead each piece gently into a loaf shape. Place each loaf, round side down, in a pan. Then turn the loaf, round side up, so it is completely oiled. Cover the loaves with a towel until double in size.

Bake for 45 minutes. After removing the bread from the oven, brush the top with melted butter to give a softer crust, then sprinkle with coarse kosher salt and chopped fresh dill. Cool before slicing.

VARIATIONS: This dough also makes pizza crust or pizza bread. Roll it out to between a ¼–½-inch thickness and top with olives, sun-dried tomatoes, and mushrooms, or other toppings of your choice, before baking for 25 minutes.

Papa took a walk every day to survey the farm.

APPLE TARTE HÉLÈNE

This tart, named for Maman, really represents for me the essence of what cooking should always be. Seasonal, full-flavored ingredients are combined in a way that presents elegance through simplicity.

8 SERVINGS

½ cup applesauce (see Basics, page 391)

1 recipe short pastry dough, partially baked (see Basics, page 382)

4 large Granny Smith or Golden Delicious apples, peeled, cored, quartered, and thinly sliced

¼ cup apricot preserves

Preheat the oven to 400°F.

Spread the applesauce on the bottom of the partially baked pastry dough. Fan the sliced apples out in a circular pattern on top of the applesauce.

Heat the apricot preserves until melted, then brush the tops of the apples with syrup. Bake for approximately 35 minutes, or until the apples are soft and well glazed.

VARIATIONS: Mix in an assortment of nuts with the applesauce before spreading it in the tarte.

- This can also be glazed with warm honey or maple syrup.

- One tablespoon of brandy can be added to the apricot glaze before warming.

- Reserve the apple peels to make applesauce.

CHOCOLATE WALNUT CAKE

This is a very easy cake to make. I use walnuts in September, when a good walnut cake should be made as close to when the nuts arrive at the market as possible. As nuts age, they begin to lose moisture, concentrating their flavor. But the freshest walnuts have a sweet and mild taste that goes so well with chocolate.

12 SERVINGS

CAKE:
4½ ounces semisweet chocolate
¾ cup powdered sugar, sifted
4 egg yolks
1 teaspoon vanilla extract

4 egg whites
⅓ cup cake flour
¾ cup toasted ground walnuts

GANACHE:
1 cup cream
24 ounces semisweet chocolate, shaved
4 ounces bittersweet chocolate, shaved
3 tablespoons unsalted butter

GARNISH:
2 cups toasted walnuts, coarsely chopped
Chocolate leaves

Preheat the oven to 350°F. Butter and flour a 9-inch springform pan.

To make the cake, melt the chocolate in a double boiler, stirring to prevent burning. Remove from the heat and keep warm.

Beat ½ cup of the powdered sugar with the egg yolks until light and fluffy. Stir in the vanilla and melted chocolate.

Beat the egg whites until frothy, then add the remaining ¼ cup sugar and beat until stiff peaks form. Combine the cake flour with the ground walnuts.

Fold the egg whites into the yolk mixture, alternating with the flour. Pour the batter into the springform pan, smooth out the top until even, then bake for 40 minutes. The center will be dry when done. Remove from the pan and cool.

Meanwhile, prepare the ganache. In a saucepan, bring the cream to a simmer, then add all the chocolate. Beat vigorously until all the chocolate is melted. Remove from the heat and continue beating for a few minutes until the mixture cools slightly. Cover the top and sides of the cake with the ganache. Press the chopped walnuts into the sides of the cake. Top with **chocolate leaves.**

VARIATIONS: Other nuts, like almonds, hazelnuts, pecans, and even pistachio nuts, combine well with the chocolate.

♥ *Monique's Touch:*

Chocolate leaves are a simple and elegant way to decorate cakes. Melt 4 ounces of semisweet chocolate. While still warm, use a brush to coat the waxy side of a leaf with the chocolate. Use two coats, if necessary, to cover the leaf. Refrigerate until the chocolate sets, then carefully peel back the green leaf. It is important to use waxy leaves, such as ivy, lemon leaves, camellia leaves (all purchased from a florist), or lime leaves, which can be purchased in Asian grocery stores. Rinse in soapy water and dry completely before using.

OCTOBER

My sister Marie-Hélène (left), *her husband Michel,*
my sister Madeleine (center right), *and Papa,*
after a successful forage for mushrooms.

In the same way I think of April as the beginning of the culinary year, I think of October as the end of it. Everything in nature is quieting down and getting ready for winter. We're not quite ready to go indoors, so we snuggle into warm woolen sweaters as the wind blows colder out of the north. A couple of weeks ago a walk in the woods was a noisy affair, with leaves crackling and skipping under our feet. Now the leaves are silent and damp, and a soft carpet of green moss cushions our step. September's hunt for wild berries to go into pies gives way to the foraging of pungent mushrooms, which will complement the braised meats and rich soups our taste buds are telling us to serve now. Turnips, parsnips, onions, carrots, leeks, pumpkins, winter squash, and cabbage are the last vegetables of the garden. They are hardy squash and root vegetables, grown close to the ground or burrowing into it for the last warmth of the year. Now they are harvested and either enjoyed fresh one more time or put up for the coming winter.

The entire pace of life on our farm slowed considerably during October. It was time to survey what repairs were needed on tools and machinery, a time to make warm clothing, and a time to cut enough wood to heat the house during the cold season ahead. In October our Sunday noon lunches moved indoors, where a feeling of gentle family coziness replaced the often raucous activity found at our outdoor summer table.

This gentleness carried over to meal preparation in October. The dishes we cooked in the fall were not as elaborate as what the bounty of summer called for. Grilling and roasting were replaced by braising and simmering. It was not yet time for heavy stews, but we could already taste a hardy satisfaction in the simple soups, roasts, and vegetables Maman served. Smells were warm and earthy. A favorite Sunday meal might include a beautiful pork roast braised with prunes or onions, cabbage flavored with caraway, and a big mound of creamy mashed potatoes. Or we might have a root vegetable soup in a very nice broth accompanied by a slice of pâté. Always on the table was a loaf of crusty bread, a plate of cornichon pickles made the summer before, and a big bowl of nuts for cracking after the meal. Many times Maman cooked both a soup and a roast on Sunday and then strained the vegetables out of the soup broth to serve with the meat. The next day she would slice a thin piece of day-old bread, put it in the bottom of a soup plate, and pour the broth over it. The lingering full flavor of mature vegetables gave the broth a wonderful taste, and the bread made it filling. Combined with a slice of cheese and a pear for dessert, it was our Monday evening meal. As always, today's fare turned into tomorrow's supper.

As cozy as October was, not much time was spent sitting around the table after lunch because Sunday afternoons were set aside for my father and brothers to go hunting. As soon as the meal was finished, my father would throw a leather satchel over his shoulder, whistle for our hunting dog, and off he would go with one of my brothers. For them hunting was a relaxing chore, but it was never done strictly for pleasure. Our bargain with nature was that she provided us with food, but we never took more than was needed. We depended on the game for the coming winter, because meat that wasn't eaten right away was braised and put up for stews in January, or was canned into pâtés and the bones cooked for soup stock. Papa was an expert at tracking, amazing us all when he could reveal by the crush of grass where a rabbit rested or tell by a scattering of leftover seeds in a field where ducks fed on their migration south. As practiced by my father, hunting was an art that drew him closer to nature and the birds and small animals he loved.

Today we don't hunt for survival, but we have other ways of linking ourselves to the changes going on in nature during October. This is the time to take off from the city and go to the country for a day to feel invigorated one more time as nature gets ready to sleep. October is the biggest month of the year for apple picking, so take an afternoon to discover the apples grown in your area. Certainly we have Washington apples year-round at the market, but now is the opportunity to sample local apples that may not be suitable for shipping or long-term storage. Or this year, instead of buying a Halloween pumpkin at the grocery store, make a family excursion of going to a local pumpkin patch to pick out the perfect jack-o'-lantern. There are hundreds to choose from, and all are lying right in the field where they grew.

Notice the change in produce at the farmers' markets. Artichokes are back for their second appearance of the year, but this time with a mellower, buttery taste. This is because the growing temperature for the plants is reversed from the spring harvest, but the cooking methods we use are the same. It's only a matter of substituting seasonal ingredients to create an artichoke variation that will taste right for this time of year. Sweet, heavy grapes appear, their beautiful purple color making a striking contrast against the orange and yellow winter squash. Except for sage, all of the herbs are past. Luckily, the squashes and root vegetables have so much flavor that not much is needed to enhance them. When we cook, it's time to move toward seasoning dishes with herb seeds like caraway, dill, and fennel. Also, using flavored vinegars will give sauces a piquant taste to match the sharp October air. Most of all, listen to your body. You want deeper flavors, a little heartier bread, a more substantial soup.

At home, start doing things to mark the change in the season. Serve warm apple cider spiced with cinnamon instead of cold juice as an after-school snack. Toast pumpkin seeds or make taffy apples to go along with the cider. Use Halloween as a way to create a family memory, perhaps by making a yearly tradition of serving my tasty and nutritious Trick-or-Treat Supper before sending the goblins out the door. Serve meals in front of a fireplace, if you have one. Or make dinner special just by setting a basket of colorful leaves in the center of the table. The most important thing is to take the time to celebrate October with family and friends. A laughing, talking group of loved ones sharing the experience of the meal is the best way to be in harmony with nature's cycle.

OCTOBER RECIPES

Wild Rice and Mushroom Chowder

Carrot and Ginger Soup

Purée of Butternut Squash with Roasted Hazelnuts

Fresh Herb–Crusted Fish

Chicken with Red Wine Vinegar

Pheasant with Grapes

Halloween Meat Loaf

Pork Chops Charcutière

Braised Cabbage with Caraway

Pumpkin au Gratin

Salsify with Dill Butter

Baked Potato with Capers and Olives

Wild Rice Salad

Roasted Hazelnut and Mixed Green Salad

Upside-Down Apple Cake

Pear Frangipane Tart

TRICK-OR-TREAT SUPPER

Halloween Meat Loaf

Pumpkin au Gratin

Braised Cabbage with Caraway

Toasted Pumpkin Seeds

Hot Mulled Apple Cider

WILD RICE AND MUSHROOM CHOWDER

Mushrooms can be found nearly year-round, but they vary greatly by season when it comes to flavor. Fall brings the wonderful, rich intensity of wood mushrooms, which include chanterelles, shiitake, trumpet, cèpe, and Portobello. My father would often bring back a basket of mushrooms gathered while hunting in the woods near our farm. On the rare occasion a specimen we didn't recognize would appear, the strange mushroom was immediately taken to the local pharmacist, who was licensed to test mushrooms for poison.

4 SERVINGS

1 tablespoon arrowroot
2 cups chicken stock (see Basics, page 375)
1 small baking potato, peeled and diced
1 cup milk
1 tablespoon olive oil

2 garlic cloves, peeled and minced
¼ cup each diced onion, celery, and leeks
¼ pound mushrooms, mixed variety
1 cup cooked wild rice
1 tablespoon chopped fresh parsley
Salt and pepper

Dilute the arrowroot in a small amount of cold water until it makes a paste. Bring the chicken stock to a simmer and add the arrowroot paste, stirring and simmering until the stock thickens. Add the potato and cook 10 minutes, or until the potato is tender. Take off heat and stir in the milk. Set aside.

In a shallow pan, heat the olive oil and sauté the garlic, onion, celery, and leeks until soft but not brown. Sauté the mushrooms separately, just until their juices are released and they are tender. Add the vegetables, mushrooms with their juice, and rice to the stock. Blend well and bring to a simmer. Cook for 10 minutes. Adjust the seasoning and sprinkle with parsley before serving.

CARROT AND GINGER SOUP

The addition of ginger to classic carrot soup updates this easy favorite. The ginger's fire intensifies and brings out the sweetness of mature carrots.

8 SERVINGS

1 leek, tough green end trimmed, sliced

2 tablespoons unsalted butter

2 pounds carrots, trimmed and sliced

2 garlic cloves, peeled and pressed

2 tablespoons grated fresh ginger

5 cups chicken stock (see Basics, page 375)

1 cup cooked rice

3 tablespoons chopped fresh celery leaves

Salt and pepper

In a large pot, sauté the leek in the butter until translucent but not brown. Add the carrots and toss for 2 minutes on low heat. Add the garlic, ginger, stock, and rice. Bring to a boil, then lower to a simmer. Cover and cook gently for 20 minutes, or until the carrots are soft.

Strain the soup, reserving the broth. Purée the vegetables and **rice** in a food processor, then add back to the broth. Salt and pepper to taste. Reheat and sprinkle with celery leaves before serving.

VARIATIONS: Any combination of autumn root vegetables can be used in this recipe, such as parsnip, turnip, rutabaga, celery root, and parsley root.

♥ *Monique's Touch:*

Whenever root vegetables are used for a purée or puréed soup, use cooked **rice** or a potato as a binder. Root vegetable juices have a tendency to separate from the pulp after cooking, making the dish runny. The starch in rice or potatoes will hold the pulp and juice together.

PURÉE OF BUTTERNUT SQUASH
WITH ROASTED HAZELNUTS

This soup has very few ingredients, allowing the smooth natural flavor of the butternut squash to come through. Taking the extra time to roast the squash first brings out a wonderful nutty flavor.

8 SERVINGS

1 large butternut squash, halved
1 quart chicken stock (see Basics, page 375)

1 cup roasted hazelnuts
Salt and pepper
Freshly ground nutmeg

Preheat the oven to 375°F.

Place the **squash** halves facedown on a baking sheet and roast 30 minutes, or until soft. Cool.

Scoop out the squash seeds and discard. Scoop out the pulp and mix with the stock in a large saucepan. Bring to a boil and simmer for 10 minutes.

Strain the squash, reserving the stock. Purée the squash in a food processor with the hazelnuts. Add back to the stock. Blend well and season with the salt and pepper and nutmeg.

VARIATIONS: Instead of adding the puréed squash and hazelnuts back to the stock, serve the purée as a vegetable side dish. Dot with 2 tablespoons of unsalted butter before serving.

- Use the squash purée as a quiche filling. Bake in a tart shell at 350°F for 30 minutes.

- Use the squash purée as a filling for handmade ravioli.

♥ *Monique's Touch:*

To properly cut any **squash,** make 2 separate cuts. Starting in the center, cut toward the blossom. Starting in the center again, cut toward the tail. It's important to cut along the length of the squash to expose enough of the meat for roasting and to ensure the heat will be distributed evenly. Large squash pieces keep nutrients from leaching out during cooking, so keep the pieces large until done, then cut into the proper size for the dish.

FRESH HERB–CRUSTED FISH

This has always been the last fresh herb dish of the year in my family. All the herbs we enjoy through the spring and summer seasons are either in bloom or about to hibernate for the winter, making their flavors less intense. Instead of highlighting one particular herb flavor, a mixture of herbs are rubbed together to get the last breath of summer before the garden goes to sleep.

6 SERVINGS

½ cup chopped mixed savory,
    oregano, and dill
¼ cup finely ground blue corn chips
½ teaspoon salt
¼ teaspoon freshly ground black
    pepper

¼ teaspoon cayenne pepper
Six 4-ounce fillets of bass, halibut, or
    salmon, about ½ inch thick
1 tablespoon olive oil

Mix together the herbs, corn chips, salt, black pepper, and cayenne. Rub the fillets on both sides with the mixture. Wrap tightly in plastic wrap and refrigerate for at least 30 minutes.

Remove the fillets from the plastic wrap and drizzle both sides lightly with olive oil. Place on a hot grill and cook for 2 minutes on each side. Let rest for 5 minutes on a hot serving platter before serving.

VARIATIONS: The rule of thumb for cooking fish by any method is to cook it for 8 minutes total for every inch of thickness. For herb-crusted fish try the following:

- To poach: Prepare the fish as above until the grilling step. Omit the olive oil. Keep the fish wrapped in plastic and lower it into simmering water for 8 minutes.

- To steam: Prepare the fish as above, but instead of grilling, place it in a steamer for 8 minutes.

- To sauté: Prepare the fish as above until the grilling step. Heat 1 tablespoon of olive oil in a pan and brown the fillets for 2 minutes on each side. Place the pan in a preheated 400°F oven for 4 minutes. Let rest 2 minutes before serving.

CHICKEN WITH RED WINE VINEGAR

Vinegar, particularly cider vinegar, is a common cooking liquid in Brittany. Besides adding a brisk note to sauces, vinegar is useful as a tenderizer during braising. Vinegar acts as an acid to break down the fibers that make aged chicken or meat tough, and it will do this even if cooking time is short. In this recipe we combine the two uses—adding vinegar to make the chicken almost velvety in the mouth as well as to impart a slight tartness to the natural flavors.

6 SERVINGS

One 3-pound chicken, cut into 8 pieces
2 tablespoons unsalted butter
2 tablespoons olive oil
1 small onion, peeled and chopped
2 tablespoons chopped shallots
3 garlic cloves, peeled and minced

½ cup red wine
½ cup red wine vinegar
1 cup chicken stock (see Basics, page 375)
2 tablespoons chopped fresh parsley
Salt and pepper

Rinse and pat each piece of chicken dry with a paper towel. Season lightly with salt and pepper. In a large skillet, heat the butter and olive oil until it sizzles. Brown the chicken on both sides. Lower the heat to medium, cover, and cook for 20 minutes. Remove the chicken and keep warm. Discard any fat.

Add the onion, shallots, and garlic to the pan and sauté until the onion is soft and lightly brown. Add the red wine and vinegar, and simmer for 2 minutes to reduce by half. Add the stock and simmer for about 4 minutes. Place the chicken back in the sauce, cover, and cook for 10 minutes. Adjust the seasoning, if necessary. Serve on a platter with the parsley sprinkled over the top of the chicken.

PHEASANT WITH GRAPES

After the work of summer harvest was finished, the fall hunting season began. Nature was allowing us time after the busy harvest and before cold weather to gather our stores for the winter. Today we can enjoy pheasant, rabbit, deer, and other tasty meats without hunting ourselves. However, we can still be a part of the cycle of nature by buying meat in season from producers who reject chemical feeds and allow the animals to naturally develop flavors through free-range feeding.

4 SERVINGS

Two 2-pound pheasants
4 slices lean bacon, halved
1½ pounds white grapes and 1 small
   bunch grapes, reserved
2 tablespoons unsalted butter
½ cup cognac
8 shallots, peeled

8 juniper berries
1 cup white wine
1 cup chicken stock (see Basics, page
   375)
4 tablespoons crème fraîche (see
   Basics, page 379)

Bard the pheasants with the bacon.

In a food processor, purée the grapes. Strain and reserve the juice.

In a heavy dutch oven, melt the butter and brown the pheasant on all sides. Add the cognac and flambé (see Sidenote, page 179). Add the shallots and juniper berries, tossing until the aroma of the berries is released. Stir in the wine, stock, reserved grape juice, and crème fraîche. Cover and simmer gently on low heat for about 45 minutes, or until the pheasant is fork-tender. Remove from the pan and keep warm.

Reduce the sauce by half, simmering about 10 minutes. Remove the bacon from the pheasant breast and discard. Quarter the pheasants and place on a serving platter. Spoon the sauce over the pheasant and garnish with the reserved bunch of grapes. Serve.

VARIATIONS: Pork roast or chicken can be substituted for pheasant. Eliminate the bacon, as barding is not necessary to keep those meats moist.

SIDENOTE:
Pheasant, partridge, guinea hen, and any very lean fowl or birds that have had the skin removed benefit from barding before roasting. Barding, or covering the bird with a layer of fat, keeps the bird moist during cooking. To bard a fowl, cover the

breast completely with a ¼-inch layer of salt pork or bacon, cut into 3-inch pieces. Secure the barding to the bird with twine. Discard the barding after cooking.

My father's mother, Marie Jamet.

HALLOWEEN MEAT LOAF

American meat loaf reminds me of pâté chaud, or hot pâté, which Maman served on cold autumn nights when we wanted something to warm us up without making us feel stuffed. I found it to be the perfect meal to feed my children on Halloween night before they went out and the temptation of too many sweets ruled the night. The secret to a good meat loaf is a balance of meats—beef to give it juiciness, pork for flavor, and veal because it is lean. My recipe uses sausage already seasoned with garlic to save time. This recipe is enough to feed a good-sized crowd of goblins.

8 SERVINGS

1 pound ground beef
1 pound ground veal
¾ pound garlic sausage, with casings, if any, removed
½ teaspoon allspice
1 teaspoon each dried oregano and thyme
½ teaspoon salt
2 teaspoons freshly ground black pepper

1 tablespoon unsalted butter
1 cup chopped onion
2 eggs, beaten
1 cup toasted bread crumbs
1 cup coarsely chopped fresh tomatoes, drained
½ cup chopped fresh parsley
3 tablespoons tomato paste

Preheat the oven to 375°F. In a large bowl, mix the beef, veal, sausage, allspice, oregano, thyme, salt, and pepper. Refrigerate for at least 1 hour but preferably overnight.

Melt the butter and sauté the onion until tender but not brown. Cool. Add the eggs, bread crumbs, and tomatoes to the meat mixture and mix well. Add the onion and the parsley.

Fill a 6-cup loaf pan with the meat mixture and brush the top with tomato paste. Cover with aluminum foil and place in the oven to bake for 20 minutes. Uncover and finish baking for another 30 minutes, or until the juice runs clear when pressed in the center. Serve hot or cold as an entrée or a sandwich.

VARIATIONS: If nongarlic sausage is used, add 3 cloves minced garlic to the seasonings before mixing.

- Add 1 cup fresh chopped spinach during the final mixing.

- Substitute the bread crumbs with a mixture of 1 cup crushed blue corn chips and ¼ teaspoon red pepper flakes, and substitute ½ cup chopped cilantro for the parsley to give the meat loaf a south-of-the-border flair.

- Add ¼ cup chopped pecans and ¼ cup peeled and chopped apple during the final mixing for a nice autumn touch. This is best done if the meat loaf is to be served as an entrée, since the nuts and apple make slicing for sandwiches difficult.

SIDENOTE:

To get the best value when buying ground meat, select the choicest cut of meat available and have the butcher grind it for you. Choose either a lean shoulder blade, also called chuck, or a lean round piece, which is cut from the leg. Because the leg and shoulder areas of the animal are exercised heavily, the lactic acid released into the muscle gives these less expensive cuts high flavor. The piece should be bright red in color, and any fat on it should be white.

PORK CHOPS CHARCUTIÈRE

Pig butchering was a huge job that was always a family project. One entire day each spring and fall was devoted to the task, and everyone had a job appropriate to their age. Even the smallest child could scrub and sterilize the jars and pots needed to cure the meat after the work of dispatching the hog had been done by the adults. It was hard work, but we were rewarded for our efforts. While most of the meat was salted, smoked, or turned into pâtés for the coming winter, on butcher days Maman always made a satisfying braised pork tenderloin or pork chops.

4 SERVINGS

4 lean pork chops, trimmed
1 tablespoon freshly ground black
   pepper
3 tablespoons olive oil
4 shallots, peeled and minced
1 small onion, peeled and finely
   chopped

½ cup dry white wine
1 cup brown stock (see Basics, page
   376)
2 tablespoons Dijon-style mustard
2 tablespoons chopped fresh celery
   leaves or parsley

Rub both sides of the chops with pepper. Heat the oil in a heavy skillet and brown the chops on both sides. Remove from the pan and keep warm. Discard excess fat.

Add the shallots and onion to the pan and sauté for 1 minute. Add the wine, swirling to loosen the brown bits on the bottom. Simmer for 3 minutes, then add the stock. Place the chops back in the sauce and cook for 5 minutes, or until the chops are light pink in the center. Place the chops on a serving platter and keep warm.

Stir the mustard into the sauce and simmer for 5 minutes until thickened. Spoon the sauce over the chops, sprinkle with celery leaves or parsley, and serve.

VARIATIONS: Replace the mustard with 2 tablespoons of chopped cornichon pickle and 2 tablespoons of cider vinegar for a more piquant flavor.

- Pork tenderloin, pork roast, chicken, and turkey all work well with this recipe.

BRAISED CABBAGE WITH CARAWAY

Raising cabbage is similar to raising a child in that the cabbage has three distinct "person-ality" changes in its life. Early summer finds the cabbage young and sweet, quite supple, and uncomplicated in flavor. The teenage years come in late summer, when cabbage has a strong, rebellious, and sometimes bitter taste. Finally, after the first frost brings up a cabbage's sugar content, it becomes the fully mature and once again the sweet cabbage that we loved so well in June.

6 SERVINGS

2 tablespoons unsalted butter
1 onion, peeled and thinly sliced
8 cups shredded cabbage
1 cup chicken stock (see Basics, page 375)

2 tablespoons caraway seeds, crushed
3 tablespoons chopped fresh parsley
Salt and pepper

In a heavy skillet, melt the butter and sauté the onion until tender but not brown. Add the cabbage and sauté lightly. Add the chicken stock and caraway seeds, tossing gently to mix. Cover and simmer until the cabbage is tender, about 20 minutes. Add the parsley, salt and pepper to taste, and serve.

VARIATIONS: If red cabbage is used, add 3 tablespoons of red wine vinegar after the cabbage is sautéed to retain the red color.

- The cabbage can be braised in quarters, but add 5 minutes to the cooking time.

- One pound of Brussels sprouts in the fall or 1¾ pounds of kale in the spring and summer can be substituted.

SIDENOTE:
Cabbage Varieties

Green and Red:
The most common available, they have the strongest flavor. The only difference between the two is color.

Savoy:

Includes all the curly varieties of cabbage. Very tender and the mild flavor does not require blanching prior to cooking.

Chinese:

Sweeter than green cabbage and the leaves can be shredded for stir-fry.

PUMPKIN AU GRATIN

Pumpkin is one of the most versatile of winter squashes, but it has only been recently that people are discovering its wonderful nutty flavor. Often markets carry pumpkins only in October, since almost everyone buys a pumpkin once a year to make a jack-o'-lantern for Halloween. This year experiment with toasting the seeds and using the trimmings left over after carving for this delicious side dish. If buying pumpkin specifically for this gratin, use small ones because they are meatier.

6 SERVINGS

2 tablespoons unsalted butter, softened
6 cups cleaned, peeled, and sliced pumpkin from 1 small pumpkin and jack-o'-lantern trimmings
2 cups grated Cheddar or Swiss cheese
1 cup cream
Salt and pepper
Freshly ground nutmeg

Preheat the oven to 375°F. Completely coat the inside of a 14 × 9-inch baking dish with the butter.

Arrange one layer of **pumpkin** in the bottom of the dish. Sprinkle with half the cheese, then arrange another layer of pumpkin on top. Sprinkle with the remaining cheese. Pour the cream over all. Season with salt and pepper and freshly ground nutmeg. Cover with aluminum foil and bake for 15 minutes. Remove the foil and continue baking for another 15 to 20 minutes, or until the pumpkin is fork-tender.

VARIATIONS: Alternate the layers of pumpkin with potatoes, sweet potatoes, or other squash.

- To make soup, purée leftover pumpkin au gratin and heat through before serving.

♥ *Monique's Touch:*

Toasted seeds, from **pumpkin** or any other squash, are a nutritious snack that is easy to make. Sprinkle a heavy skillet with kosher or sea salt. Wash the seeds, carefully removing all the strings. Do not dry. Add the seeds to the skillet and flip the seeds until they are toasted but not dried out. Store in a brown paper bag.

SALSIFY WITH DILL BUTTER

In mid-October we always looked forward to salsify. Because of salsify's long, tapered shape and mild flavor, Maman referred to it as "autumn's asparagus." I like this image because it reminds me that even as asparagus is one of the earliest vegetables to poke its tender shoots aboveground to reach for the first warm rays of the spring sun, salsify burrows downward, a late root vegetable searching for the last bit of warmth left by the autumn sun. Salsify can have a creamy-colored flesh, or it can come in a deep purple-brown variety called scorzonera.

6 SERVINGS

1½ pounds whole salsify, stems
   removed
1 lemon, halved
2 tablespoons unsalted butter,
   softened

1 tablespoon chopped fresh dill
1 tablespoon chopped fresh parsley

In a large pan, cover the salsify and lemon with water. Bring to a boil, then lower to a simmer for 25 minutes or until tender. Drain. When cool, rub the salsify between your fingers to easily slip the skin off. Discard the skin. Cut the salsify in half.

Heat a pan over high heat, add the butter, dill, and parsley. Add the salsify and toss gently for 1 minute. Serve.

VARIATIONS: Substitute chives or ½ teaspoon of dried thyme or savory instead of dill.

- Toss with 2 tablespoons of yogurt or sour cream before serving.

BAKED POTATO WITH CAPERS AND OLIVES

The capers Americans are familiar with are grown in California or the Mediterranean region on bramblelike shrubs. When I was a child, we made capers from nasturtiums. In the spring, buds were picked while still tight and then pickled. During the summer we picked the blossoms often, to encourage a mass of edible blooms that found their way into colorful salads. Come fall, the seeds were gathered to be pickled just as we did in the spring, bringing to a close one more cycle of the culinary year.

6 SERVINGS

6 baking potatoes, cut into eighths
4 tablespoons capers
½ cup Kalamata olives, chopped

4 garlic cloves, peeled and minced
4 tablespoons olive oil

Preheat the oven to 375°F.

Place the potatoes on a baking sheet. Mix together the **capers,** olives, and garlic, crushing the capers as they are mixed. Add the olive oil.

Sprinkle the caper mixture over the potatoes. Bake for 30 minutes, or until the potatoes are soft and the skins crisp.

♥ *Monique's Touch:*

Nasturtium **capers** are easy to make. While the nasturtium buds are still closed in the spring, pick off the smaller ones from the plant. Wash the buds under a gentle spray of cold water. Drain and sort them to discard any blemished buds. Fill a small glass jar with the buds, along with a sprig of fresh dill or a tablespoon of dillseeds. Cover the capers with a good-quality white wine or cider vinegar. Close tightly and let ripen in a cool place for 3 weeks. In the fall, nasturtium seeds can be made into capers as well. Blanch the seeds for 5 seconds in boiling water, then cool in ice water. Drain and pat dry. Proceed as for nasturtium buds.

WILD RICE SALAD

Wild rice is not a food I grew up with, but it is one I have happily adapted to many recipes that originated in Maman's kitchen. It is actually not a rice at all, but a tall grass indigenous to the lake areas of northern Wisconsin and Minnesota that ripens in the fall. The Native Americans who primarily raise the grass watch for the right time to harvest the crop from the paddies and then pick it by hand. It is then set out to cure and dry over an open fire. The husk is removed the traditional way by beating it while the grain hangs from a frame.

6 SERVINGS

SALAD:

2 cups wild rice, rinsed
6 cups water
1 cup slivered almonds, toasted
2 scallions, wilted stems and roots
   trimmed, chopped
¼ cup chopped fresh parsley
1 Red Delicious apple, diced
1 Golden Delicious apple, diced
6 red lettuce leaves
6 slices Red or Golden Delicious
   apple, for garnish

DRESSING:

¼ cup balsamic vinegar
1 tablespoon Dijon-style mustard
Juice of 1 lemon
¾ cup olive oil
Salt and pepper

In a saucepan, combine the rice and water and bring to a boil. Cover and simmer over very low heat for about 45 minutes, until the water is absorbed. The rice will look like miniature popcorn when it's done. Remove the cover and let any extra moisture evaporate.

Mix together the rice, almonds, scallions, parsley, and diced apples. Refrigerate until ready to use.

To prepare the dressing, in a bowl, blend together the vinegar, mustard, and lemon juice. Slowly whisk in the olive oil. Adjust the seasoning with salt and pepper. Toss with the rice before assembling the salad.

To assemble, place 1 lettuce leaf on each serving plate. Divide the wild rice among the plates and garnish with an apple slice.

VARIATIONS: Any rice may be used, as well as any toasted nut.

- To make an Oriental version, replace the almonds with toasted sesame seeds and add 3 tablespoons of shredded coconut. For the dressing, replace the red wine vinegar with rice wine vinegar, the ⅓ cup of olive oil with sesame oil, and add 2 teaspoons of soy sauce.

ROASTED HAZELNUT AND MIXED GREEN SALAD

The hazelnut bush serves as a hedgerow in the farmlands of Brittany, and every fall we would harvest these pretty nuts by shaking them off their tall branches. In the cool climates of northern Europe, the hazelnut is as ubiquitous in regional dishes as the almond is to Mediterranean cuisine. The hazelnut is gaining popularity in the United States, but if it is unavailable, try substituting walnuts, pecans, pistachios, or macadamia nuts.

4 SERVINGS

DRESSING:
¼ cup red wine vinegar
1 scallion, wilted stems and roots trimmed, finely chopped
2 garlic cloves, peeled and minced
¾ cup olive oil
Salt and pepper

SALAD:
6 cups curly endive, torn into bite-size pieces
6 cups escarole, torn into bite-size pieces
1 cup roasted hazelnuts
4 thin slices French bread, toasted
4 slices goat cheese

To make the dressing, mix the vinegar, scallion, and garlic in a mixing bowl. Slowly whisk in the olive oil until the ingredients are combined and thickened. Season with salt and pepper to taste.

To prepare the salad, mix together the endive and escarole, and divide between 4 plates. Drizzle the dressing over the greens and then sprinkle with hazelnuts. Serve with the French bread toast and cheese.

SIDENOTE:
Hazelnuts may be purchased prepackaged, already peeled and blanched, or they can be sold raw and in bulk. To roast hazelnuts before use, place the nuts on a baking sheet and roast in a 375°F oven for 5 minutes until they brown. Wrap the hazelnuts in a towel. Rub the towel against the countertop between two hands until all the nut skins are rubbed off. Discard the skins and store the nuts in a plastic or paper bag.

UPSIDE-DOWN APPLE CAKE

Green Granny Smith apples are the last apples to be harvested. They are perfect for my version of the American favorite, pineapple upside-down cake. This cake has a moist texture from the juice of the apples, blending well with the smooth feel of the caramel.

ONE 10-INCH CAKE

CARAMEL:
- 3 tablespoons unsalted butter
- 2 tablespoons sugar
- 4 firm Granny Smith apples, peeled, cored, and quartered

CAKE:
- 6 tablespoons unsalted butter, softened
- 1 cup sugar
- 4 egg yolks
- Zest of 2 lemons, grated
- 1 teaspoon baking powder
- 1½ cups flour
- 4 egg whites

Preheat the oven to 375°F.

To make the caramel, place a 10-inch cake pan over medium heat and melt the butter and sugar in it until a light brown caramel forms in the bottom of the pan. Place the apple quarters in the pan and continue to heat and stir until the apples are completely brown. Remove from the heat and cool.

To make the cake, cream the butter and sugar in a mixing bowl until light and fluffy. Add the egg yolks and mix well. Mix in the lemon zest. Add the baking powder to the flour. Blend the flour into the batter a little at a time, beating well.

Beat the egg whites until soft peaks form, then gently fold the egg whites into the batter. Pour the batter over the apples and caramel. Place the pan on the middle rack of the preheated oven and bake for 30 to 40 minutes, or until the center tests dry with a toothpick. Remove from the oven and immediately turn upside down onto a serving plate. The cake can be served as is or with whipped cream or ice cream.

VARIATIONS: Plums and pears are also good fall variations of this cake, or use peaches, apricots, and nectarines in the summer and traditional pineapple in the winter.

PEAR FRANGIPANE TART

In late September I was off to boarding school at a nearby convent. Before we left, my brothers, sisters, and I would spend a day gathering unripe wild pears from hedgerows surrounding neighboring farms. We each would hide our stash in a secret place in the barn, burying the pears in a haystack, knowing the heat of the hay would slowly ripen our treat over the next month. Of course, when we came home at the end of October for All Saints' Day, we never could find the pears and spent the first hours home accusing each other of theft. Maman always anticipated the outcome of our treasure hunt and solved the whole problem by baking this delicious pear tart. The buttery flavor and flaky crust soon made us forget our lost pears, which were usually found the following spring, a shriveled reminder of autumn.

6 SERVINGS

1 recipe sweet short pastry dough
   (see Basics, page 384)
1 cup sugar
4 cups white wine
Zest of 1 lemon, grated
Juice of 1 lemon
1 vanilla bean or 1 teaspoon vanilla
   extract

3 Anjou or Bosc pears, peeled, with
   stems left on
¼ pound unsalted butter
1 egg
1 cup finely ground almonds
3 tablespoons dark rum
1 teaspoon almond extract
1 tablespoon flour

Preheat the oven to 375°F. Line a 10-inch tart pan with the sweet short pastry dough. Refrigerate until needed.

To poach the pears, combine ½ cup of the sugar, the wine, lemon zest, lemon juice, and vanilla bean or extract in a large saucepan. Bring to a boil and simmer for 20 minutes. Add the pears to the poaching liquid. The pears should be fully immersed, so add water, if necessary. Bring to a boil and simmer for 20 minutes, or until the pears can be pierced with a fork but are still firm.

Remove the pears from the poaching liquid. Continue simmering the syrup for 20 minutes, or until reduced to 1 cup. Cool.

Cream the butter and remaining ½ cup of sugar until light and fluffy. Add the egg, almonds, rum, almond extract, and flour. Beat until smooth. Spread the mixture in the chilled tart shell.

Cut the pears in half and completely pull out the stems and cores. With the cut side down, slice the pear into ½-inch slices on the diagonal, keeping the slices in the pear shape. With a spatula, lift the pear halves intact and place them around the edge of the tart with the narrow tip toward the center, pinwheel fashion. Bake for about 45 minutes, or until the tart shell is golden brown and the almond filling has puffed and is lightly browned. With a pastry brush, gently coat the tart with the syrup. Serve at room temperature.

VARIATIONS: Poached pears are delicious served alone or with a chocolate or custard sauce, raspberry coulis, or ice cream.

SIDENOTE:

If you plan to make a pear tart for Saturday, buy the pears on Wednesday. Pears are sold at the market still underripe by about 3 days. Look for pears that are firm to the touch with a slight greenish yellow color on the bottom. Store pears before use in a basket or bowl covered by a towel. This will keep heat in to hasten ripening but will not promote moisture and bacteria. Ripe pears give when pressed, releasing a sweet, pleasing aroma.

NOVEMBER

Gathering together on All Saint's Day
to remember family and friends.
I am seated far right.

November is the evening of the year. It's time to begin to settle in, a time to prepare for a rest period during the long night of winter. But just as evening light throws everything around it into shadows, smoothing and flattening out movement so our surroundings can appear quiet and still, November can fool us into thinking nature has died until spring, when, in fact, it is still very much alive. Life is only more hidden, more of it taking place inside. On farms most of nature's work moves underground as the soil replenishes itself with the old vegetation plowed under when the fields are readied for winter. People have less inclination toward physical activity, so we start to bend toward our inner selves. Our pace slows down, but time is not wasted. We are hunkering down, using our energy to nurture our spirit. The way we cook also slows as a craving for stews melded from long hours of simmering gradually overtakes us. But even the indolent stew is not what it seems to the casual eye. A stew does not require much effort to be assembled, but to succeed in coaxing out the complicated layering of flavors and nuances that can be detected in the mouth, it must be given enough time to do its work.

Slower rhythms took over the farm in November as a cast of winter settled over us. Papa brought the animals in from the pastures and plowed the fields for the first time, turning up great big chunks of rich earth to face the slate sky. He spent a lot of time in the barn sorting through the crop of potatoes, saving the best seedlings to start next year's crop with. The cider had been fermenting in the barrels since the September apple pressing and would be bottled soon, so steamy afternoons were spent in the cold cellar washing the bottles in boiling water. Maman counted over our winter stores one more time, making sure there was enough food to last the winter. Like Papa in the fields, she readied the potager for next year, turning the bare earth until it looked like a brown blanket with its edges bunched around the base of the leeks left to winter over. There was work to be done, but at this time of year the urgency to race against nature was missing.

In November the kitchen hearth became the center of our life. During the warm weather the fire was lit only for cooking and would die down during the day. But now the fire burned continually. The chores done out in the cold barn brought us all in early, eager for a bowl of hot cider and a hearty meal next to the fire. The sun set by four o'clock in the afternoon, and our hunger was for food as thick and dark as the night itself. Cassoulet—a synthesis of beans, duck, lamb, and sausage, all cooked down to fork-tenderness—could take the chill off our bones and keep our stomachs full through the night. The broths and chowders we enjoyed during fall did not satisfy the burgeoning hunger of winter, so they were replaced by stews simmered all day in cooking liquids of strong stock and gutsy red wine. The colors of the dishes Maman created took on different tones as the muted rusts, maroons, and golden browns of autumn vegetables gave place to the nutty dark browns of chestnuts, dried mushrooms, and game braised in rich sauces. The only greens left in the garden before the first hard frost were a few cabbages and the Brussels sprouts, which stood straight and spiky, as if they were guards in front of a deserted palace. Maman still had a few root vegetables harvested the month before, which she served roasted, to bring out their natural sweetness. As the smells in the kitchen became heavier and smoky vapors filled the air, we were grateful for a successful harvest and a full larder.

Conversations over dinner were different during November. During most of the year talk was of crops, the markets, and the weather. But in November very often the talk turned to days gone by. All Saints' Day, a holiday to remember relatives who have passed on, took place the first week in November. After a visit to the cemetery and a church service, all the family gathered at my grandmother's home. We shared a simple meal and spent a relaxed time telling stories about the past. It was how we children learned about our family and understood our place in it. Perhaps a funny story would be told by my grandmother about an eccentric aunt, or a heart-stopping tale of bravery during the war was related by my father about his brother, or my mother reminisced about the kindness of her grandfather—all were told over again year after year. As the years went by, stories about our own growing up were added to the family lore.

Besides thinking of our relatives, November sparked in my family an awareness of our luck when a good crop had been harvested. We were thankful a cozy winter was ahead of us. In the United States we take time to reflect on our fortunes on Thanksgiving. It's also the celebration when, many times, stories are shared around the dinner table and, purposefully or not, the family history is passed on to the next generation. The tradition of passing on the oral family history to the children ensures that the past lives on inside each of us, even when those who peopled it appear to be grown or gone. November, when nature is quiet on the outside so that we may reflect on the inside, is the perfect month to remember what came before as we move on to a new year.

NOVEMBER RECIPES

Caramelized Pear and Endive Soup

Chicken and Sage Soup

Cabbage-Wrapped Pike with Cider

Sautéed Scallops with Jerusalem Artichoke

Roasted Thanksgiving Turkey with Sage

Versatile Bread Stuffing

Rabbit Braised with Mustard and Chestnuts

Tournedos with Portobello Mushrooms

Le Cassoulet à ma Façon

Potato-Leek Tourte

Winter Roasted Vegetables

Belgian Endive au Gratin

Escarole, Turnip, and Apple Salad

Cranberry-Pear Relish

Pumpkin and Spice Roulade

Bourbon Pecan Pie

Pumpkin Custard with Butterscotch Caramel Sauce

FAMILY DINNER

Caramelized Pear and Endive Soup

Rabbit Braised with Mustard and Chestnuts
Beaujolais

Winter Roasted Vegetables
Fall Greens of Curly Endive, Escarole, and Spinach
Basic Vinaigrette Dressing

Pumpkin and Spice Roulade
Sauvignon Blanc

CARAMELIZED PEAR AND ENDIVE SOUP

In the fall we often think of using cabbage or late spinach as the basis of a soup and forget the other greens in season during this time. Endive is here, along with turnips and mustard greens. Adding fruit to the soup balances the bitter flavor common to fall greens. Many old farm recipes call for the use of the outer leaves of lettuce heads, which we in the city usually overlook. I have developed this recipe with those throwaways in mind.

6 SERVINGS

¼ cup honey

3 Bartlett pears, peeled, cored, each cut into 8 wedges

1 head Belgian endive, halved

3 shallots, peeled and finely chopped

3 cups coarsely chopped outer leaves curly endive

3 cups chicken stock (see Basics, page 375)

1 cup milk

2 tablespoons pear brandy

Salt and pepper

Heat the honey in a large sauté pan. Add the pears, stirring to coat each wedge with honey. Continue heating for 3 to 5 minutes, stirring occasionally, until the pears are caramelized evenly. Remove from the pan, setting aside 6 wedges for garnish. Place the remaining pears in a large saucepan.

Add the Belgian endive to the honey, heat for 3 minutes to caramelize, lowering the heat, if necessary, to prevent scorching. Transfer to the saucepan.

Heat the shallots and curly endive for 1 minute in the honey. Stir in the stock, scraping up the honey from the pan bottom. Transfer the stock, shallots, and endive to the saucepan. Bring to a boil. Lower to a simmer for 15 minutes.

Transfer the soup to a food processor and purée until smooth. If necessary, pass through a strainer to remove any fiber. Return to the saucepan, add the milk, and adjust the seasoning. Heat through, but do not boil. Stir in the pear brandy. Ladle the soup into bowls and top each serving with a pear wedge. Serve at once.

VARIATIONS: Maple syrup instead of honey may be used, or 3 tablespoons of sugar may be substituted.

- Use fall apples instead of pears, or a half-and-half combination of apples and pears.

- Ginger or curry can be used for flavoring instead of brandy.

My father's father, Louis Jamet.

CHICKEN AND SAGE SOUP

Making a soup from the broth a hen cooked in was one way Maman turned today's fare into tomorrow's supper. Meat from the hen was served with a cream sauce for lunch, then the next day the extra meat was shaped into little meatballs and served with the broth as a soup for supper. It was our version of chicken noodle soup. Soup is a good way to use up bits and pieces of ingredients left from other recipes that by themselves might be of little use. In this recipe, leftover egg whites, some chicken meat, a couple of bread slices, and an odd carrot or celery stick combine with stock made from a chicken carcass to make a delicious soup.

6 SERVINGS

1 pound ground chicken
2 egg whites
2 tablespoons chopped fresh sage
2 slices bread, torn into small pieces
4 garlic cloves, peeled and minced
½ cup chopped shallots
2 tablespoons unsalted butter

5 cups chicken stock (see Basics, page 375)
1 large carrot, trimmed, halved lengthwise, and thinly sliced
1 celery stalk, thinly sliced
5 ounces vermicelli
Salt and pepper

In a mixing bowl, combine the chicken, egg whites, sage, bread, garlic, and shallots. Mix with your hands until all ingredients bind and are well mixed. Cook a teaspoon of the meat mixture to taste for seasoning and adjust with salt and pepper, if necessary. Refrigerate for at least 1 hour. Form into thirty ½-inch meatballs.

Melt the butter in a pan, then evenly brown the meatballs. Set aside.

In a large pot, combine the chicken stock, carrot, and celery. Simmer gently for 20 minutes. Add the meatballs and cook for 5 minutes, then add the vermicelli and cook for another 5 minutes. Adjust the seasoning and serve at once.

VARIATIONS: The meatballs can be done with turkey or lean fish.

- Summer herbs that have been stored in the freezer can be used instead of sage, or use spice powders for different flavors.

- Serve the meatballs by themselves with a favorite sauce or over pasta.

Medieval tradition claims that a strong woman rules the household of a garden where sage is grown. The name sage even suggests wisdom and longevity, and over the centuries sage has become increasingly valued for its culinary uses. Sage is the last of the summer herbs, sustaining itself long into the cold winter after other herbs have gone to sleep. The flavor is particularly compatible with rich meats and stews. The woody branches can be soaked in water, then burned in the grill to impart a smoky sage flavor.

CABBAGE-WRAPPED PIKE
WITH CIDER

Pike, along with trout, was the very first fish we ate as children. Maman didn't hesitate to serve it to us even though it is very bony. She taught us how to eat fish safely by rubbing the meat against the palate with our tongue to separate out the bone, then to politely place the bone on the edge of the plate. Of course, we turned it into a game, and for us it was just another excuse to be as silly as possible at the table!

6 SERVINGS

6 cabbage leaves
2 tablespoons unsalted butter
¼ cup chopped shallots
½ teaspoon celery seeds, crushed
3 cups apple cider

Six 4-ounce pike fillets
½ cup cream
3 tablespoons chopped fresh celery
  leaves
Salt and pepper

Bring 1 quart of lightly salted water to a boil. Immerse the cabbage leaves and blanch for 10 minutes. Drain and set aside.

In a sauté pan, melt the butter, then sauté the shallots until tender and lightly brown. Add the celery seeds and the cider, simmering until reduced by half, about 7 minutes.

Meanwhile, season the pike with salt and pepper, then wrap each fillet individually in a cabbage leaf. Set the fillets in the pan with the cider sauce. Cover and simmer over low heat for 10 minutes. Remove the fish and keep warm.

Whisk the cream into the sauce and reduce until the sauce coats the back of a spoon. Arrange the pike on a serving platter, spoon the sauce over, and top with the chopped celery leaves.

VARIATIONS: Napa cabbage is a sweeter cabbage that can be used.

- Red snapper, bass, talapia, and grouper are good substitutions.

SAUTÉED SCALLOPS WITH JERUSALEM ARTICHOKE

During the cold months, when scallops were their most plump and succulent, they were often served as the first course at Maman's Sunday table. She had many ways of preparing them, but the combination of scallops with Jerusalem artichokes is unusual. I think she was trying to disguise the taste of the Jerusalem artichokes, as Papa didn't care for them. One of his brothers kept a grocery store in Paris, and I believe he thought the Jerusalem artichoke far too citified for our proud table. To me the taste of the Jerusalem artichoke is reminiscent of the flavor of artichoke bottoms, with the soft bite of a water chestnut.

6 SERVINGS

2 tablespoons olive oil
1½ pounds sea scallops
½ pound Jerusalem artichokes,
    peeled and cut into ⅛-inch
    slices

2 tablespoons chopped fresh parsley
1 tablespoon curry powder
1 cup cream
1 cup bread crumbs
Salt and pepper

Preheat the oven to 375°F.

In a heavy skillet, heat the oil over high heat and sauté the scallops for 1 minute on each side. Add the Jerusalem artichokes, parsley, and curry, and toss gently. Off heat, stir in the cream and season with salt and pepper.

Divide the scallops among 6 individual ceramic au gratin dishes or spoon into a 12 × 6-inch baking dish. Top with bread crumbs and place in the top third of the oven for 5 minutes, or until golden.

VARIATIONS: Assorted shellfish, like shrimp, mussels, and clams, can replace or be mixed with the scallops.

- This can also be done with diced chicken or turkey breast.

- The bread crumbs can be replaced with grated Swiss, Gruyère, or Emmentaler cheese.

ROASTED THANKSGIVING TURKEY WITH SAGE

Thanksgiving is a time for family and a time to celebrate the harvest. It can be a melting pot in which traditions from the past harmoniously blend with patterns being formed around life today. My Thanksgiving table always holds memories of meals shared with my family during childhood, when All Saints' Day served as the catalyst for giving thanks for the harvest and for reminiscing about good days shared before. It is with pleasure that I have adopted the very American Thanksgiving turkey as the centerpiece for our meal, reminding me that change today carries forward the family traditions of yesterday.

14 SERVINGS

One 16–18-pound turkey
24 sage leaves
2 tablespoons olive oil
1 sprig thyme
1 sprig sage

1 carrot, coarsely chopped
1 celery stalk, coarsely chopped
1 small onion, peeled and quartered
2 garlic cloves, peeled and crushed
Salt and pepper

GRAVY:
Neck and giblets from turkey
1 small onion, peeled and diced
   small
1 tablespoon unsalted butter
1 carrot, trimmed and diced small
1 celery stalk, finely chopped

2 quarts cold water
1 sachet (see Basics, page 374)
2 cups white wine
3 tablespoons flour
Salt and pepper

Preheat the oven to 450°F.

Rinse the bird, inside and out, under cold running water. Pat dry.

Separate the skin of the turkey from the breast and thighs by running your fingers under the skin, breaking any fibers between the two. Insert the sage leaves underneath the skin, lying them flat against the turkey meat. Lightly press the skin back in place. Rub the turkey all over with the olive oil.

Fill the cavity of the turkey with the thyme and sage sprigs, carrot, celery, onion, and garlic. Fasten the legs close to the body by tying the drumsticks together with kitchen twine. Season with salt and pepper.

Place the turkey in the oven for 25 minutes, then lower the temperature to 350°F. **Roast** until the juices run clear between the thigh and breast when pierced with a fork, or until the internal temperature registers 150°F with a meat thermometer. Cooking time will vary according to the size of the turkey, but will be about 5 hours for an 18-pound bird.

Meanwhile, in a saucepan, prepare the gravy. Brown the neck, giblets, and onion in butter. Add the carrot and celery. Add the water and sachet, and bring to a boil. Let simmer over low heat during the time the turkey is roasting, adding more water, if necessary.

When the turkey is done, remove the vegetables from the cavity and discard. Transfer the turkey to a serving platter and keep warm. Place the roasting pan over high heat until the fat separates from the brown bits. Pour off as much fat as possible, then add the wine, scraping the bottom of the pan to loosen the brown bits. Simmer for 5 minutes until reduced by half.

With a slotted spoon, lift the neck, giblets, and vegetables from the stock and discard. Add 4 cups of stock to the roasting pan and simmer for 5 minutes. Dilute the flour with a little cold water to make a smooth paste. Whisk the paste into the stock until thickened. Adjust the seasoning with salt and pepper, and serve with the turkey.

♥ *Monique's Touch:*

You may notice this method of **roasting** does not require basting. It is a misconception that basting a turkey (or any other fowl) helps keep the bird moist. The skin prevents any of the juices from penetrating the meat, making it impossible to infuse a turkey with moisture. It also interferes with the caramelization process, which gives a turkey an even golden brown appearance. I also dislike spending any more time than necessary in the kitchen, especially if I have guests, and basting takes a lot of time. The secret to moist turkey is to seal in the juices with high heat in the first 25 minutes of cooking, then turn the oven temperature down to continue cooking.

VERSATILE BREAD STUFFING

Stuffing is traditional with Thanksgiving turkey, but I like to serve it during the year with many other dishes. Maman often used stuffing as a way to stretch a meal, varying the seasonings according to what was available. What never varied, however, was her use of day-old bread. Day-old bread is drier, so it absorbs flavors and holds its shape better than fresh bread.

14 SERVINGS

2 cups mixed chopped onions, leeks, and shallots
3 tablespoons olive oil
1 pound day-old bread, cubed
1 cup hot chicken stock (see Basics, page 375)
2 eggs, lightly beaten

3 tablespoons chopped fresh parsley
1 tablespoon chopped fresh winter savory or thyme
3 tablespoons chopped fresh sage
1 cup raisins
1 cup chopped walnuts
Salt and pepper

Preheat the oven to 350°F.

Sauté the onions, leeks, and shallots in the olive oil until translucent but not brown. Cool.

In a large bowl, combine the bread, stock, and eggs. Blend well. Mix in the onion mixture, herbs, raisins, and walnuts. Sauté a tablespoon of **stuffing**, taste for seasoning, and adjust, if necessary. Bake the stuffing in a greased loaf pan for 45 minutes.

VARIATIONS: Add brandy or other liquor to the stuffing for flavor.

- Dried fruits are a traditional ingredient for stuffing. Use cranberries, cherries, blueberries, blackberries, or raisins.

- Ground meat, sausage, or oysters can be used instead of bread, but bake an additional 15 minutes to thoroughly cook the meat.

♥ *Monique's Touch:*

I believe the reason **stuffing** is usually served only at holiday time is because we think it must be cooked inside the turkey, but that is not so. Many home cooks still cook turkey stuffing inside the roasted bird, but this practice has been given up in professional kitchens because of the dangers of bacterial contamination. I recommend baking the stuffing separately from the turkey and moistening it with the turkey drippings, if necessary.

RABBIT BRAISED WITH MUSTARD AND CHESTNUTS

Cultural symbols can be powerful, and nowhere is this more evident than in the United States when we talk about rabbit. On our farm rabbits were either hunted or raised in hutches for winter food and fur without a sentimental thought. This was the way of pioneers here, too, when survival was the creative force behind every cook. As our affection for Peter Rabbit and the Easter Bunny grew, our appetite diminished, so the succulent rabbit stew sadly passed outside the realm of popular food culture. Perhaps we are more sophisticated today, or perhaps our interest in a wider variety of foods is leading us back to our roots, but rabbit is once again gaining popularity. Rabbit braised in mustard is a classic French country dish, and is an excellent way to introduce this "new" winter game to your family.

6 SERVINGS

One 3-pound rabbit, cut into 6 pieces
3 tablespoons stone-ground mustard
3 tablespoons unsalted butter
1 large onion, peeled and coarsely chopped
1 large carrot, trimmed and cut into ¼-inch slices

1 cup red wine
2 cups brown stock (see Basics, page 376)
1 pound fresh chestnuts, blanched and peeled
3 tablespoons chopped fresh parsley

Preheat the oven to 350°F. Cut a piece of parchment paper the size of a dutch oven.

Rub each piece of rabbit with mustard. In the dutch oven, melt the butter, then sauté the rabbit until brown on both sides. Set aside. Add the onion and cook for 1 minute, or until light brown. Add the carrot and toss gently. Swirl in the red wine, then simmer for 2 minutes to reduce by half. Add the stock, chestnuts, and parsley. Set the rabbit over the vegetables. Cover with parchment paper and the dutch oven lid. Braise in the oven for 20 minutes, turn the rabbit on the other side, and continue braising, covered, for another 20 minutes, or until the meat flakes off the bone when touched with a fork.

Remove the rabbit pieces to a serving platter. Reduce the sauce, if desired, to thicken. To serve, ladle the sauce over the rabbit.

VARIATIONS: Cut-up chicken, pheasant, or 6 turkey legs are good variations from rabbit.

- Instead of chestnuts, try combining Jerusalem artichokes and walnuts.

SIDENOTE:

Chestnuts are wild and majestic trees, hardy enough to produce luxuriant crops of nuts for generations. Some chestnut trees in Europe are estimated to be a thousand years old. Good chestnuts can be found in glass jars at gourmet food shops, but there is nothing to compare with the taste of freshly roasted or blanched chestnuts. They are easy to prepare and well worth the effort.

Roasting:

Cut an X into the round side of the chestnuts and soak overnight in enough water to cover. Place in a wire basket over hot coals until soft, about 5 minutes. Transfer to a brown bag and shake to loosen the skin. Cool and peel.

Blanching:

Cut an X into the round side of the chestnuts. Drop into enough cold water to cover, then bring to a full boil for 10 minutes. Transfer to a bowl of cold water to cool. Peel away the outer skin and the inner white skin. Use as directed in recipes.

TOURNEDOS WITH PORTOBELLO MUSHROOMS

Usually beef dishes served at Maman's table came to our large family made into economical pot roasts or beef stews. Cuts like beef tenderloin were enjoyed only on very special occasions or at civic functions such as a dinner honoring the town's mayor. Later, when my parents visited me in the United States, I liked to serve tournedos with Portobello mushrooms. The preparation is simple but dramatic, and never failed to delight Maman and Papa as they became the honored guests.

6 SERVINGS

¼ cup balsamic vinegar
½ cup basic vinaigrette (see Basics, page 381)
6 small Portobello mushroom caps
One 2-pound beef tenderloin, cut into 6 fillets

3 tablespoons chopped shallots
1 cup red wine
1 cup brown stock (see Basics, page 376)
2 teaspoons cornstarch
2 tablespoons chopped fresh parsley

Preheat the oven to 450°F.

Mix the balsamic vinegar with the vinaigrette and rub the mushroom caps on both sides. Marinate for 20 minutes.

Heat a heavy-bottomed sauté pan (I prefer cast iron) until very hot. Sear the mushrooms on both sides until brown. Set aside on a serving platter and keep warm.

Sauté the fillets until brown on both sides, then finish in the oven to taste. Keep warm with the mushroom caps. Add the shallots to the pan and toss gently for a few seconds, then add the mushroom marinade and red wine. Reduce by half.

Stir the brown stock and cornstarch together, then whisk into the sauce until it binds with the cornstarch and thickens slightly.

To serve, place a fillet in the center of a mushroom cap and spoon the sauce over and around the tournedo.

VARIATIONS: The same can be done with pork tenderloin, pork loin, or duck breast.

- The mushrooms can be sliced before sautéeing, if preferred, but leaving them whole makes preparation faster and gives a more dramatic presentation.

Cooking times for seared meats are always given assuming the cut of meat is fresh. Times will vary depending on the quality of cut, thickness, temperature, how long and by what method the meat has been stored. Meats left overnight in the refrigerator or frozen and thawed lose juices in storage, so cooking time will be less. Meats that are intended to be served rare to medium-rare should not be less than 1 inch thick. Sear on high heat until the meat is well caramelized and a pearl of red juice appears on the top. Turn to the other side and sear until brown. Finish in the oven and test for doneness by touch. Rare will be soft in the center, medium-rare will be slightly soft, medium-well firm but not tough. Practice this method and soon experience will be your guide for perfectly cooked meat every time.

LE CASSOULET À MA FAÇON

There are as many variations for cassoulet as there are cultures to cook it, but no kitchen in Brittany is respectable without making a version of its own. The ingredients that go into any cook's cassoulet may vary according to what is available in the region, but the style of cooking is always the same. The flavor of the finished dish will depend on which meats are used and the way they are roasted beforehand. The type of sausage can give various flavors to a cassoulet. Even the choice of beans is variable. White beans are used in the French version, but Brazilians favor a cassoulet-style dish made with black beans. Use your imagination and let taste be your guide. My version is a simple one that can be embellished by personal taste or creative whim.

10–12 SERVINGS

½ pound salt pork or bacon, diced
1 large onion, peeled and sliced
2 cups diced canned tomatoes
½ cup chopped fresh parsley
6 garlic cloves, peeled and minced
2 pounds great northern white
  beans, cooked
One 3-pound duck, roasted,
  removed from the bone, and cut
  into 2-inch pieces
1 pound shoulder of lamb or pork,
  roasted and cut into 2-inch pieces

1 pound garlic sausage, cooked and
  cut into 2-inch pieces
3 quarts brown stock (see Basics,
  page 376)

CRUST:

2 cups chopped fresh parsley
1 cup bread crumbs
6 garlic cloves, peeled

Preheat the oven to 375°F.

Sauté the salt pork or bacon until crisp. Reserve 1 teaspoon of fat, then discard the rest. Sauté the onion in the same pan until translucent, then stir in the tomatoes, parsley, and garlic. Mix together with the beans.

Combine the duck, lamb or pork, and sausage. In a large earthenware pot, alternate layers of beans and meat, finishing with a top layer of beans. Moisten the cassoulet by filling the pot two thirds of the way up with stock. Set the rest of the stock aside to moisten the cassoulet during braising.

To make the crust, blend together the parsley, bread crumbs, and garlic in a food processor. Spread the crust mixture over the cassoulet. Cover with aluminum foil and place in the oven. Cook for 45 minutes, remove the foil, and continue baking for another 35 minutes. Add more stock, as necessary, to keep from drying.

To serve, spoon the beans on a plate, arrange the meat on the beans, and top with a small piece of crust. Serve piping hot with toasted French bread.

Maman's family church in the nearby village of Roudouallec.

POTATO-LEEK TOURTE

A tourte is a savory country pie that can be filled with almost any variety of vegetables or meat. Mémé Kerzon, my maternal grandmother, often served potato-leek tourte when we came to visit because it serves a large gathering easily and is very simple to make.

6 SERVINGS

1 large russet potato, baked and peeled

1 recipe short pastry dough, partially baked in a 9-inch pie shell (see Basics, page 382)

3 cups chopped leek, white and light green part only

1 tablespoon unsalted butter

½ cup cream

2 eggs

½ teaspoon salt

¼ teaspoon freshly ground pepper

¼ teaspoon freshly ground nutmeg

Preheat the oven to 375°F.

Gently crush the potato with a fork in the bottom of the pie shell. Sauté the leek in the butter until translucent. Transfer to the pie shell. Mix together the cream, eggs, salt, pepper, and nutmeg to make a custard. Pour over the onion and potato, and place in the preheated oven, baking for 45 minutes, or until the tourte is golden brown and the custard set.

VARIATIONS: Cheeses can be sprinkled on top of the custard prior to cooking. Use goat cheese, ricotta, Gruyère, or any good Swiss cheese.

- Add smoked salmon between the layer of potato and leeks.

WINTER ROASTED VEGETABLES

One of the biggest chores on the farm this time of year was the sorting and storing of winter vegetables. This was always done quickly after the first cold snap brought the sugars in the root vegetables to full sweetness. After being pulled from the ground, the vegetables were sorted and arranged in baskets in the barn, where they kept cool and dry through the winter, covered in straw. Cut and bruised vegetables, too damaged for long storage, were winnowed out during the initial sorting. The discards immediately went into this simple and quick-roasted dish, the pure natural flavors and mellow colors of the vegetables making a welcome supper after a long day.

6 SERVINGS

Zest of 2 lemons, grated
Juice of 2 lemons
½ cup olive oil
½ cup chopped fresh parsley
1 tablespoon paprika
1 yellow turnip, peeled and cut into 8 wedges
1 large baking potato, cut into 6 wedges

2 carrots, peeled and cut into ¼-inch slices
1 parsnip, peeled and cut into ¼-inch slices
1 large sweet potato, peeled
Salt and pepper

Preheat the oven to 375°F.

In a mixing bowl, blend the lemon zest and juice with the olive oil, parsley, and paprika. Salt and pepper to taste. Add all the vegetables to the bowl and toss to thoroughly coat. Lift with a slotted spoon and arrange in a single layer on a baking sheet. Bake until vegetables are soft, about 25 minutes. Some vegetables may cook faster than others, depending on their ripeness and moisture content. The turnip will take the longest, followed in order by the baking potato, carrots, parsnip, and sweet potato. Remove the vegetables as they finish cooking.

VARIATIONS: Crushed red or black pepper added to the oil mixture before coating the vegetables adds a robust taste.

BELGIAN ENDIVE AU GRATIN

Belgian endive naturally grows to about two feet, spreading out leafy greens when left on its own in the garden. Because the very bitter taste of endive greens was too strong for us, Papa used the greens as feed for the farm animals. Then at the beginning of October he would dig up the roots and bury them under two feet of sawdust and soil mixed in a cold frame. They lay moist and dark in the cellar all winter, forced to produce small tightly packed heads that Maman called chicons *and we know here as Belgian endive. She cut and used the chicons in salads and casseroles. Come spring, the endive roots would go back to the garden to grow so they could nourish our animals, starting the process of nature once again.*

6 SERVINGS

6 large Belgian endives

3 tablespoons olive oil

1 medium onion, peeled and cut into ¼-inch dice

½ pound baking potatoes, baked, peeled, and cut into ¼-inch slices

1 tablespoon fresh dillweed

1 teaspoon dillseed, crushed

2 tablespoons chopped fresh parsley

½ cup bread crumbs

3 tablespoons clarified butter

Preheat the oven to 375°F. Butter a 12 × 6-inch baking dish.

Bring a pot of lightly salted water to a boil and blanch the endives for 10 minutes to remove some of the bitterness. Drain in a nonaluminum colander, heads down. Cool, then cut each in half lengthwise.

Heat the oil in a pan and sauté the onion until translucent. Add the endives, cut side down, and brown.

Arrange the potatoes at the bottom of the baking dish. Spread the endives and onions on top of the potatoes.

In a small bowl, mix the dillweed, dillseed, and parsley together with the bread crumbs. Spread over the top of the endive. Drizzle with **clarified butter** and bake for 10 minutes, or until golden brown. Serve very hot.

VARIATIONS: To make this hearty enough for a main supper dish, put ham in between the layers of potatoes and endive, then top with a grated cheese, such as Cheddar, Swiss, or Parmesan, instead of bread crumbs. A mix of grated cheese is a good way to use up small bits of cheese that may be left from other recipes.

♥ Monique's Touch:

Clarified butter is butter that has its milk products removed before using, which gives the butter a desirable, clear, fresh taste. To clarify butter, heat a stick of butter until melted, allowing it to bubble and foam. The butter will separate into 3 layers, with foam on top, butter in the middle, and milk solids settling on the bottom. Skim the foam off the top and pour the butter into a dish before refrigerating. When it firms, lift the butter out of the dish and the milk solids will remain behind. Keep covered in the refrigerator for 3 to 4 weeks.

SIDENOTE:

When choosing Belgian endive at the farmers' market or store, look for heads that are plump and tight, colored white to pale yellow. If any green color is present, the heads will be bitter because they have been exposed to too much light.

ESCAROLE, TURNIP, AND APPLE SALAD

Winter salads such as this one would often be on the supper menu with a bowl of boiled chestnuts and a cup of hot cider. Late fall and early winter greens almost always have a sharp, pungent taste. Escarole, chicory, radicchio, and the endives appeal to our appetite this time of year and throughout the winter because they cleanse our body and palate to make way for the rich texture of winter meals. This salad has a nice harmony between the bitterness of the escarole and the sweetness of the apple and turnip.

6 SERVINGS

4 tablespoons cider vinegar
4 tablespoons walnut oil
1 tablespoon chopped fresh parsley
1 medium white turnip, coarsely
   grated
2 small Golden Delicious apples,
   diced with peel

½ cup crumbled blue cheese
½ cup walnut pieces
1 head escarole, torn into bite-size
   pieces
Salt and pepper

In a salad bowl, whisk together the vinegar, oil, and parsley. Salt and pepper to taste. Mix together the turnip and apples, and toss with the dressing. Top with the cheese and walnuts.

Divide the escarole between 6 plates. Serve the turnips and apples on a bed of escarole.

CRANBERRY-PEAR RELISH

Relishes were always part of the fall and winter season on the farm. While apples could be stored in our attic throughout the cold months, pears were usually put into relishes because they were too perishable to last long. Maman liked to mix raisins with pears, but here I've used cranberries to add a bit of holiday tradition. The lovely red berries seem to sparkle against the mellow pears. The sweet-and-sour taste of the relish complements almost any fowl or game.

4 CUPS

1 tablespoon unsalted butter
1 cup chopped onions
1 cup red wine
2 cups fresh cranberries
Zest of 1 lemon, grated
Juice of 1 lemon

2 Anjou, Bartlett, or Bosc pears, peeled and cored
¼ cup walnut pieces
6 whole allspice berries or ¼ teaspoon ground allspice

In a heavy saucepan, melt the butter. Sauté the onions for 1 minute until translucent but not brown.

Add the red **wine** and reduce for 5 minutes. Add the cranberries, lemon zest, lemon juice, pears, and walnuts, and cook, covered, for 15 minutes, or until the pears are soft.

Store in a container and refrigerate overnight. Serve hot or cold, or use as a spread for turkey sandwiches.

♥ *Monique's Touch:*

As a rule, it is recommended to cook **wine** for 5 to 20 minutes prior to adding ingredients such as fruit or fish. The cooking mellows the intensity of the wine, and much of the alcohol is evaporated instead of being absorbed by the food. Consequently, the flavors of the delicate fruits and seafood are not disturbed, but the flavor essence of the wine adds a lovely note to the dish.

PUMPKIN AND SPICE ROULADE

When the occasion called for fancy baked goods, Maman usually depended on a good patisserie rather than take the time to make them herself. However, roulades, or jelly-roll cakes, were often part of her table, because they are not time-consuming or difficult. They are less dependent than most cakes on perfect rising because jelly-roll cakes are baked thin and flat. They can be made as plain or elaborate as you like, with a variety of creams and fillings. They are fun to do and a good way to include children in the kitchen.

12 SERVINGS

CAKE:

6 egg yolks	6 egg whites
⅓ cup sugar	⅔ cup flour
4 tablespoons honey	½ teaspoon allspice
Zest of 1 lemon, grated	½ cup powdered sugar

FILLING:

1 tablespoon gelatin	½ cup milk
½ cup water	1 tablespoon vanilla extract
2 tablespoons cognac	1 cup chilled heavy cream for
2 eggs	whipping
2 cups cooked pumpkin purée or	Pinch each salt and freshly ground
canned pumpkin	nutmeg
2 tablespoons honey	

Preheat the oven to 350°F. Lightly butter the bottom of a jelly-roll pan, then line with parchment paper. Lightly butter and flour the parchment paper.

To make the cake, in a mixing bowl, beat the egg yolks, sugar, and honey until light. Add the lemon zest. In a separate bowl, beat the egg whites until stiff.

Sift together the flour, allspice, and powdered sugar, then alternate folding the egg whites and dry ingredients into the egg mixture. Pour into the prepared pan and spread evenly. Bake for 15 minutes, or until light golden in color.

Sprinkle a small amount of powdered sugar on a large cotton towel, then invert the cake onto the towel as soon as it comes out of the oven. Pull the parchment paper away and tightly roll the cake lengthwise in the towel. Cool.

Meanwhile, prepare the filling. Soften the gelatin in the water for 3 to 5 minutes. In a large saucepan, blend together the cognac, eggs, pumpkin, honey, milk, and vanilla. Sprinkle in a pinch of salt and nutmeg for flavor. Stir constantly over gentle heat for 5 minutes. Do not boil. Off heat, blend in the dissolved gelatin. Set aside.

Beat the whipping cream until firm. Mix one third of the whipped cream into the pumpkin mixture. Gently fold in the rest. Cool at least 1 hour in the refrigerator.

On a clean work surface, roll out the cake and spread with the pumpkin filling. Roll the cake up once again and place, seam side down, on a long serving platter. Chill overnight.

To serve, trim the ends evenly and sprinkle with confectioners' sugar before cutting.

VARIATIONS: The pumpkin filling can be chilled in individual ramekins and served with a custard or cranberry sauce.

- Line a round soufflé mold with ladyfinger cookies. Pour the filling into the mold and chill overnight. Unmold before serving and garnish with whipped cream.

BOURBON PECAN PIE

I grew up with a similar pie made with fresh walnuts, which are abundant in Brittany during the fall. Many a rainy day was spent in the attic shelling nuts, the sharp ping of rain striking the roof competing with the plunking sound of tender nuts striking the pan. I'm sure Maman was thankful she had a task that kept several housebound children occupied, but to us it was more than a way to keep busy. It was a chance to talk, share stories, and really get to know one another. While it takes more time to shell nuts yourself than to buy them, the effort shows in the fresh taste of the finished pie. Once nuts are shelled, they begin to lose some of their moisture and taste. Set aside an hour or two once a season to shell as many nuts as possible, then freeze them in plastic bags, as nuts will keep their delicate flavor when properly stored.

6 SERVINGS

2 cups pecan halves
3 eggs
¾ cup dark brown sugar
¾ cup corn syrup
4 teaspoons bourbon

1 tablespoon vanilla extract
3 tablespoons unsalted butter, melted
1 recipe short pastry dough, blind baked (see Basics, page 382)

Preheat the oven to 375°F.

Spread the pecans on a baking sheet in the oven and toast for 3 minutes. Choose 24 of the nicest halves and set aside.

In a mixing bowl, beat the eggs with the sugar until creamy. Add the corn syrup, bourbon, vanilla, butter, and the remaining pecan halves. Mix well, then pour into the pie shell. Arrange the 24 reserved pecan halves on top in a circular patter. Bake for 50 minutes, or until the center is almost set but still slightly soft. Cool on a rack before slicing. Top with whipped cream, if desired.

VARIATIONS: For chocolate pecan pie, add 3 ounces of melted chocolate to the egg mixture.

- For pumpkin pecan pie, add 1 cup of pumpkin purée to the eggs and replace the corn syrup with ¾ cup of heavy cream.

PUMPKIN CUSTARD WITH BUTTERSCOTCH CARAMEL SAUCE

Butterscotch caramel was often the only candy we had as children, and we were very good at making it last all day. Maman washed empty clam shells and filled them with caramel spooned straight from the cooking pot. After the candy cooled and stiffened we licked it out of the shells all through the day, storing them in our pockets when we were busy playing.

8 SERVINGS

1½ cups water
1¾ cups sugar
1½ pounds pumpkin, peeled and
    diced
2 whole eggs
6 egg yolks
1 tablespoon maple syrup
⅛ teaspoon allspice
2 cups cream

BUTTERSCOTCH CARAMEL SAUCE:
1 cup sugar
¼ cup corn syrup
½ cup water
4 tablespoons unsalted butter
1 cup cream

Preheat the oven to 350°F.

Combine the water and 1½ cups of the sugar in a large saucepan and bring to a boil. Lower to a simmer for 10 minutes, or until the sugar is dissolved. Add the pumpkin to the syrup and cook gently for 20 minutes, or until soft. Remove the pumpkin and drain.

Purée one third of the pumpkin and set aside. Place the remaining diced pumpkin in a 2-quart round ceramic dish, or divide among 8 individual baking dishes.

In a mixing bowl, cream together the whole eggs, egg yolks, and the remaining ¼ cup of sugar until fluffy and light. Add the puréed pumpkin, maple syrup, allspice, and cream. Blend well. Pour the mixture over the diced pumpkin.

Place the custard in a hot-water bath (see Monique's Touch, page 32) and bake in the oven for 15 minutes. Lower the temperature to 325°F and continue baking until the custard is set, or a toothpick inserted in the center comes out clean, about 1 hour. The timing will depend on how deep the baking dish is, or if individual dishes were used. The smaller or shallower the baking dish, the less time will be needed.

To make the butterscotch, combine the sugar, corn syrup, and water in a saucepan. Stir well as the mixture comes to a boil. Lower the heat and cook until a candy thermometer registers 290°F. Remove from the heat and add the butter, 1 tablespoon at a time. Stir each addition until melted before adding the next.

In a separate pan, heat the cream until warm but not bubbling. Off heat, slowly stir the cream into the syrup until well blended. Transfer to a bowl and cool slightly. Serve warm, spooned over the custard.

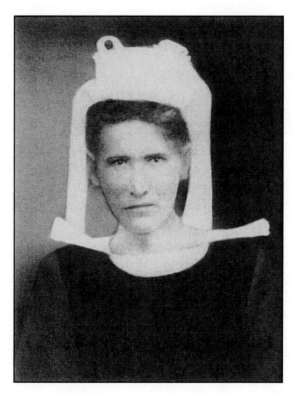

My mother's mother, Marie Corbel,
known to us as Mémé Kerzon.

DECEMBER

Monique's parents' wedding party in 1926.
Maman and Papa stand, center front row.

December announces itself with every breath we take. Our heads swell with the sting of resinous pine in our nostrils, the odor of snow-damp wool, the pristine smell of lemons and oranges washing the air, and the sweet, moist scent of a child's flushed face on Christmas Eve. After the hard work of the fall harvest, we spend November in a reflective doze, but the odors of December slowly awaken in us an anticipation of the holidays that will soon overtake the month in a fevered frenzy of celebration. The food in December is unlike that of any other time of the year. The abundance and richness of the pâtés and foie gras, the roast goose with its skin glistening like polished mahogany, the decadence of chocolate truffles rolled in hazelnut, shiny glazed cakes, and the spun-sugar fantasy of a golden *croquembouche*—all are indulgences that can delight the eye and tempt our resolve. Whether we navigate snow-covered roads or tropical waterways in December, the air swirling around our lives reminds us it has been a long year and now it's time to give ourselves over to festooned gaiety. December comes once a year. With a happy sigh we give in.

The anticipation of the Christmas holidays permeated the farm in December. The excitement played out like a piece of music that begins quietly with a fluttery piccolo riff and ends in a cacophony of crashing cymbals. Perhaps because the emphasis at Christmas was not on exchanging gifts but on sharing a special meal with our family that the excitement built slowly. A lot of time was spent preparing for the supper we would have on Christmas Eve and the big dinner to be served on Christmas Day. Early in the month Maman began making her special cognac-flavored Christmas pâté. She set us a task of preparing the pounds of chestnuts that would be needed, some for stuffing the goose and others for her wonderful chestnut cake. Maman gave us twice as many nuts as she calculated would be needed. After the chestnuts were roasted in a pan, we all tossed several back and forth on our fingers to take the sting of the coals out of the nuts, then peeled each one and popped them into our mouths. We always ate as many chestnuts as we prepared. We were only slightly more disciplined the two weeks before Christmas, when the baking began in earnest. The *bûche de Noël,* fancy cookies, pans of caramel and chocolate candies were made ahead of time, as well as the puffs needed for the croquembouche that would be served a week later on New Year's Eve. The sisters, from oldest to youngest, helped with the baking, and this was the rare time when all of us worked together at the same chore. We enjoyed slipping into comfortable companionship and taking the opportunity to know each other better.

The week leading up to Christmas was used to get the house ready for the celebration. Our home smelled of starch and beeswax as the linens were pressed before being slipped onto the freshly polished oak table. Our best china was brought out and cleaned until it sparkled. The decorations we put up in the country were simple but loved no less than the most glittering display found in Paris. There were wreaths made from dried fruits, flowers, and vines gathered in the summer and fall. One or two days before Christmas Eve a pine tree Papa cut in the woods was set on a table for us to decorate. Paper snowflakes, bits of colored string, and candles pinched onto the boughs were our ornaments. Beginning in December, clementines from Morocco were available at the market, and Maman cleverly showed us how to use them as decorations. We carefully segmented the meat of the small orange citrus without fully peeling it, leaving the white center fiber upright in the middle of the skin "bowl." Cooking oil was poured into the half-globe, and the fiber was lit as a wick. A dozen or so clementine lights circled the tree, the heat of the flames sending up wafts of orange perfume to mix with the pine.

Shortly before Midnight Mass on Christmas Eve, Maman served all of us a light meal of oyster chowder potage. Then, after Mass, the Christmas celebration began in earnest with the commencement of the *réveillon.* The réveillon is a Christmas supper beginning after church services and lasting into the small hours of Christmas Day. The food Maman served was simple but of the best quality. The table was spread with fresh oysters, perhaps tuna braised with lemon, duck rillettes, pâtés, loaves of bread, and an assortment of cakes and cookies. There was cider and mulled wine for the adults, and the night was spent playing games and singing songs.

The highlight of the réveillon came when my grandmother told the Christmas story against the light of the fire and candles burning on the tree. The youngest children, by now exhausted with excitement and good food, placed their wooden shoes on the hearth for Père Noël to find and went to bed around two o'clock in the morning. The adults continued making merry for a couple more hours before retiring. As kids do all over the world on Christmas morning, we were up not long after the adults had gone to bed. There was much excitement as we raced to see what was under the tree. Gifts were not extravagant—a pink marzipan Baby Jesus and a piece of chocolate found in our shoes from Père Noël, or perhaps a needed pair of gloves or a scarf knitted by Maman.

Around noon on Christmas Day my grandparents arrived, and we all sat down to dinner. We began the meal with an appetizer of liver pâté, followed by a cabbage or beet soup. The fish course came next, perhaps steamed scrod with a cream sauce. After the fish came the main course, which was always a big, fat goose, surrounded by a wreath of turnips and potatoes. The meal lasted for hours, with breaks between courses to play cards or to hear a story from my grandfather. Late in the afternoon friends and other relatives began dropping by for coffee and to taste one of several desserts offered by Maman. When special friends arrived, they were sometimes given a small gift of a handmade brandy or a jar of fruit preserves from our kitchen. The day was lingering and relaxed, with an emphasis on sharing our joy of the day at the table with family and friends.

Over the years I have made many changes in the way I celebrate Christmas, adapting old traditions to new life situations. We all have a tendency to rush through December, crowding our calendars with obligations, feeling a pressure to create the perfect Christmas, and complicating the season until it's no longer enjoyable. I have many friends to see through the holidays, and I rarely go to someone's home without a small gift. I like to carry on Maman's tradition of giving a jar of preserves or perhaps a bottle of the herb-flavored vinegars I make in the late summer. It's nothing expensive, nor does it take extra effort at a time of year when my time is limited. But my friends always appreciate my little gifts. If you put up your own wonderful salsa in the late summer, think ahead and make extra jars to give at Christmas. People enjoy receiving gifts that speak of the giver, and nothing is more eloquent than a gift of food from your kitchen.

My family still celebrates with a réveillon and a traditional Christmas Day dinner, complete with a big, fat goose. However, I know my time is more limited, so I use many convenient items on the market today to make our celebration special. I pick one traditional thing that I want to do myself and then find ways of filling in with items from nearby specialty shops. For me, I usually like to take the time to make a bûche de Noël with my sons. I then visit a patisserie to buy cookies and pastries to go along with it. We often roast chestnuts over the fire on Christmas Eve, but I don't have the time to shell nuts for my holiday cooking. My solution is to splurge on good-quality jarred chestnuts from a gourmet cooking shop. Relieve the pressure on yourself by taking advantage of the best of the gourmet items available.

Let simplicity be the gift we give ourselves in December.

DECEMBER RECIPES

Four Onion Soup with Garlic Toast

Oyster Chowder Potage

Country Pâté with Cognac

Duck Rillettes

Gently Braised Tuna with Lemon

Poached Cod with Saffron Sauce

Crisp Halibut Steak with Walnuts

Traditional Christmas Goose

Christmas Goose Stuffing

Buckwheat with Roasted Garlic and Mushrooms

Brussels Sprouts and Mandarin Oranges

Red Lentils with Crème Fraîche

Monique's Pasta au Gratin

Velvet Ganache Truffles

Simply Elegant Florentines

Bûche de Noël

Gingerbread Cookies

Golden Croquembouche

CHRISTMAS CELEBRATION DINNER

Country Pâté with Cognac

Pinot Noir

Poached Cod with Saffron Sauce

Sancerre

Traditional Christmas Goose

Christmas Goose Stuffing

Buckwheat with Roasted Garlic and Mushrooms

Brussels Sprouts and Mandarin Oranges

Bordeaux

Bûche de Noël

Simply Elegant Florentines

Velvet Ganache Truffles

Riesling

FOUR ONION SOUP WITH GARLIC TOAST

Traditional onion soup—rich, dark brown, and filling—meant winter had arrived at the farm just as surely as having tomatoes in July meant summer was in full swing. Originally, onion soup was a simple sustainable farm food made to feed hardy people. Today onion soup is served in the most elegant restaurants. My version is lighter, making it a perfect first course to Christmas dinner.

6 SERVINGS

3 tablespoons olive oil
1 small leek, cleaned and coarsely chopped
1 Spanish onion, peeled, quartered, and cut into ¼-inch slices
1 red onion, peeled, quartered, and cut into ¼-inch slices
4 shallots, peeled and coarsely chopped

2 garlic cloves, peeled and minced
5 cups chicken stock (see Basics, page 375)
1 sachet (see Basics, page 374)
6 teaspoons sherry wine (optional)
6 slices French bread, ½ inch thick
1 garlic clove, peeled and halved lengthwise
Salt and pepper

Preheat the oven to 400°F.

In a heavy saucepan, heat 2 tablespoons of oil, then sauté the onions and garlic together until soft and brown. (You will need a total of approximately 5 cups cut onions.) Add the stock and sachet and simmer for 20 minutes on medium heat.

Brush both sides of the French bread with the remaining tablespoon of olive oil. Stroke the halved garlic over one side of each slice. Toast in the oven for 1 minute, turn, and toast 1 minute more, until the bread is light brown.

Discard the sachet from the soup and correct the seasoning with salt and pepper. Ladle the soup into warmed bowls and add 1 teaspoon of sherry to each bowl before serving, if desired. Serve with the toasted bread.

VARIATIONS: Using chicken stock gives the soup a golden color and mellow taste. Brown stock may be substituted for a richer brown color and added flavor depth.

- Personalize this basic recipe by using different combinations of onions. Choose one or more of the onions above, or substitute other varieties like Vidalia onions, which have a sweeter taste.

OYSTER CHOWDER POTAGE

Early in the evening on Christmas Eve we children feverishly polished our wooden shoes so that Père Noël would find them clean and sparkling in front of the fireplace Christmas morning, enticing him to fill them with a treat or two. After our cleaning ritual we reluctantly went down for a nap. Around ten o'clock that night we awoke and joined the adults for a supper of oyster chowder potage and bread before composing ourselves for the midnight church services ahead. As excited as I was to see what delights the next morning would bring, somehow eating this hot delicious soup filled me with a sense of calm and peace that lasted through the night.

6 SERVINGS

14 oysters, shucked, liquor reserved
¼ pound bacon or salt pork, diced
1 large leek, tough ends trimmed, minced
3 medium baking potatoes, peeled and diced

1½ quarts vegetable stock or fish stock (see Basics, page 377)
2 garlic cloves, peeled and minced
2 tablespoons chopped fresh parsley
Ground white pepper

Preheat the oven to 350°F. Spread the oysters on a baking sheet and place in the preheated oven for 5 minutes until they open. Remove the meat from the shells and set aside. Discard the shells.

In a large saucepan, sauté the bacon or salt pork until light brown. Set aside, discarding the fat. Add the leek and potatoes, tossing together to begin heating. Do not brown. Add the vegetable or fish stock, garlic, and reserved oyster liquor, then simmer for 15 minutes until the potatoes are tender.

Remove half the vegetables and set aside. Add half the reserved oysters to the potage and simmer for 5 minutes. Coarsely chop the remaining oysters.

In a food processor, purée the potage, then return to the pan with the reserved vegetables, chopped oysters, and parsley. Simmer for 5 minutes more. Adjust the seasoning with white pepper.

VARIATIONS: To make a richer potage, stir in 1 cup of milk or cream with the reserved vegetables and chopped oysters.

- One quarter cup each of diced carrot and celery added with the leeks gives a slightly sweeter taste and adds texture.

- One teaspoon of sherry may be added to each bowl at serving time.

COUNTRY PÂTÉ WITH COGNAC

For the holiday season Maman always made her special pâté to serve with several other varieties she purchased from the village charcuterie. Since goose liver pâté was too dear for our purse, she made her own pâté a little more elegant by grinding it finer than usual and adding a touch of cognac for flavoring. Maman watched it very closely in the wood-burning stove, a look of satisfaction brightening her face when she judged the brown crust of the pâté just right. Pâté making is an art taking practice to balance all the ingredients, but this simple recipe is easy for anyone to start with.

12 SERVINGS

1 tablespoon unsalted butter
4 shallots, peeled and chopped
¾ pound veal shoulder, ground
1¼ pounds pork shoulder, ground
¼ cup cognac
2 garlic cloves, peeled and minced
¼ teaspoon *quatre-épices* (see Sidenote, page 262)

1 teaspoon dried thyme
½ teaspoon salt
¼ teaspoon pepper
2 eggs, slightly beaten
½ pound bacon strips
2 bay leaves

Preheat the oven to 350°F.

In a heavy pan, melt the butter, then sauté the shallots until translucent but not brown. Cool to room temperature.

In a mixing bowl, combine the veal, pork, cognac, garlic, quatre-épices, thyme, salt, pepper, and shallots. Mix well, cover, and refrigerate overnight.

Add the eggs to the cold meat mixture and mix well. To **test for seasoning,** sauté a teaspoon of the pâté in a hot pan before tasting. Adjust seasoning, if necessary.

Line a 1-quart oval or rectangular ovenproof terrine with the bacon, letting the tips hang over the sides of the pan. Fill the terrine with the pâté mixture. Firmly tap the terrine on the counter several times to remove any air pockets. Place the bay leaves on top of the pâté, then fold the bacon ends over the top of the terrine.

Cover the terrine with aluminum foil and place in a hot-water bath (see Monique's Touch, page 32). Bake for approximately 1 hour and 15 minutes, or until a meat thermometer registers 160°F or the pâté has pulled ¼ inch away from the sides of the terrine.

Remove from the hot-water bath. Pour out the water and return the terrine to the pan. Cut a piece of cardboard to the size of the terrine and wrap it in plastic. Place the cardboard on top of the pâté and weigh it down with a few cans or a brick. Refrigerate several hours until cool.

To serve, discard the bay leaves before cutting into thin slices. Serve cold with mustard and sour pickles.

VARIATIONS: Meats that make good pâté are chicken, rabbit, duck or other game.

- The taste of a pâté can be varied by adding nuts, mushrooms, or flavored liquors in place of the cognac.

- Use pâté as a sandwich filling.

♥ *Monique's Touch:*

When **testing for seasoning** by sautéeing foods that will be served cold, as with this terrine, remember they should taste a little saltier when tested hot. Some of the strength of the seasoning flavor will be lost during cooling.

SIDENOTE:
"Quatre-épices," meaning "four spices," is a traditional blend of spices the French use for seasoning pâtés, sausages, soups, and braised dishes. The mixture keeps well in a jar near the stove and is a wonderful way to correct seasoning in the final minutes of cooking. To make quatre-épices, blend 3 parts ground black pepper with 1 part each ground nutmeg, allspice, and ginger.

DUCK RILLETTES

Rillettes are different from pâtés in that rillettes are very rich spreads served on dense rye bread as hors d'oeuvres. Pâtés are firm and served in slices, making a meal in themselves when served with bread. Every French country household has its own special recipe for rillettes made of duck, pork, or sometimes salmon. A crock of this flavorful duck rillettes is always part of my holiday table.

8 SERVINGS

One 5-pound roast duck, skinned
    and boned, drumsticks reserved
    for another use
1 pound pork back fat, diced
6 ounces pork loin
1 medium onion, halved
1 carrot, trimmed, peeled, and
    halved lengthwise

1 garlic clove, unpeeled
1 tablespoon mixed dried thyme,
    rosemary, savory, and sage
1½ cups dry white wine
1 teaspoon green peppercorns
Salt and pepper

Remove approximately ¾ cup of duck fat from the skin and cut into very small dice. Cut the duck flesh into strips 1½ inches long and refrigerate until ready to use.

Place the duck and pork fat in a large saucepan with enough water to cover. Set over medium heat, cover, and cook gently until the water has evaporated, about 30 minutes. Stir occasionally to prevent sticking.

Add the pork loin, duck meat, onion, carrot, garlic, and herbs to the fat. Pour in 1 cup of the wine and bring to a boil. Cover, set over low heat to a bare simmer for 3 hours. The meat should be very tender.

Leaving the meat and fat in the pan, remove and discard all vegetables and herbs. Add the remaining ½ cup of wine and the peppercorns. Cover the saucepan with a damp cloth, being careful not to let the cloth touch the meat. Cool to room temperature.

After the meat is cool, use a fork to shred it into the fat. Mix well until a creamy, spreadable consistency is reached. Correct the seasoning with salt and pepper before molding the rillettes in a terrine. Cover with waxed paper laid directly on top of the rillettes and store in the refrigerator for up to 4 weeks.

GENTLY BRAISED TUNA
WITH LEMON

A can of tuna would never be found in my mother's cupboard, nor do I keep any in mine. Fresh tuna, readily available today, is far superior in taste and texture. Braising brings out the flavor while keeping the tuna moist. The recipe below can be adapted endlessly using seasonal herbs, and I always make extra to turn into tuna salad the next day.

6 SERVINGS

3 tablespoons olive oil
1 large onion, thinly sliced
1 tablespoon cider vinegar
1 tablespoon crushed black pepper
2 bay leaves
3 sprigs fresh parsley

One 1½-pound tuna steak
1 cup white wine
Zest of 2 lemons, finely grated
Juice of 2 lemons
3 tablespoons unsalted butter

In a nonaluminum pan, mix together the oil, onion, vinegar, pepper, bay leaves, and parsley. Place the tuna in the marinade and coat on both sides. Let stand in the refrigerator for at least 1 hour or overnight.

Heat a heavy-bottomed pan until very hot. Remove the tuna from the marinade and sear quickly until brown, turn, then sear the second side. Add the marinade to the pan. **Cover** and simmer gently for 30 minutes over low heat.

Remove the tuna from the pan and keep warm. Swirl in the wine, lemon zest, and lemon juice. Add the butter to the sauce and blend well. To serve, ladle the sauce on the bottom of a serving platter, then place the whole tuna steak on top. Cut into serving pieces at the table.

VARIATIONS: This can be done with any firm, thick fish, like halibut or swordfish.

- In the summer diced fresh tomatoes can be added during the last 5 minutes of braising.

- The bones can be used to make fish stock (see Basics, page 377), and the leftover sauce can be used to flavor soup broth.

♥ *Monique's Touch:*

Covered braising is best done in a pan with a tight-fitting lid in which the ingredients fit snugly. When braising in a pan that is a little too large for the recipe, create a tight braise by laying parchment paper or aluminum foil directly on top of the contents, tucking in the edges all around, then cover with the pan lid. Thus the "lid" is lowered, allowing the parchment paper or foil to keep the moisture close to the braising food.

POACHED COD WITH SAFFRON SAUCE

Whenever we received family at home for dinner, fish would be the first course. Because of its abundance, cod was usually the choice Maman served. Today I rarely have time to serve dinner in courses, but I continue to rely on this favorite recipe because the vegetables cook along with the cod. Served with a winter green salad, it makes a quick, simple but elegant supper.

6 SERVINGS

4 cups court bouillon (see Basics, page 378)

1 small onion, thinly sliced

1 carrot, trimmed, peeled, and thinly sliced

2 garlic cloves, peeled and crushed

Six 4-ounce cod fillets

1 cup white wine

2 tablespoons tomato paste

½ teaspoon saffron threads

1 cup cream

2 tablespoons chopped fresh parsley

In a large saucepan, combine the court bouillon, onion, carrot, and garlic. Simmer for 10 minutes, or until the carrots are tender. Immerse the fillets and poach over low heat for 5 minutes. Remove the fillets, strain the vegetables, and set both aside, keeping warm. Return the poaching liquid to the saucepan.

To make the sauce, blend the white wine, tomato paste, and saffron into the liquid. Simmer approximately 10 minutes, or until reduced to 2 cups. Stir in the cream and parsley, and continue simmering for 5 minutes, or until the sauce is reduced by half. Arrange the cod fillets and vegetables on a serving platter and top with half the sauce. Serve with the additional sauce on the side.

VARIATIONS: Other fish fillets that make suitable substitutes are halibut, sole, bass, hake, grouper, or mahi mahi.

- Curry powder, ginger, or lemongrass may be used instead of saffron.

CRISP HALIBUT STEAK
WITH WALNUTS

On rainy or cold days I played with my sisters and brothers in the attic among the trays of walnuts being stored there for the winter. The stacks of trays made perfect room dividers for our playhouse. Eventually, when we tired of our rambunctious games, our play evolved into a quiet afternoon of shelling nuts. At the end of the day we took a bowl of nuts down to Maman to use in that night's supper. Maman liked mixing crushed walnuts with bread crumbs to add flavor to sautéed fish. It gives a crusty texture that is reminiscent of fried fish, and the delicate scent of the walnuts is very inviting.

6 SERVINGS

2 egg whites
½ cup milk
½ cup bread crumbs
1 scallion, wilted stems and roots
　　removed, minced
3 tablespoons chopped fresh parsley
½ cup crushed walnuts

Six 4-ounce halibut steaks
1 cup basic vinaigrette (see Basics,
　　page 381)
4 shallots, chopped
6 lemon slices
Salt and pepper

Preheat the oven to 375°F.

Beat the egg whites and milk together. In a separate bowl, mix the bread crumbs, scallion, parsley, and walnuts together. Salt and pepper the halibut steaks on both sides.

Heat a heavy pan until hot, then add ⅓ cup of the **vinaigrette.** Pass each halibut steak through the egg-white mixture, then coat each side with bread crumbs. Quickly brown on both sides, then finish inside the oven for 10 minutes.

Remove the pan from the oven to the top of the stove over medium heat. Set aside the steaks and keep warm. Swirl the shallots and the remaining ⅔ cup of vinaigrette in the pan. Transfer the halibut steaks to a serving platter and top with the sauce, then serve each portion with a slice of lemon.

VARIATIONS: Firm fish fillets such as pompano or grouper can be substituted, as well as whole fish such as sea bass or trout.

- Serve with a light tomato sauce made from tomatoes preserved during the summer months.

♥ *Monique's Touch:*

I always keep several cups of basic **vinaigrette** on hand. Besides being a wonderful dressing for salads, I like to use it as a cooking oil, as in the recipe above. A whiff of infused herbs enhances the flavor of whatever I am sautéeing without the heaviness of adding dry winter herbs, and in the summer I am saved the time of chopping fresh herbs. It is an easy, creative way to simplify your daily cooking.

TRADITIONAL CHRISTMAS GOOSE

We did not have goose every year for Christmas, but the years we did are most memorable. We all trailed along when Papa went to buy the bird from our neighbor and kept quiet as he surveyed the flock, taking care to find just the right one. The geese preened and strutted in front of us, not realizing their vainglorious beauty would land them on the Christmas table the next day. What a feast it was to be able to taste a well-prepared goose, cooked slowly so the meat always came out juicy and tender! Even in the fat-conscious era of today's kitchen, I indulge in the pleasure of a fine braised goose with plenty of chestnuts for our very special Christmas dinner.

8 SERVINGS

One 8-pound goose, giblets cut into small pieces
4 cups stuffing (see Christmas Goose Stuffing, page 271)
½ pound cooked chestnuts, peeled (see Sidenote, page 236) (optional)
2 tablespoons unsalted butter

2 carrots, diced
1 medium onion, diced
3 tablespoons flour
4 cups hot brown stock (see Basics, page 376)
3 cups dry white wine
½ cup port wine (optional)
Salt and pepper

Preheat the oven to 400°F. Rinse the goose in running cold water, inside and out, then pat dry. Salt and pepper the cavity.

Stuff the goose with alternating layers of stuffing and **extra chestnuts.** Truss the goose and set in a large roasting pan. Salt and pepper the outside of the bird and roast for 20 minutes, or until the skin starts to turn golden brown.

Melt the butter in a saucepan, then brown the giblets, carrots, and onion until the onion begins to brown. Add the flour and mix well for approximately 1 minute, or until the flour is absorbed. Slowly add the stock, stirring constantly. Bring to a boil and simmer for 20 minutes, or until the sauce is reduced by a third. Remove the goose from the oven and lift it from the pan. Pour off the fat. Swirl the wine in the pan, scraping the brown bits to blend. Pour the giblet sauce into the pan, return the goose, and cover with aluminum foil. Lower the oven temperature to 350°F and continue braising the goose for 2 hours.

Transfer the goose to a large serving platter and keep warm. Skim the excess fat from the sauce, then simmer 10 minutes to thicken. Add the port wine, if desired, and adjust the seasoning.

To serve, carve the goose into serving pieces. Pass with the sauce.

♥ *Monique's Touch:*

The **extra chestnuts** I layer my stuffing with are included purely for my family's taste. Many Americans are not accustomed to the flavor of chestnuts, so you may wish to adjust the amount you use or omit them entirely from your recipe.

CHRISTMAS GOOSE STUFFING

Bretons compliment a cook by saying, "There must be fairies in your caldron!" and I think that was true whenever Maman made her goose stuffing. Christmas was for splurging, so she liked to use a meat stuffing instead of bread. I never saw her follow a recipe, yet people raved about the excellence of her stuffing. Sorcery was hardly the secret in her cooking, but she did take care to check that the flavors, texture, and seasonings were balanced just right. Her recipe, which I've adapted below, is not fussy or complicated. The real magic at her fingertips was the pride of simplicity that came out in her while cooking.

FOR ONE 8-POUND GOOSE

1½ pounds cooked chestnuts, peeled
   (see Sidenote, page 236) or one
   and a half 15-ounce jars chestnuts
3 shallots, minced
½ cup cognac
¾ pound lean veal, ground

1¼ pounds pork shoulder, ground
2 eggs, slightly beaten
3 garlic cloves, peeled and minced
1 tablespoon dried thyme
Salt and pepper

Combine all the ingredients in a large bowl and mix well. Sauté 1 teaspoon of stuffing to taste for seasoning and adjust, if necessary. Refrigerate until ready to use.

Prior to cooking, stuff the cavity of the goose with the stuffing mixture. Proceed as directed in the goose recipe.

SIDENOTE:

While it is recommended to cook stuffing outside a turkey, cooking a stuffed goose is very safe. The reason is that there is less meat around the cavity of a goose, so the moist heat from a braised goose penetrates to the center of the stuffing quickly and stays at a sufficiently high heat for a long enough period of time to destroy bacteria.

BUCKWHEAT WITH ROASTED GARLIC AND MUSHROOMS

Buckwheat is something I grew up with, and many long winter nights our tummies were warmed by crispy buckwheat cakes cooked on a griddle over an open fire. Buckwheat was a staple of Breton cooking and is most widely known through our buckwheat crêpes. It all but disappeared from the table during the last thirty years as Brittany became more influenced by global culinary fashions. Recently buckwheat has once again become popular, since people in Brittany have begun reviving their roots and celebrating their regional cuisine. In this recipe I have taken traditional buckwheat and combined it with popular ingredients of today.

6 SERVINGS

1 cup dried shiitake mushrooms
4 cups chicken stock (see Basics, page 375)
1 small leek, cleaned and coarsely chopped

2 tablespoons olive oil
2 cups buckwheat groats
1 head of garlic, roasted, pulp extracted (see Sidenote, page 24)
1 cup freshly grated Parmesan cheese

Soak the mushrooms in the chicken stock until soft, about 30 minutes. Drain, reserving the stock. Thinly slice the mushrooms and set aside.

Sauté the leek in the olive oil until translucent. Add the mushrooms and buckwheat, gently mixing to coat the buckwheat with oil.

Turn the heat to low and stir in the reserved chicken stock. Cook, covered, until the grains are slightly soft in the center, about 15 minutes.

Add the garlic pulp, mix well, then transfer to a deep serving dish. Top with Parmesan cheese and serve immediately.

VARIATIONS: Arborio or regular rice can be used. Adjust cooking time according to package directions.

- Couscous makes an excellent quick variation. Shorten the cooking time to 5 minutes.

BRUSSELS SPROUTS AND
MANDARIN ORANGES

Foods found in season have a seasonal life within their own species. The progression of winter brings a parade of bright citrus fruits from the orange family, starting with the naval orange toward the end of November in very early winter. The first weeks of December bring the mandarin orange, which meant to us children that the Christmas season was about to begin. Clementines signaled the very imminent arrival of Père Noël, while blood oranges arrived around the New Year and were a treat almost until Lent.

6 SERVINGS

1 quart water, lightly salted
1½ pounds Brussels sprouts, outer
    leaves trimmed, bottoms trimmed
    and scored with an *X*
1 small onion, diced
1½ cups celery root, coarsely grated

2 tablespoons olive oil
Zest of 3 mandarin oranges, finely
    grated
3 mandarin oranges, peeled and
    sectioned

Bring the water to a boil. Blanch the Brussels sprouts for 15 minutes, or until tender. Transfer to a colander to drain.

Sauté the onion and celery root with the olive oil for 5 minutes. Add the Brussels sprouts and orange zest, cover, and simmer for 5 minutes. Gently toss in the orange segments until heated through. Serve immediately.

VARIATIONS: Because Brussels sprouts are a member of the cabbage family, any cabbage type can be used in this recipe. Broccoli and kohlrabi make particularly interesting variations.

RED LENTILS WITH CRÈME FRAÎCHE

Meatless dinners were served at home many nights between holidays during December. Lighter meals were needed to give the body a rest from the richness of festive fare, and lentils are filling without being heavy. We ate lentils much like people here eat chili—alone, ladled over rice or pasta, or with more stock added to make a soup. Lentils keep well in the refrigerator and don't take long to cook, an added bonus during the busy weeks of celebration.

6 SERVINGS

1 medium onion, diced
2 tablespoons olive oil
¾ pound red lentils or any type
    lentil, rinsed and sorted
1 garlic clove, peeled and minced
2 tablespoons cider vinegar
2 tablespoons chopped fresh parsley
3 cups chicken stock (see Basics,
    page 375)

1 bay leaf
1 cup canned diced tomatoes,
    drained
½ cup crème fraîche (see Basics, page
    379)
Salt and pepper

In a deep saucepan, sauté the onion in the oil until translucent but not brown. Add the lentils, garlic, vinegar, parsley, stock, and bay leaf. Cover and let simmer over medium heat for 15 minutes. Add the tomatoes and season with salt and pepper. Simmer over low heat for another 10 minutes, or until the lentils are tender. Most of the liquid will be absorbed. Remove from the heat and stir in the crème fraîche. Serve immediately.

VARIATIONS: Dried split peas can be used instead of lentils.

- Hot pepper sauce to taste gives creamed lentils a spicy flavor, or a tablespoon of chopped cilantro during the last 10 minutes of cooking is good.

MONIQUE'S PASTA AU GRATIN

This was our version of macaroni and cheese, which we loved as children as much as American kids do. It is one of the first dishes I learned to cook, as Maman felt learning to make a good basic white sauce was fundamental to cooking in her kitchen. Pasta au gratin is a very simple dish to make, easily adaptable to whatever is at hand, and perfect with a mixed green salad for a light supper when your family needs a break from too many holiday dinner parties.

6 SERVINGS

3 tablespoons unsalted butter

2 tablespoons flour

1½ cups warm milk

2 pounds rotini pasta, cooked according to package directions

1 cup grated Gruyère and Swiss cheese, mixed

Salt and pepper

Freshly ground nutmeg

Preheat the oven to 350°F. Butter a 2-quart ovenproof baking dish with 1 tablespoon of the butter.

In a saucepan, melt the remaining 2 tablespoons of butter. Stir in the flour until smooth, then cook for 1 minute. Do not brown. Slowly add the milk, stirring constantly. Season with salt and pepper and nutmeg.

Layer a third of the pasta in the bottom of the baking dish. Pour ½ cup of the sauce over the pasta, then top with a third of the grated cheese. Repeat the layers twice.

Bake for 15 minutes, or until the top is golden and the cheese melts.

VARIATIONS: Shredded cooked meat like turkey, ham, or chicken can be added to the layering.

- One cup of shredded spinach can be added to the sauce with the milk.

- Other cheeses can be substituted or combined, like Cheddar, goat, Parmesan or Romano cheese.

VELVET GANACHE TRUFFLES

In my family truffles were given at Christmastime when we went visiting. My grandmothers were particularly fond of them, and looked forward with anticipation to discovering which flavorings my mother would choose to use each year. While truffles are quite elegant, they are very simple to make. Since they are made from regular ganache filling used in cakes at this time of year, they take little extra time in the kitchen to make when doing the holiday baking. Truffles can also be made ahead of time and frozen, kept handy for when unexpected gifts are needed.

2 DOZEN

½ cup cream
10 ounces bittersweet chocolate, shaved
4 tablespoons unsalted butter
1 tablespoon vanilla extract
½ cup unsweetened cocoa powder

In a saucepan, bring the cream to a boil, then remove from the heat. Immediately add the chocolate, butter, and vanilla. Beat the mixture until the chocolate is completely melted and the texture becomes smooth. Transfer to a bowl, cover, and chill overnight.

Take about 1 tablespoon of the chocolate and quickly roll it in your hands to form a ball. Repeat until 2 dozen truffles are rolled. Chill for at least 30 minutes, or until the truffles are firm. To finish the candies, roll each truffle in cocoa until it is completely coated.

VARIATIONS: Instead of vanilla extract, Grand Marnier, raspberry liqueur, cognac, or Armagnac make excellent flavors for truffles.

• The truffles can be finished in powdered sugar, shaved coconut, or crushed nuts.

SIDENOTE:
There are many types of chocolate on the market, and understanding the differences can help recipes come out just right. The quality of the chocolate used is also important. Chocolate should break easily and cleanly, be uniformly dark, with a sheen to the surface. The aroma should smell strongly of chocolate. Store in a dark, dry place at a temperature no higher than 75°F. Do not refrigerate or freeze.

Unsweetened:
Used for baking and also known as baking or bitter chocolate.

Semisweet:
Made from chocolate liquor obtained from grinding cocoa beans, cocoa butter, sugar, and vanilla. Less expensive chocolate will use a vanilla substitute called vanillin.

Bittersweet:
Made from chocolate liquor with added cocoa butter and sugar. The quality and intensity of flavor will depend on the quality of cocoa beans and how much cocoa butter is added. A good chocolate is balanced. Can be used interchangeably with semisweet chocolate.

Sweet:
Same as semisweet but with more added sugar.

Milk:
Same as semisweet with the addition of milk powder and other flavorings. Some manufacturers use higher amounts of added sugar.

White:
Made from cocoa butter extract with sugar and powdered milk added. Good quality, has high cocoa butter content.

SIMPLY ELEGANT FLORENTINES

Just as we do today, Christmastime in our village meant there was a lot of coming and going, much visiting and many friends stopping by. Bretons by nature are a private people, so even friends who came by to visit were likely to find themselves chatting in the courtyard instead of inside our house. When the ultimate sign of friendship and hospitality was extended and they were invited in for coffee, Maman always served these delicate little cookies to her special guests.

3 DOZEN

1 cup unsalted butter, softened
½ cup corn syrup
½ cup toasted and crushed hazelnuts
½ cup sugar
1 cup flour

Preheat the oven to 350°F. Butter and lightly flour a cookie sheet.

Combine all the ingredients in a bowl and blend well. Place 4 to 6 teaspoon-size balls of cookie dough on the sheet, leaving about 2 inches in between to allow for spreading. Bake for 5 minutes, or until light golden brown in the center. **Mold** into shapes, if desired, while warm. Cool completely.

♥ *Monique's Touch:*

This is a fun cookie to make because it can be **molded** to any shape you like while still warm. When the cookies are cool enough to handle but still pliable, sometimes I fold them around the handle of a wooden spoon to make slender cylinder cookies. Florentines can also be molded into little baskets by shaping the warm cookie around the base of a small teacup or muffin tin.

BÛCHE DE NOËL

The bûche de Noël (Yule log) is the classic French Christmas Day dessert and was always the crowning end to our holiday meal. There was a strict protocol in our kitchen for the making of the Yule log. All the girls gathered around the kitchen table a few days before Christmas and were assigned different tasks according to age. Beginning with the youngest, whose job it was to lick the bowl, all the way up to the oldest, who had the honor of assembling the confection, we each took part in creating the annual festive cake. The afternoons my sisters and I spent in the kitchen making our cake each year are vivid in my mind when my sons and I make our own bûche de Noël.

8–10 SERVINGS

1 recipe mocha French buttercream (see Basics, page 389)
1 recipe chocolate French buttercream (see Basics, page 389)
1 jelly-roll cake (see Pumpkin and Spice Roulade, page 247)

2 tablespoons rum
Meringue mushrooms (see Meringue Nests, page 92)
1 teaspoon powdered sugar
1 teaspoon unsweetened cocoa powder

Bring the buttercreams to room temperature at least 1 hour before assembling the log. Beat the buttercream to fluff it with air before using.

Unroll the jelly-roll cake on a work surface. Sprinkle with rum. Spread three fourths of the mocha buttercream on top. Reroll the cake, placing the seam side down on a serving platter.

Cover the top and sides of log with chocolate buttercream. Trim the ends at an angle, setting the trimmings on top of the log to simulate stumps. Finish the cut ends by frosting with mocha buttercream. With a fork, draw wavy lines through the frosting all over the log to simulate the bark of a tree.

Place the remaining mocha buttercream in a pastry tube. Use it to write "Joyeux Noël" or "Merry Christmas" on the cake. Arrange meringue mushrooms around the base and on top of the log to simulate mushrooms growing out of the log. Sprinkle the log with powdered sugar to look like a light dusting of snow, and the mushrooms with cocoa powder to simulate soil. Refrigerate until ready to serve. Let stand at room temperature 1 hour before serving.

GINGERBREAD COOKIES

When my children were small, we began hosting a children's Christmas party every December to diffuse some of the excitement that built up during the month. We entertained everyone by making a traditional gingerbread house, and each year we added more elements until one year we built a whole village during one party. The gingerbread village was perhaps an inevitable extension of a custom we had as children in Brittany. We always shaped our gingerbread cookies into hearts and figures of the people who were part of the village—the woodcutter, the shepherd, the baker, and others. It was a reminder that the spirit of Christmas is truly found in the hearts of the people who touch our lives every day of the year.

2 DOZEN

½ cup honey
½ cup molasses
¾ cup sugar
¼ pound unsalted butter
1 egg, slightly beaten
3½ cups flour
2 teaspoons baking powder
¼ cup ground almonds

1 teaspoon each cardamom, ginger,
 cloves, nutmeg, and cinnamon
2 teaspoons grated orange zest
2 teaspoons grated lemon zest

GLAZE:
½ cup honey
2 tablespoons water

Preheat the oven to 375°F.

In a saucepan, stir together the honey, molasses, and sugar. Heat to a boil, stir well, and remove from the heat. Let cool for 20 minutes, then stir in butter. Let cool another 20 minutes, then beat in the egg.

In a separate bowl, mix the flour, baking powder, almonds, spices, orange and lemon zests. Slowly add the dry ingredients to the sugar syrup, stirring to blend well. Let rest overnight in the refrigerator.

Roll out the dough so that it is between ⅛–¼ inch thick. Cut into shapes with cookie cutters. Place on a buttered cookie sheet and bake for 15 minutes. Remove from the oven.

To glaze, combine the honey and water, and brush the cookies while still hot. Cool to room temperature before storing in an airtight container.

VARIATIONS: Ground candied oranges and lemon, found in the market, can be added for taste and color.

- This recipe makes a soft and spongy cookie. For harder cookies, lower the oven temperature to 325°F and bake for an additional 15 minutes.

GOLDEN CROQUEMBOUCHE

During the holiday season I always enjoyed walking past the patisserie, where an elaborately decorated croquembouche commanded center stage. The croquembouche makes a spectacular centerpiece for a New Year's celebration. Traditionally 365 tiny cream puffs, one for each day of the year just passed, are piled like a pyramid and held inside a web of golden spun sugar. Guests pull the puffs off the pyramid in the sharing spirit and toast the coming year with champagne. Although the croquembouche looks elaborate, it is really quite easy to do, as it can be made in advance and assembled shortly before the party. The recipe below is enough to make a small pyramid of about forty-eight puffs, enough for three per person.

14 SERVINGS

CARAMEL SYRUP:
3 cups sugar
¼ cup light corn syrup

Double recipe puff paste (see Basics,
    page 386)
1 recipe custard cream (see Basics,
    page 388)

Before assembling, make the caramel syrup by combining the sugar and corn syrup in a saucepan. Heat slowly until a candy thermometer reaches 317°F and the syrup is amber-colored. Remove from the heat at once and carefully plunge the bottom of the pan into cold water for a few seconds to stop the cooking, but do not cool completely or the caramel will stiffen.

To assemble the croquembouche, make a small hole in the back of each puff with a sharp knife. Fill a pastry bag fitted with a ¼-inch tip with custard cream, then pipe approximately 1 to 2 tablespoons of cream through the hole in the puffs.

Dip the filled cream puffs, one by one, into the caramel syrup and arrange the first layer of the croquembouche on a round 9–11-inch cake board or plate. Graduate the number of puffs used in each layer until a pyramid cone is formed. The caramel will hold the puffs together.

To finish, dip a fork in the syrup, then draw it around and around the croquembouche, draping the puffs in thin threads of caramel.

VARIATIONS: Sugar almonds, candied flowers and fruits, small pieces of dried fruit or candies can be sprinkled over the croquembouche for a more decorated look.

JANUARY

*This is the type of folk dancing, in traditional
Breton costume, that took place at home
during a January* veillée.

January is as welcome as an afternoon nap the day after a raucous party. The first week of the new year is given over to a sleepy slowness as we begin to recover from the lush celebrations of the month before. There is almost a sense of relief that the flashy foods of December have lost their appeal, and even the idea of eating can make us want to pull the covers over our head and groan. But by the second week of January our appetite is beginning to rouse again. Against the backdrop of a bleak January day we find ourselves hungering for the comfort of a good meal, and we ask ourselves, "Now what do we do?"

The foods of January cleanse out the richness of December. We are no longer interested in buttery sauces and extravagant meats. The bitter bite of Belgian endive, the tartness of a winter grapefruit, or a sauce cut with the clean taste of vinegar seem right to us as we try to balance out the overly sweet and fat-rich flavors we've indulged in. At the same time, it's not the perkiness of a summer salad we desire. A primitive voice inside calls us to soothe ourselves during the lonesome night of winter with slow-simmering stews and braised dishes that will fill us up and make us feel protected.

In January the seasonal cook looks for a satisfying depth of flavor from foods put up or gathered during the harvest that have had time to develop their texture. Mature root vegetables are wonderfully pulpy and softer to the touch in winter. Because moisture is lost during storage, these vegetables do not hold their shape as attractively when roasted or quickly cooked whole. They are perfect for turning into a thick potage or smooth purée. Stored nuts develop a pleasing intensity as they lose moisture and add a pleasing texture to dishes. Mushrooms can be coaxed back to life once more in the stewpot, their strong taste as prevalent as when they were picked and dried in the fall. All the flavors of January have a true, mature personality that lingers long in the mouth and are very satisfying.

January on the farm was cold and wet. When we weren't in school, we stayed close to the house and fireplace, playing games or helping Maman with the knitting and mending that she had no time for in the busy summer. On most days a fine mist veiled the glow of the sun and fused the short days and long nights together. It seemed to bring with it a quiet that permeated the countryside as thoroughly as the damp air. Outside, the animals huddled close in the barn, munching the hay and oats stored for them during the hot August harvest. Yet even in the cold stillness, work continued. Papa and my brothers cleaned the animal beds regularly and then spread the old straw and manure across the bare fields to fertilize them. They were looking ahead to spring, giving back to the soil so it would in turn provide us with another year of living.

Maman was looking to her stores of root vegetables, apples, pears, nuts, dried and canned foods to provide for our meals. Just as she did at the peak of the summer season, she thought about the flavor and texture of ingredients when deciding how to prepare them to best take advantage of what she had. The flavor of the potatoes, carrots, cabbages, and winter squashes she stored in the barn had grown stronger as they aged. She tended them slowly in a corner of the hearth, combining dried beans or bits of smoked meat with the vegetables until the low heat of the coals caused the flavors to develop into velvety layers. The strong flavors of the stews were gently accented with the dried herbs Maman deftly added to the pot. She allowed the natural aging of her stored ingredients to supply the flavor.

The way we ship and store food today has changed dramatically from even thirty years ago, stunting the natural aging process of produce. Produce departments no longer follow the seasons. Most fruits and vegetables are grown on commercial farms in California and Florida, where long growing seasons allow them to supply consumers with most produce up to nine months of the year. To fill in the gap, suppliers ship in produce from other countries whose growing season is opposite that of North America. All the fruits and vegetables are picked before ripening, shipped thousands of miles, and placed in cold, low-oxygen storage. Many of them, like apples, turnips, cucumbers, and rutabagas, are coated with paraffin to prevent further maturation and bruising during transport or when being handled in the store. After sitting for as long as months in storage, they are piled high in colorful displays at the supermarket, each perfectly shaped and colored piece the same as the next. The result of turning our markets into year-round gardens is produce that is bred for appearance and transport. The sugars and acids naturally found in fruits and vegetables, causing them to ripen and mature with wonderful flavors, are reduced to minimal levels. Most of the taste from mass-grown produce is bland, and we are missing the opportunity to experience the true flavor of what a winter-overed carrot or apple should have. In addition, flavor has much to do with the amounts of food we consume. If flavors are fully developed, our sense of taste signals that our hunger is deeply satisfied more quickly. When flavors are bland or indistinguishable from one another, we continue eating, often to excess, to try to quench our craving for satisfaction. We spend more money and devote more time today to preparing exotic food combinations to tempt the palate, but we don't find what we are looking for when we sit down at the table.

It is still possible to bring seasonal flavors into your kitchen during the winter. First, be aware of what produce is actually in season. A tomato in January is tasteless because it doesn't belong and has been raised for retail, not flavor. Second, when buying produce in the winter, look for organically grown fruits and vegetables. Sometimes people are put off by the look of organic foods because they have odd shapes or the color is not uniform, and we are used to seeing picture-perfect produce in our supermarkets. But the way organic vegetables and fruits look is the way of nature. They have been raised without chemicals and harvested shortly before coming to market, with as little intervention as possible. Organic foods will mature closely to the way nature intended, allowing the flavors to develop. Lastly, we need to make better use of the produce we buy in the stores. Understand that if a carrot feels soft or a cabbage has wilted leaves on the outside, it does not indicate an ingredient is past using. Peel away the wilted outer leaves and put the heart of the cabbage in the pot when braising a pot roast. Combine the soft carrot with other root vegetables to make a delicious purée. Savor the fully developed flavors that fully mature vegetables have to offer.

The winter flavors of vegetables and the simplicity of one-pot meals, such as a pot-au-feu, combine to make cooking in January not only delicious but easy. At first glance the pot-au-feu requires a lot of ingredients. But once put together, the pot-au-feu needs little attention and can be turned into at least three meals. The first night serve the meat and half of the vegetables with some of the sauce ladled over for a substantial dinner. The second day serve more of the vegetables beside an omelet and a slice of crusty bread for a light supper. On the third day the remaining sauce, meat, and vegetables can be added to stock and turned into a hearty soup for lunch. The depth of flavor found in recipes during winter works for us to minimize kitchen time as it maximizes mealtime satisfaction.

January begins with appetites dulled by the glittery repasts of December. It seems sleepy and uninspired, a month to be tolerated instead of celebrated. But if we listen to the seasons, we begin to realize that January is full of flavorful and comfortable meals that help us live through the depths of winter. January is a month of satisfaction, to be enjoyed as it slowly propels us toward spring.

JANUARY RECIPES

Fireside Cabbage Soup

Garbanzo Beans and Roasted Garlic Soup

Salmon Gravlax with Mustard Sauce

Sea Scallops with Oranges and Cracked Pepper

Scaloppine of Turkey with Green and Black Olives

Chicken in Calvados

Le Pot-au-Feu à la Sauce Piquante

Black-Eyed Peas with Chorizo

Smoked Meat Potée with Cabbage and Chestnuts

Potato Lyonnaise

Rutabaga and Quince Mash

Endive and Pink Grapefruit Salad

Thumbprint Lemon Cookies

Galette des Rois

Orange and Honey Madeleines

DEEP WINTER NIGHT'S SUPPER

Black-Eyed Peas with Chorizo

Crusty Country Bread

Apple Cider

Endive and Pink Grapefruit Salad

Thumbprint Lemon Cookies

Orange and Honey Madeleines

Coffee

FIRESIDE CABBAGE SOUP

It was on dark nights, when the penetrating damp of a Breton winter fell around us, that my grandfather Pépé took the time to visit. To warm himself on the outside when he came in from the cold, he settled on a bench placed just inside our enormous stone fireplace, which was large enough for a grown man to stand in. To take the chill off his insides, he ladled helpings of this cabbage soup over thick bread into a wooden bowl, the hot soup sending up aromatic clouds of steam curling around his head.

6 SERVINGS

1 pound lean ham
3 medium russet potatoes, quartered
3 quarts cold water
1 pound cabbage, thinly sliced
1 sachet (see Basics, page 374)
3 garlic cloves, peeled and crushed
2 medium onions, thinly sliced

1 small cabbage head, cored and cut into 6 wedges
1 teaspoon dillseeds, crushed
1 teaspoon celery seeds, crushed
1 cup chicken stock (see Basics, page 375)
Salt and pepper

In a large pot place the meat, potatoes, and water. Bring to a boil, lower to a simmer for 20 minutes. Skim off any foam that rises to the top. Add the sliced cabbage to the pot, along with the sachet, garlic, and onions. Return to a boil, then lower to a simmer for 30 minutes.

Meanwhile, in a medium saucepan, sprinkle the cabbage wedges with the crushed dillseeds and celery seeds. Add the chicken stock, cover, and simmer over low for 15 minutes, or until the cabbage is tender.

Remove the meat from the pot, set aside, and keep warm. Discard the sachet. Purée the cabbage slices and cooking broth in a food processor until smooth. Adjust seasoning with salt and pepper. Return to pot and heat through.

To serve, slice the meat. Place a wedge of cabbage in a deep soup plate, top with some of the meat, and pour the hot puréed soup over.

GARBANZO BEANS AND ROASTED GARLIC SOUP

Garlic is usually always associated with southern French cooking, but twisted ropes of garlic hanging inside windowsills and from barn rafters are a common sight throughout the Breton countryside. Garlic is used differently in Brittany than in other parts of France, less as a powerful flavor and more as a subtle seasoning. To flavor bean soups, Maman liked to take the skin of a roasted head of garlic after the pulp was extracted and wrap it in cheesecloth. She tied the bag to the pot handle and dangled the garlic into the soup while it simmered. Before serving, she pulled out the garlic skin, thereby giving a hint of garlic without allowing the nutty flavor of the beans to be overshadowed. My family, having grown up in the States, where the strong flavor of garlic is desired in much of our cooking, prefers that the pulp of the roasted garlic be added directly to the soup. Experiment with both methods to discover how using ingredients in different ways can change the character of a dish.

6 SERVINGS

3 cups garbanzo beans

2 tablespoons olive oil

1 onion, diced

1 leek, cleaned, cut in half lengthwise, and diced

2 carrots, diced

6 cups chicken stock (see Basics, page 375)

3 sprigs fresh parsley, stems removed, chopped

1 sachet (see Basics, page 374)

1 large head of garlic, roasted (see Sidenote, page 24)

1 cup diced preserved roasted tomatoes (see Oven-Roasted Tomatoes Mylène, page 184) or canned tomatoes, drained and diced

Salt and pepper

Soak the garbanzo beans in enough water to cover overnight. Drain and rinse. Add water to 2 inches over the beans and bring to a boil. Cook for 25 minutes, or until tender. Drain.

In a large pot, add 1 tablespoon of the olive oil, the onion, and leek. Sauté until translucent, but do not brown. Add the carrots, and cover for 1 minute. Gently toss in the beans. Add the stock, half the parsley, and the sachet. Wrap the garlic head in cheesecloth and add to the soup. Season with salt and pepper, and simmer, covered, for 20 minutes. Add the tomatoes and simmer for 5 minutes more.

Remove the garlic and 2 cups of the beans and vegetables. Set aside. Unwrap the garlic head and cool. Squeeze the pulp from each clove and add back to the soup. Discard the skin.

In a food processor, purée the soup until smooth. Pass through a fine strainer to remove any fibers. Return to the pot, stir in the reserved beans, vegetables, and parsley. Heat through and serve while hot.

VARIATIONS: In Brittany, flageolet beans are often used for this recipe, but black beans, kidney beans, or great northern white beans are also used.

SALMON GRAVLAX
WITH MUSTARD SAUCE

Along with the croquembouche, Maman always served some sort of cured or smoked fish on her New Year's table. Most often she favored trout or eel, as it was readily available from nearby river waters. As my experience with food widened during my training in Europe, I came to love the delicate salty flavor of cured salmon. I carry on the tradition of my childhood by serving fish on New Year's Day, but it is always salmon, which reflects the preferences and tastes of my life today.

6 SERVINGS

2 pounds salmon fillet, skin and
    bones removed
1 cup kosher salt
1 tablespoon white peppercorns,
    crushed

½ cup sugar
½ cup dried dill
4 tablespoons Dijon-style mustard
2 tablespoons red wine vinegar
¾ cup olive oil

Gently pound the salmon fillet to an even thickness. Mix together the salt, peppercorns, and sugar. Reserving 1 tablespoon of the dill for the mustard sauce, mix in the rest. Rub each side of the salmon with the mixture, then wrap tightly in plastic wrap.

Place the salmon in a roasting pan, fitting a second pan on top, like a sandwich. Weigh the pans down with a 5-pound bag of flour or several cans from the pantry, then set in the refrigerator to cure for 48 hours.

Gently rub the salt and dill off the salmon fillet and then rinse under a light spray of cold water. Pat dry. Carefully slice the salmon on the bias into paper-thin strips and place on a serving platter.

Combine the mustard, red wine, and reserved dill. Slowly whisk in the olive oil until well blended. Spoon some of the mustard sauce over the salmon before serving. Serve with crackers or small rye bread slices with the mustard sauce on the side.

VARIATIONS: Any dried herb or mixture of herbs may be used, according to taste.

- In the summertime fresh herbs should be used instead of dried.

SEA SCALLOPS WITH ORANGES AND CRACKED PEPPER

Fresh winter scallops were always a part of our Sunday meal, each week bringing a different preparation, as they are so versatile. I have always favored this dish because I like the slightly bitter taste of the wilted winter greens against the sweetness of the oranges and scallops.

6 SERVINGS

2 pounds sea scallops, about 24 pieces
7 teaspoons olive oil
4 tablespoons cracked black peppercorns
2 naval oranges, peeled and segmented, with juice reserved
3 cups chopped broccoli rabe
3 cups chopped outer leaves curly endive
Zest of 2 naval oranges, grated
1 cup dry white wine

Pat the scallops dry and drizzle with 6 teaspoons of the oil. Roll each scallop in the peppercorns to coat well.

Lightly oil a heavy skillet with the remaining oil. Heat over a very high flame until hot. Sear each scallop for 1 minute on each side. Set aside. Discard any excess oil.

In the same pan, sear the orange segments and set aside.

Rinse the broccoli rabe and endive in cold water, but do not dry. Add the greens to the pan and toss gently until wilted. Stir in the orange zest and reserved juice. Transfer the greens to a serving platter and arrange the scallops on top.

Add the wine to the pan and simmer for 2 minutes to reduce the sauce by a third. Spoon the sauce over the scallops and garnish with the orange segments.

VARIATIONS: Sliced boneless chicken breast or medallions of pork tenderloin may be substituted.

- A variety of greens may be used in this recipe. Use kale or savoy cabbage as a fall seasonal variation.

- For a richer sauce, whisk in 1 cup of cream after the wine and simmer for 5 additional minutes.

SIDENOTE:

To segment citrus fruit, cut each end of the fruit to make a flat top and bottom. Stand the fruit on a cutting board, and with a small, sharp knife, cut away the peel and white pith from top to bottom. Turn the fruit upside down and trim away any remaining peel and pith. Holding the fruit in your hand over a bowl to capture the juice, gently cut the membrane close to the fruit to free the segment. Remove the segment and continue around the fruit until all the segments are removed. Squeeze the membrane to extract the remaining juices.

SCALOPPINE OF TURKEY WITH GREEN AND BLACK OLIVES

Maman looked forward to relaxed Sunday lunches in January, as it was the only month of the year when chores were light and the garden was sleeping at the same time. There was time to linger in town after church, so Papa usually headed to the café for a glass of wine. While he passed time with the other village men, Maman, we children close at heel, stopped at the patisserie to buy a dessert for that day's table. Afterward we all headed home, where Maman made up a scaloppine, favoring it for Sunday lunch because it is quick and easy to do. Here I have used turkey with green and black olives for a contemporary version of Maman's dish, which she would have made with veal and chopped cornichon pickle. Try either for a delicious and simple meal.

6 SERVINGS

1½ pounds turkey breast, cut into scaloppine (see Sidenote)
2 tablespoons flour, seasoned with salt and pepper
2 tablespoons olive oil
2 tablespoons unsalted butter
½ cup chopped shallots
6 garlic cloves, peeled and minced

½ cup chopped green olives
½ cup chopped black olives
1 cup white wine
1 cup chicken stock (see Basics, page 375)
¼ cup bread crumbs
½ cup chopped fresh parsley

Pat the scaloppine dry, then lightly dredge through the flour to coat on both sides.

Heat 1 tablespoon each of oil and butter in a large skillet until hot. Place the scaloppine pieces in the pan and brown 1 minute on each side. Do not crowd the pan. Add the rest of the oil and butter as needed to keep the scaloppine from sticking to the pan. Set aside after browning.

Add the shallots, garlic, and olives to the pan and toss gently. Add the white wine and simmer for 3 minutes to reduce by half. Add the stock, swirling to loosen any brown bits in the bottom of the pan. Add the bread crumbs and parsley. Return the scaloppine to the pan and turn a few times to coat well with the sauce as it heats through. Arrange on a serving platter and serve at once.

VARIATIONS: Chicken breast, veal, or pork work as scaloppine.

- Mushrooms or artichoke hearts may be substituted for, or added with, the olives. Using chopped cornichon pickle is a classic Breton preparation, but the pickles should substitute for the olives rather than be added in with them.

- In the summer a cup of diced fresh tomatoes may be added, or use canned tomatoes in winter.

SIDENOTE:

To prepare the scaloppine, cut a boned turkey breast into ¼-inch diagonal slices. Slip the slices, a few at a time, into a plastic bag. With the flat side of a meat mallet, pound the turkey slices until very thin, about ⅛ inch.

CHICKEN IN CALVADOS

This is a great dish to have late in January, when winter feels endless and summer is only a ghost hanging suspended in the frozen air. Whatever the time of year, the cooking technique is very adaptable to ingredients that are at hand, but this version is particularly welcome in winter. I use tomatoes preserved in August as a reminder of summer to come, brightening everybody's spirits, if not the weather. The apple brandy and cider lighten the texture, providing a break from traditional winter stews and the heaviness of the season.

6 SERVINGS

One 3-pound chicken, cut into 8 pieces
2 tablespoons unsalted butter
2 tablespoons olive oil
1 large onion, halved and thinly sliced
¼ cup Calvados or domestic apple brandy
1 cup sparkling apple cider or 2 cups apple juice
1 cup diced preserved roasted tomatoes (see Oven-Roasted

Tomatoes Mylène, page 184) or canned tomatoes, drained and diced
1 teaspoon Dijon-style mustard
⅛ teaspoon freshly ground pepper
1 tablespoon flour
1 tablespoon water
½ cup cream
3 tablespoons chopped fresh parsley

Pat the chicken dry. In a heavy pan, melt the butter with the oil until hot. Brown each piece 2 minutes on each side. Remove and drain on paper towels. Discard the excess fat from the pan.

Sauté the onion until soft. Return the chicken to the pan and add the Calvados or apple brandy. Light the Calvados or brandy with a match to flambé (see Sidenote, page 179). When the flame dies down, add the apple cider or juice. Simmer for 15 minutes, or until the liquid is reduced by half. Cover and simmer for 25 minutes, or until the chicken is fork-tender.

Remove the chicken pieces and keep warm. Add the tomatoes, mustard, and pepper to the pan. Dilute the flour in the water and stir until a smooth paste forms, then add slowly to the sauce to thicken. Cook for 5 minutes on high heat until the sauce thickens. Stir in the cream. Return the chicken to the pan and heat for 5 minutes. Sprinkle with the parsley and serve at once.

VARIATIONS: Pork chops, rabbit, and duck may be used.

- Cognac or less expensive brandy may replace the Calvados.

My grandmother Jamet spinning wool outside the manoir.

LE POT-AU-FEU À LA SAUCE PIQUANTE

Maman never had to call us to table when she made her version of pot roast. The kitchen filled with the aromatic vapors of winter vegetables and dried herbs, announcing to everyone exactly what was for dinner. As with most French cooks, presentation of her meals was always important to Maman. Her method of bundling the vegetables together helped keep their shape during cooking and made it easy to pull the vegetables from the pot. She always arranged them on the platter in attractive groupings around the sliced meat, with sauce ladled over all. Flavor, color, and texture were always in balance, and one didn't exist without the others.

12 SERVINGS

One 2-pound brisket
One 4-pound round pot roast, with bone
8 cups cold water
2 cups brown stock (see Basics, page 376)
1 large onion, loose skin removed and halved
1 large whole onion, unpeeled
2 cloves
1 head of garlic, loose skin removed
1 sachet (see Basics, page 374)
8 small carrots, trimmed and peeled
8 small white turnips, peeled
4 leeks, cleaned and halved lengthwise
1 small cabbage, cored and cut into 6 pieces
6 potatoes, skin on and halved

SAUCE:
1 small onion, diced
1 tablespoon unsalted butter
¼ cup cornichon pickle juice
½ cup tomato paste
½ cup tomato purée
1½ cups brown stock (see Basics, page 376)
½ cup chopped cornichon pickles
2 tablespoons chopped fresh parsley

Soak the brisket and the roast in the water for 1 hour. Remove, then bring the water to a boil. Return the meat to the pot and blanche for 3 minutes, then remove and rinse in cold water. Skim the foam off the top of the soaking water before returning the meat to the pot. Add the stock and bring to a boil, then lower to a simmer.

Heat a pan until very hot and place the onion halves cut side down, and sear until dark brown. Wrap in cheesecloth and add to the meat pot. Stud the unpeeled onion with the cloves and add to the pot, along with the garlic and sachet. Simmer gently for 2½ hours.

Make 2 cheesecloth bundles with 4 carrots and 4 turnips in each. Make 2 cheesecloth bundles with 4 leek halves and 3 cabbage pieces in each. Add all the bundles to the pot, along with the potatoes, and continue simmering over medium heat for another 40 minutes.

To make the sauce, sauté the diced onion in butter for 1 minute until transparent. Add the pickle juice, tomato paste, tomato purée, and stock, then blend well while bringing to a boil. Lower the heat to simmer for 15 minutes. Pass the sauce through a fine strainer, return to the pan, and stir in the pickles and parsley.

To serve, remove the meat and vegetables, discarding the cheesecloth bags. Slice the meat before arranging the meat with the vegetables on a serving platter. Spoon a ladleful of sauce on top and pass the remainder.

♥ *Monique's Touch:*

I **soak** meat in cold water prior to boiling to allow the water-soluble collagen tissue in meat to dissolve in the cooking liquid, which provides nutrition to the liquid and gives it a nice, gelatinous consistency. It also extracts the impurities in the meat that can be skimmed off the surface as it coagulates into foam. This gives the finished pot-au-feu a clear and flavorful broth to be served with the meat and vegetables.

BLACK-EYED PEAS WITH CHORIZO

January winter nights fell by four o'clock in the afternoon, and without electricity, the days were short and nights long on the farm. Luckily, January was also the month of the veillée. The veillée were informal evening gatherings during which family and friends joined to gossip and play cards. Occasionally the sound of accordion music and dancing feet filled the room, which competed with voices raised in heated discussion about current politics. Hardy dishes that fed a crowd without fuss were in order, so bean casseroles fit the casual atmosphere quite nicely. Today I serve my veillée guests by track lighting instead of candlelight, and the sound of my son's rock band practicing often competes with table conversation, but I still serve beans flavored with good-quality sausage. The components of a good veillée never change, whatever the generation—good food, good friends, and a long winter night.

6 SERVINGS

3 cups black-eyed peas, soaked overnight in enough water to cover

1 large onion, sliced

2 tablespoons canola oil

6 ounces chorizo sausage, cut into ¼-inch slices

2 ounces Canadian bacon, diced small

3 garlic cloves, peeled and minced

1 bay leaf

3 cups chicken stock (see Basics, page 375)

3 cups shredded turnip greens

3 tablespoons cider vinegar

½ cup crème fraîche (see Basics, page 379)

1 tablespoon chopped fresh parsley

Rinse the black-eyed peas under cold water and cover with water by 2 inches. After 5 minutes of soaking, discard beans that are still floating. Drain and rinse once more.

In a large pan, sauté the onion in the oil until lightly brown. Add the sausage and sauté for 1 minute, then add the bacon and toss gently. Add the black-eyed peas, garlic, bay leaf, and stock. Bring to a boil, then lower to a simmer. Cover and cook for 35 minutes, stirring occasionally and adding more stock if the peas become dry.

Heat a pan over medium heat until hot. Rinse the turnip greens in cold water, but do not dry. Toss a handful of greens at a time into the hot pan, letting the rinse water steam the greens until wilted. Stir the greens and vinegar into the black-eyed peas 5 minutes before the peas are finished cooking. Ladle the peas and sausage into serving bowls and top with a dollop of crème fraîche. Sprinkle with the parsley and serve.

VARIATIONS: Black beans, kidney beans, and great northern white beans may be used.

- Instead of turnip greens, kale, spinach, shredded cabbage, or greens left from other recipes that might be discarded may be used.

- Chorizo is a pungent sausage, but other sausages may be used as well. The fennel in Italian sausage, or the garlic in Polish sausage, or any good smoked sausage adds variety and expands the versatility of the dish.

SIDENOTE:

Often pebbles or small bits of dirt are mixed in with dry beans, so remember to sort and discard any foreign material. Discard beans still floating after 5 minutes of soaking, as these beans were probably spoiled prior to drying. Do not use the water the beans soaked in as cooking liquid because impurities that are carried on the dry beans leach into the water.

SMOKED MEAT POTÉE WITH CABBAGE AND CHESTNUTS

Potée is a word meaning "everything in one pot," and this recipe certainly has everything necessary to make a substantial meal without a lot of work or time. A potée can have as many ingredients as are available or desired. I'm particularly fond of adding chestnuts to mine because their aroma can bring back for me a sense of warmth, probably from the many afternoons I spent in front of the fire peeling chestnuts with my brothers and sisters. Whatever you decide to put in your own pot, remember the secret to an excellent potée is to introduce at least one smoked meat to the mix.

12 SERVINGS

One 3-pound green cabbage, outer
    leaves removed
2 tablespoons unsalted butter
Four 4-ounce center-cut pork chops
1 large onion, sliced
4 slices smoked ham, ¼ inch thick,
    halved
½ pound smoked sausage, cut into
    1-inch pieces

2 pounds chestnuts, blanched and
    peeled
1 sachet (see Basics, page 374)
4 juniper berries, crushed and added
    to sachet
4 carrots, peeled and cut into
    3 × ¼-inch sticks
2 small turnips, peeled and quartered
2 cups apple cider

Preheat the oven to 375°F.

Bring a pot of lightly salted water to boil. Blanch the cabbage whole for 10 minutes. Let stand in a colander to drain and cool. Cut into 6 wedges, then slice very thin.

Melt the butter, then sauté the pork chops for 2 minutes on each side. Set aside. Add the onion and cabbage to the pan and sauté until the cabbage begins to soften.

In a dutch oven or ovenproof earthenware pot, layer the bottom with a third of the cabbage. On top arrange 2 pork chops, 2 slices of ham, half the sausage, and half the chestnuts. Next, place the sachet on top. Repeat the layers, omitting the sachet, ending with a layer of cabbage. Arrange the carrots and turnips on top of the cabbage and pour the cider over all. Cover and bake in the oven for 45 minutes. Serve at once.

VARIATIONS: Thirty-two ounces of canned sauerkraut may be used instead of fresh cabbage. Rinse the sauerkraut under cold water before using to reduce the salt content.

• Chicken stock or white wine may be used instead of cider.

- The meat in the recipe can be varied according to taste and availability, such as chicken, sliced Canadian bacon, or any type of sausage. To retain the traditional flavor, include at least one smoked meat.

SIDENOTE:

Anyone living in the country close to colder climates, where game is a traditional meat, will be familiar with the aromatic juniper berry. Many game dishes use the tiny bluish-black berry as a flavor ingredient. Juniper berries come from an evergreen shrub pine found in Europe and England. It is the main flavoring for gin, and it used to be believed the berry would heal snakebites. The flavor is reminiscent of resin and slightly bitter. Besides game, it is a great seasoning for roasts, stews, braised meats, and as an ingredient in marinades. To use, crush first to detect the potency. Start by adding 6 to 8 berries to a recipe, then increase, if desired.

POTATO LYONNAISE

Potatoes were a staple for our dinners during this time of the year. One of our favorite ways to eat them was simply boiled, then dressed with fresh cream scooped off the top of the milk pail. The cream sat on top of the pails for three or four days between the days we churned butter, maturing as cheese would, so the cream developed a sour flavor very close to crème fraîche. This is a variation of that memory, with onion added Lyonnaise-style for extra flavor.

6 SERVINGS

6 medium baking potatoes, peeled and covered in cold water until needed
1 bay leaf
2 cups milk
3 shallots, finely chopped
¼ teaspoon salt

⅛ teaspoon freshly ground pepper
⅛ teaspoon freshly ground nutmeg
1 large onion, halved and cut into ⅛-inch slices
½ cup crème fraîche (see Basics, page 379)
2 tablespoons unsalted butter

Preheat the oven to 375°F.

Immediately prior to cooking, **cut the potatoes** into ⅛-inch slices. In a large saucepan, place the potatoes, bay leaf, and milk. Bring to a boil, then lower to a simmer for 5 minutes. Gently stir in the shallots, salt, pepper, and nutmeg. Simmer for another 10 minutes until the potatoes are semi-tender.

Remove the bay leaf and discard. Using a slotted spoon, transfer half the potatoes to a 1-quart baking dish. Lay half the onion slices on top, spread with half the crème fraîche. Repeat with the remaining potatoes, onions, and crème fraîche. Dot the top with butter.

Bake for 15 minutes, or until the potatoes are brown on top. Serve immediately.

VARIATIONS: Instead of onion, grated Swiss or Gruyère cheese can be spread between the potato layers.

- Instead of using crème fraîche, reduce the milk that the potatoes cooked in by half. After the potatoes and onions are layered, pour the milk to the top of the dish and bake as directed.

♥ *Monique's Touch:*

Potatoes peeled in advance should be soaked whole in water to prevent discoloration, but I wait to **cut the potatoes** for this recipe until the very last moment. This preserves as much of the starch on the potato surface as possible, which acts as a thickening agent as the potatoes bake.

RUTABAGA AND QUINCE MASH

The quince has often been called the ugly duckling of the apple family, but my younger sister Danielle and I thought they were lovely. Through the summer we worked our own baby garden under the quince tree close to the big kitchen garden. We watched as the green, furry fruit grew pear-shaped through the summer, then we harvested them for storage in the fall. Come the middle of winter, the quince had turned reddish pink, and we were ready for their buttery flavor to tame the sharpness of the mature rutabaga.

6 SERVINGS

1 large or 2 medium rutabagas,
   peeled and cut into ½-inch dice
3 tablespoons unsalted butter
2 small quince, peeled, cored, and
   cut into ½-inch dice

¼ cup chopped fresh parsley
¼ cup bread crumbs
Salt and pepper

Preheat the oven to 400°F.

Bring a pot of lightly salted water to a boil. Blanch the rutabaga for 3 minutes. Drain.

Melt the butter and sauté the quince for 3 minutes, add the rutabaga, and continue cooking for 3 minutes more, or until both are tender. Transfer to an ovenproof baking dish, then coarsely mash with a fork. Salt and pepper to taste.

Mix the parsley and bread crumbs together and sprinkle over the rutabaga and quince. Bake for 15 minutes. Serve immediately.

VARIATIONS: Other root vegetables, like white turnips and celery root, can be combined with quince.

ENDIVE AND PINK GRAPEFRUIT SALAD

Once the oranges had passed through their winter season, grapefruit from Morocco and Spain began appearing sporadically at the market. But even though the grapefruit was familiar to us, Maman never used them, because they were a scarce and a costly treat for such a large family. Then in the early '60s my older brother and sister were the first of the family to immigrate to the United States, where grapefruit is domestic, plentiful, and cheap. On their first return visit home, they prepared grapefruit salad for Maman, who decided right then that some treats in life were well worth the cost, and she enjoyed grapefruit regularly from then on.

6 SERVINGS

3 heads Belgian endive, whole leaves
    separated
1 large pink grapefruit, sectioned,
    juice preserved (see Sidenote,
    page 294)
½ cup chopped walnuts
2 tablespoons cider vinegar

2 tablespoons chopped fresh parsley
2 small shallots, chopped
1 tablespoon Dijon-style mustard
1 teaspoon freshly ground black
    pepper
½ cup canola oil

Arrange the endive leaves on a large serving platter. Garnish with the grapefruit segments and sprinkle with walnuts.

In a small bowl, mix together the vinegar, parsley, shallots, mustard, and pepper. Whisk in the oil until the dressing is well blended. Drizzle half the dressing over the salad and serve the remainder on the side.

THUMBPRINT LEMON COOKIES

Baking with so many helpers in the kitchen could have been a trial for Maman, but she usually found ways to occupy our hands so that we learned something about cooking while she kept us out of her way. Often some very interesting variations of her recipes came out of our baking sessions together, as with the cookies below. The original recipe was for classic lemon squares, but when Maman gave us a little dough to play with while she worked, we made up our own cookies. We liked to roll the dough into a ball the size of a walnut, then make an indent in the center with our thumbs. Of course, we wanted to fill the impression with custard, just as Maman spread the lemon custard over her dough. After baking, we were delighted to have invented a small treat that soon came into its own as a family favorite.

2 DOZEN

2 cups flour
½ cup sugar

8 tablespoons unsalted butter,
    cold

FILLING:
2 eggs
1 tablespoon cornstarch
5 tablespoons sugar
¼ cup lemon juice

1 tablespoon grated lemon zest
½ teaspoon vanilla extract
Powdered sugar

Preheat the oven to 350°F.

Place the flour, sugar, and butter in a food processor. Process just until the mixture resembles coarse crumbs, about 15 seconds. Transfer to a lightly floured work surface and quickly work into a ball. Let rest in the refrigerator for 15 minutes.

Roll the dough into walnut-size balls and place on a nonstick baking sheet. Gently press with the thumb to make an indentation in the center.

To make the filling, blend together the eggs, cornstarch, sugar, lemon juice, lemon zest, and vanilla extract until well mixed. Drop a little custard into each thumbprint. Bake for 10 minutes. Cool and sprinkle with powdered sugar before serving.

VARIATIONS: Add ¼ cup ground almonds or hazelnuts to the crust mixture before processing.

- To cut down the tartness of the lemon flavor, reduce the lemon juice to
  ¼ cup and add ¼ cup of orange juice.

GALETTE DES ROIS

The galette des rois, or king's cake, is always served on the twelfth night of Christmas, which falls on January 6. It is the final festival of the holiday season and given over to the children for a night of merrymaking. The dessert is called king's cake because a dry bean is baked into the cake, and whoever finds the bean is declared king of the night and crowned with a paper crown. The king then chooses a queen, and the rest of the evening is spent teasing the royal couple and making silly speeches.

12 SERVINGS

4 tablespoons unsalted butter
¼ cup sugar
1 whole egg
½ cup finely ground almonds
3 teaspoons dark rum
½ teaspoon almond extract
1½ teaspoons flour

1 package frozen puff pastry, defrosted according to package instructions
1 dried bean
1 egg yolk
1 teaspoon cold water

Preheat the oven to 400°F. Butter a large baking sheet.

In a food processor, combine the butter, sugar, whole egg, almonds, rum, almond extract, and flour. Process until smooth.

On a lightly floured work surface, roll out 1 sheet of puff **pastry.** Cut out an 11-inch circle and transfer to the baking sheet. Spread custard on the pastry within 1 inch of the edge. Place the bean anywhere in the custard.

Roll out another sheet of puff pastry and cut into a 12-inch circle. Place over the custard. Using a fork or your thumb, press around the edge to seal. Mix the egg yolk and cold water, then brush the wash over the top of the galette, making sure the egg does not drip over the edge. With the point of a sharp knife, score a decorative pattern on top of the galette. To allow steam to escape, cut a half-inch cross in the center. Refrigerate for 20 minutes.

Spritz the baking sheet with cold water before placing in the oven for 25 minutes, or until the top is golden brown. Serve warm.

VARIATIONS: A galette can be filled with almost any fruit or cream filling. Try poached seasonal berries in summer or chunky applesauce in the fall.

- Instead of preparing 1 large galette, cut the puff pastry into 6-inch circles, spread the filling over half, and fold the other half on top to make turnovers. Seal and bake as above.

♥ *Monique's Touch:*

Nothing goes to waste in my kitchen, especially if I can make a sweet treat out of something. I like to cut the leftover **pastry** trimming from this recipe into small squares and place a piece of chocolate (a chocolate kiss is the perfect size) in the center. Close the square and bake on the sheet next to the galette. If I don't have chocolate at hand, I sprinkle the squares with cinnamon and sugar before baking.

ORANGE AND HONEY MADELEINES

Madeleines are delicate little cookies immortalized by Marcel Proust in his literature and adopted everywhere throughout France as a favorite accompaniment to coffee or tea. Orange and honey madeleines were my mother's own version of the classic recipe. She baked them, as Proust described, in the traditional madeleine mold to look like little scallop shells. As a child, the puffed center always reminded me of the top of a derby hat. To this day I eat my madeleines by nibbling around the edges, saving the "hat" for last.

1 DOZEN

6 tablespoons unsalted butter
1 tablespoon honey
2 eggs
¼ cup granulated sugar

1 tablespoon grated orange zest
⅓ cup flour
Powdered sugar

Preheat the oven to 375°F.

Brush the madeleine mold with 1 tablespoon melted butter. In a small pan, melt the remaining butter with the honey and let cool.

In a mixing bowl, beat together the eggs and granulated sugar for 5 minutes, until light and fluffy and the mixture forms a ribbon when the whisk is lifted out of the batter. Sprinkle the orange zest on top, then gently fold in the flour in 4 parts. Add the butter-and-honey mixture and blend well.

Spoon the batter into the prepared mold, filling each cup two thirds full. Bake for 10 minutes until the edges are golden. Remove from the oven and cool for 1 minute. Unmold by inverting and tapping gently. Dust with powdered sugar.

VARIATIONS: Flavor with lemon rind instead of orange.

- One tablespoon of ground nuts, such as almonds or hazelnuts may be added with the flour.

- To make chocolate madeleines, replace 3 tablespoons of flour with 2 tablespoons cocoa powder.

FEBRUARY

*My mother, Hélène Jamet,
and her winter knitting.*

Winter draws a cold, deep breath at the beginning of February, bracing itself for the last stand it must make before inevitably giving way to the soft sighs of spring. We take on a certain stoicism, sensing the cabin fever we feel is an ancient man-versus-nature struggle that winter will not win, so we devise strategies to get through the last weeks of the stark season.

In February the days lengthen, and there is a gradual feeling of reawakening all around us. It's not the full-blown itching to burst out of our winter cocoons that will hit us in another month, but a gentle tickle reminding us a change is coming. By the end of the month the first thaw has arrived, and with it the first crocus and daffodil buds sporadically pierce the soil. Our mailboxes fill with dreams of summer in the form of seed catalogs. Curled up next to the still comforting fire, we begin to plan our gardens. Farmers think about the coming market season, looking at last year's production as they make their calendar for the coming year. We are all longing for the sweet taste of the first spring peas, the delicate spiciness of tiny radishes. Seedlings are started indoors as we busy ourselves with decisions about what and how much to plant. Our tastes begin to change, too, and the winter stews we still crave at the beginning of the month feel too heavy and rich by the middle of February. We begin to look for leaner fare with interesting tastes that will keep us from the boredom of the last few days of winter.

The farm began to stir in February as we started to ready the fields for planting. At the beginning of the month Papa tilled the soil for the first time since fall, turning under the blanket of fertilizer put down during January. The smooth expanse of fine soil lay ready for after the first thaw, when Papa and my brothers seeded the wheat fields. Inside the house, Maman also made preparations. Lent was almost upon us, a season when the call for a food sacrifice coincided with the time of year when the larder ran low after the long winter. But before that happened, we looked forward to the last celebration of the culinary year, *La Chandeleur.*

During La Chandeleur, or the Festival of Lights, people gathered formally for the first time since the holidays in celebration of an ancient French custom. Cultures all over the world are full of rituals throughout history held to assure Mother Nature will favor us with the coming of spring. In Roman times La Chandeleur was when the French country people gathered together to study the weather and moon and to ask the gods for a fruitful harvest and a blessing on the season to come. Over the centuries La Chandeleur evolved into a playful holiday, during which dozens of candles are lit and kept burning throughout the night to signify the light of spring breaking through the darkness of winter. The tradition continued as a yearly celebration in our village as neighbors and friends held parties where we always ate the traditional food of the Festival of Lights, delicious crêpes stuffed with custard and fruit sauce. As the crêpes were prepared, a legend about how the sun returns each spring was recounted to the children. It is said that if the cook takes a crêpe in which a gold coin has been laid in the center and flips it high enough, the spring songbird will soar up to catch the coin. He steals the coin to hoard for himself, but in return the songbird brings back the sun. The sun, now given to man, will bring good weather and abundant crops. Hours were passed trying to flip the crêpes high and straight, but many crêpes ended up on the floor due to the large amounts of hard cider that slipped across our tongues as we cooked. Everyone's aim seemed to grow increasingly scattered as the night wore on. The evening always ended late in good cheer and friendliness. Our spirits were buoyed, making it possible to face the last weeks of winter with more enthusiasm.

To country people who depended on the weather and fields for life, it is not surprising that during the late winter and very early spring customs developed throughout history based on prayers for a good harvest or sacrifices made so the weather would be favorable during the growing season. Our own food stores were running low by this point in the year. Perhaps our bodies respond to a primal rhythm when we begin to desire lighter meals toward spring. While on the farm there was not much danger of starvation, trying to feed a large, restless family in February was not always easy for Maman. Leaner fare was as much a necessity as it was a longing. She cooked some of the last of the potatoes, winter squashes, leeks, turnips, and other root vegetables during the month. Maman used marinades more often to tenderize tougher cuts of late winter meat and depended more on small amounts of sausages and cured meat to enhance the taste of her dishes. The flavors of the vegetables she had left to use were past their strong maturity and weakening. The sauces and broths still echoed the hearty flavors of winter, but they were lighter, with herb seeds often simmered in them to give a little extra flavor. We also found lean winter shellfish like mussels and scallops appearing on our table more often, which perfectly matched our desire for less filling dishes.

To supplement our meals and to give the food a little more spunk, Maman turned to using more citrus fruits. Oranges, limes, lemons, and pineapples were certainly not something we grew in Brittany, but they came to be part of my mother's repertoire over the years because the fruits from Morocco and other warm climates came to our market by trade during the winter season. Dishes Maman made with citrus tasted lighter and cleaner to our winter-dulled palates.

Today we have an even wider range of access when we are looking for different ways to appeal to our seasonal appetites or to simply spark up the flavor of old standby dishes when we're feeling creative. Not only do we have the best citrus fruit available in the world from Florida during the winter, but the influx of ethnic influences on the American culinary scene provides us with an exciting opportunity to try many new and different spices and flavorings. Once exotic spices are usually available in specialized food markets, by mail, and often in ordinary supermarkets. Using spices like curry and garamasala from India, ginger, and five-spice powder from China, or cardamom and saffron from the Middle East, is a good way to make the transition between the nutty, roasted flavors of winter and the clean sharpness of spring greens. Spices add heat without heaviness and reawaken our taste buds after the winter. They are not difficult to use and are fun to play with. Start off simply, perhaps with a small amount of curry in a vegetable soup. Experiment, keeping the mixture of spices within the same cultural region, just like we combine other ingredients by region and season.

Spices, like the citrus fruits Maman used, can tease the palate and keep away the doldrums that haunt February days. We may not have a need in modern times for formal rituals to move us successfully from one season to the next, but the message we get from lightening up our meals and exciting our appetites with different flavors is as old as man himself: Hurry on, spring, we're waiting!

FEBRUARY RECIPES

Cream of Vegetable Soup

Ruby Beet and Celery Root Soup

Buckwheat Blinis with Goat Cheese

Steamed Mussels and Fettuccine

Broiled Sole with Muscadet and Pineapple Sauce

Country-Style Cod with Browned Potatoes and Onions

Winter Hen with Cream Sauce

Braised Turkey Legs with Lentils

Crushed Pepper Steak

Ham and Cheese Chausson

Winter Potatoes with Italian-Style Sausage

Chunky Squash and Applesauce

Jerusalem Artichoke Beignets

Marinated Prune Tart

Almost Spring Orange Mousse

Bavarian Crêpes with Raspberry Sauce

FESTIVAL OF LIGHTS DINNER

Buckwheat Blinis with Goat Cheese

Sparkling Cider

Ruby Beet and Celery Root Soup

Winter Hen with Cream Sauce

Merlot

Bavarian Crêpes with Raspberry Sauce

Chardonnay

CREAM OF VEGETABLE SOUP

By February the root vegetables stored in our barn were in the last stages of soft maturity. When a carrot reached the stage where it could bend easily, Maman said it was "perfect to make a bow tie"—an expression I still use today when I teach. Mature root vegetables are high in natural sugar, giving them wonderful taste and high nutritional value. They save time because softer vegetables don't need to be sautéed prior to adding to soup. The next time you think your vegetables are past using, make this easy vegetable soup and savor the deep flavors only winter vegetables bring.

6 SERVINGS

1 tablespoon unsalted butter
2 cups diced carrots
2 cups diced turnips
2 cups diced potatoes
2 teaspoons curry powder
6 cups chicken stock (see Basics, page 375)

1 small leek, cleaned, trimmed, and finely chopped
1 cup cream
¼ cup chopped fresh parsley
Salt and pepper

In a large saucepan, melt the butter and add the carrots, turnips, potatoes, and curry. Stir to coat the vegetables with butter and curry, then add 1 cup of the chicken stock. Lower the heat to a simmer, cover, and cook gently for 15 minutes. Add the remaining stock and leek, then cook, uncovered, for another 15 minutes.

With a slotted spoon, transfer the vegetables to a food processor. Process until smooth. Stir the vegetables back into the broth and add the cream. Adjust the seasoning with salt and pepper. Bring the soup to a simmer before adding the parsley. Serve at once.

VARIATIONS: This recipe is good for using up stored winter vegetables, such as parsnips, rutabagas, or squash.

- Add curry powder to taste with the salt and pepper.

- After puréeing the vegetables, add precooked dried beans for taste, texture, and vitamins.

RUBY BEET AND
CELERY ROOT SOUP

At the beginning of the winter season, when we could see our breath fogging the air and felt the sharp cold of winds off the Atlantic coast, it was time to cover the vegetables that stayed in the ground year-round in our garden. The wet weather and hard frost were not good for the beets and celery root that wintered over, so a thick layer of hay was spread on top to give the vegetables enough warmth to nurture them and allow them to mature naturally. When late winter came, the beets and celery root were picked from their chilly bed as needed and turned into a hot, tasty soup that always warmed and nurtured growing children.

8 SERVINGS

1 large onion, finely chopped
1 tablespoon olive oil
1 pound beets, peeled and coarsely grated
½ pound celery root, coarsely grated
4 cups chicken stock (see Basics, page 375)
1 cup water
2 Golden Delicious apples, peeled, cored, and coarsely grated

1 teaspoon caraway seed, crushed
2 tablespoons red wine vinegar
½ cup crème fraîche (see Basics, page 379) (optional)
1 tablespoon chopped fresh parsley (optional)
Salt and pepper

In a large pot, sauté the onion in oil until translucent, about 2 minutes. Add the **beets, celery root,** stock, and water. Bring to a boil, then lower to a simmer and cook for 20 minutes. Stir in the apples, caraway seed, and vinegar. Season with salt and pepper to taste, then simmer for another 20 minutes. Serve the soup in bowls garnished with a dollop of crème fraîche and parsley, if desired.

VARIATIONS: Beets combine well with other root vegetables. Instead of celery root, turnips, parsnips, or parsley root make good flavor combinations.

- Instead of caraway seeds, other seasonings might include celery seeds or celery leaves, dillseeds or dillweed.

- Crumble bacon bits on top of the soup before serving.

- Sour cream may be used instead of crème fraîche.

♥ *Monique's Touch:*

By grating root vegetables like **beets** and **celery root** before making soup, two things are accomplished. The cooking time is cut in half and all of the sugar in the root is released quickly, which sweetens the soup naturally. Occasionally a mature root will not be as flavorful as it should, so I add a bit of sugar to taste in the pot at the beginning of the cooking time.

BUCKWHEAT BLINIS WITH GOAT CHEESE

The one day a week, usually Friday, when Maman made crêpes and blinis was a time we all looked forward to. She stood in front of a stone oven as tall as she was, spreading the batter on the pan in a thin layer for crêpes or a thicker layer for blinis. She quickly turned them, then set the finished cakes on a stack next to the fire that grew higher by the minute. The children's job was to keep bringing her wood from the shed that Papa had cut exactly to the size of the oven earlier in the week. She kept at her chore the entire afternoon, turning out enough crêpes to feed all of us lunch for a week. As ubiquitous as the peanut butter and jelly sandwich is for today's child, crêpes were our school lunches in the winter and often fed the many workmen in our fields during the summer harvest.

8 SERVINGS

1 teaspoon sugar
1 packet dry yeast
2 cups water
1 cup buttermilk
2 eggs
2 cups buckwheat flour

1 cup flour
1 teaspoon salt
¼ cup unsalted butter, melted
¼ cup vegetable oil
½ pound goat cheese

In a mixing bowl, combine the sugar, yeast, and water. Mix well and let stand for 2 minutes, or until the yeast is bubbly. Stir in the buttermilk and eggs. Add both flours and salt, and mix well. Cover with a damp towel and set in the refrigerator to rest overnight.

To prepare the blinis, heat a cast-iron griddle until very hot. In a small saucepan, heat the butter and oil together. Brush the griddle with the butter-and-oil mixture. Drop batter by teaspoonfuls onto the griddle, making several 2-inch circles. Turn when bubbles begin forming on top, then brown briefly on the other side.

When cool, spread with goat cheese and serve.

VARIATIONS: Add 3 tablespoons of chopped fresh dill to the goat cheese.

- Spread the blinis with a mixture of half goat cheese and half cream cheese.

- Top the cheese with chopped walnuts or pecans.

SIDENOTE:

Buckwheat, a staple of Breton cooking, is becoming recognized once again here as a nutritious, inexpensive, and tasty addition to a menu. Buckwheat is a branching plant with white flowers that is not a wheat or grain at all, but is closely related to rhubarb. The edible seed resembles a stout grain, and it cooks like rice or bulgur. Stripped of its hard outer shell, buckwheat is called a groat. Roasting brings out the nutty flavor of the kernels, and roasted groats are called kasha. Buckwheat flour is more perishable than other flours, and will become rancid quickly, especially in the summer. Store in the refrigerator or freezer.

STEAMED MUSSELS
AND FETTUCCINE

Mussels are one of the most abundant shellfish along the Brittany coast. Maman would never think of buying them, because we harvested them ourselves or got them from family members who lived on the coast. Either way, late winter mussels on our table were always welcome because they were a sign that spring was not far off. It was also a last chance to enjoy the mussels until early fall, as the shellfish become lean and watery during their spring and summer spawning season. We liked them steamed open in a fragrant broth as below and served with a side dish of boiled potatoes and a slice of good rye bread to sop up the broth. Here I use mussels with fettuccine to adapt an old favorite to today's popularity of pasta.

6 SERVINGS

12 ounces fettuccine, cooked
    according to package directions
Zest of 2 limes, grated
Juice of 2 limes
3 tablespoons olive oil
1 red onion, thinly sliced
Two 15-ounce cans of tomatoes,
    drained and diced
6 garlic cloves, peeled and minced

1 teaspoon fennel seed
1 teaspoon celery seed
2 cups dry white wine
1 teaspoon dried thyme
3 tablespoons chopped shallots
½ cup chopped fresh parsley
2 pounds fresh mussels, cleaned
Salt and pepper

Toss the fettuccine with the grated lime zest and lime juice. Set aside and keep warm.

In a large pan, heat the oil, then sauté the onion until tender but not brown. Gently toss in the tomatoes, garlic, fennel and celery seeds. Lower the heat and simmer for 5 minutes.

In a large nonreactive saucepan, add the wine, thyme, shallots, and half the parsley, reserving the rest for garnish. Bring to a boil, then add the mussels, cover, and let simmer about 15 minutes, or until all the mussels are open.

Remove the mussels from the wine broth. Continue simmering for 2 minutes more, or until the broth is reduced to 1 cup, then add to the tomato sauce. Simmer a few minutes longer to blend the flavors. Adjust the seasoning with salt and pepper.

Meanwhile, shell two thirds of the mussels and toss with the fettuccine. Toss the tomato sauce with the fettuccine and shelled mussels. Place the pasta on a large serving platter and garnish with the reserved mussels in the shell. Sprinkle the remaining chopped parsley on top and serve.

VARIATIONS: If done with shrimp, sauté the shrimp with the onions and proceed as directed.

- Cooked crab may be used, added at the same time as the mussels.

- Use boneless chicken or turkey breasts or tenders cut into strips. Sauté the strips with the onions and proceed as directed.

- Any pasta may be used, or the mussels can be served on a bed of rice or couscous.

BROILED SOLE WITH MUSCADET AND PINEAPPLE SAUCE

Maman prepared fish very simply to take advantage of its freshness. Sole is a mild-flavored fish that takes well to the flavors of other ingredients, and was a favorite of hers because she could be endlessly creative in how she blended different elements. Here I have taken a traditional wine-based sauce and introduced pineapple—a fruit she would have found exotic. Of course, Maman's sole was always pan-seared, since she didn't have a broiler, but broiling frees up time in the kitchen and is a method I use occasionally today. This is again an example of how recipes can be modified to reflect today's reality in the kitchen while still retaining freshness of flavor and the spirit of tradition.

6 SERVINGS

4 tablespoons chopped shallots
1 cup white Muscadet
1 cup coarsely chopped fresh
  pineapple, with juice
1 cup cream
Six 4-ounce sole fillets

3 tablespoons unsalted butter,
  melted
6 tablespoons extrafine bread crumbs
2 tablespoons chopped fresh parsley
2 lemons, each cut into 6 wedges
Salt and pepper

Preheat the broiler.

In a saucepan, combine the shallots, wine, and pineapple with the juice. Bring to a boil for 10 to 15 minutes, or until reduced to 2 tablespoons. Stir in the cream and simmer for 5 minutes, reducing the sauce by a third. Add salt and pepper to taste. Pass through a fine strainer to remove the pineapple fibers. Discard the fibers. Return the sauce to the pan and keep warm over very low heat.

Brush the fillets with the butter and season with salt and pepper. Roll each fillet in the bread crumbs, coating both sides, then shake off the excess crumbs. Place 2 inches from the broiler and cook for 2 minutes. Turn and cook for another 2 minutes.

To serve, spoon the sauce on a plate and arrange 1 fillet on top. Scatter a small amount of parsley around the plate and garnish with 2 lemon wedges.

VARIATIONS: Any lean fish, like turbot, snapper, bass, mahi mahi, or halibut, can be served this way.

- Prior to reducing the sauce for the last time, introduce other flavors, like saffron, curry, garlic, crushed toasted pine nuts, or any seasonal herb, like cilantro, basil, dill, or tarragon.

SIDENOTE:

Fresh pineapple looks intimidating, but once the proper technique for preparation is learned, canned pineapple will be a thing of the past. The ripeness of a pineapple can be judged by the color of the skin. A pineapple is ripe when its skin is dark orange to coppery red. The pineapple is delicate and does not withstand cold temperatures, so store at room temperature.

To peel a pineapple:

First twist off the green leafy top. Working from the top down, cut off the skin in strips all around to expose the eyes. The eyes follow a spiral pattern around the pineapple and should be removed by making wedge-shape cuts ¼ inch deep, working in a continuous spiral from the top downward.

Pineapple pieces:

Do not peel. Twist off the leafy green top. Cut into 4 or 6 parts from the top to the base. Make a lengthwise cut to remove the core. Cut the fruit off the skin and divide into small pieces.

Individual slices:

Do not peel. Twist off the leafy green top. Cut into slices about ¾ inch thick, working from the base up. With a small, sharp knife, cut the core from the center of each slice. To remove the skin, cut around the edge with the knife, about ⅝ inch inside the skin, to ensure the eyes will be cut away.

COUNTRY-STYLE COD WITH BROWNED POTATOES AND ONIONS

One cannot separate the Breton from cod, as it is as popular a fish in Brittany as it is in our own East Coast region. Salt cod was usually bought dried at the fish store and, after the soaking process, hung in the chimney to smoke. Come suppertime, a piece was cut off and grilled over the open fire before we all sat down to a dinner of cod, browned potatoes, and a bowl of hot cider. It was a rare night that any cod remained on the table, but if this happened, Maman mashed it with a fork and served it the next night as a spread for country bread.

6 SERVINGS

1½ pounds cured salt cod
1 large onion, thinly sliced
3 tablespoons unsalted
    butter

1 pound baking potatoes, boiled
    with peel on, peeled, and cut into
    ⅛-inch slices
3 tablespoons chopped fresh parsley

Soak the cod overnight in enough cold water to cover, to remove the salt used to cure it. Drain well and pat dry. Discard the soaking water.

In a heavy skillet, sauté the onion in butter until transparent but not brown. Add the cod and brown about 1 minute on each side. Set aside. Add the potatoes to the skillet and brown for 2 to 4 minutes until crispy. Return the cod and onions to the skillet and heat through.

Arrange the cod, potatoes, and onions on a large serving platter. Sprinkle with parsley and serve.

WINTER HEN WITH CREAM SAUCE

If I had to choose one comfort food from my childhood, hen with cream sauce would be it. As we straggled in to the kitchen from a day at school or tramping through the misty, rainy fields, we cupped our hands over the steam rising from the pot, capturing the rich, sustaining aroma close to our frozen noses and breathing in the smell of home. Soon breath from our constant chatter mingled with the steam from the pot and lay sparkling against the kitchen window. It was a palette inviting little fingers to draw pictures on the glass, and soon a crowd of grinning faces, horned goblins, and whiskered animals stared down at my family seated around the table. Maman never complained about the extra work our watery art would cause when she had to clean the windows. I think she considered our characters simply more friends who came by for supper.

8 SERVINGS

One 4–5-pound stewing hen
3 leeks, cleaned, tough ends
    trimmed
4 carrots, peeled and cut into ¼ ×
    2-inch sticks
4 small turnips, peeled and quartered
1 large onion, peeled and quartered
2 sachets (see Basics, page 374)

SAUCE:
4 tablespoons unsalted butter
6 shallots, finely chopped
1 Belgian endive, finely chopped
4 tablespoons flour
3 cups chicken broth from the hen
1 cup cream
¼ cup sherry wine
½ cup chopped fresh parsley
Salt and pepper

Place the stewing hen in a large stockpot and cover with cold water. Bring to a boil, then simmer, uncovered, over low heat for 1 hour. Add the leeks, carrots, turnips, onion, and sachets, then simmer for another hour, or until the hen pulls easily off the bone. Remove the hen from the broth and let cool. Reserve 3 cups of the broth and half the vegetables for the cream sauce, refrigerating the rest of the broth and vegetables to make chicken noodle soup another day (see Variations). Cut the hen into 1-inch pieces and set aside. Reserve the carcass to make stock.

To make the sauce, melt the butter in a saucepan, then sauté the shallots and endive for 1 minute. Do not brown. Stir in the flour and cook on low heat for 1 minute. Slowly add the broth and then the cream while stirring constantly. Simmer for 10 minutes.

Gently stir in the hen, sherry, and parsley. Season with salt and pepper. Serve over rice or egg noodles with the reserved vegetables.

VARIATIONS: To make a quick and delicious chicken noodle soup, cook 3 ounces of egg noodles according to package directions. Heat the reserved chicken broth and vegetables from the recipe above. Stir in the noodles and 2 tablespoons of chopped fresh parsley.

- For a beautiful presentation, bundle the vegetables in cheesecloth (see Le Pot-au-Feu à la Sauce Piquante, page 299) prior to adding to the pot. Remove the vegetables from the cheesecloth when finished and arrange around the chicken pieces on a platter for serving.

- Lemon complements the flavor of the vegetables well, particularly late in the winter season. Instead of sherry, stir in ½ cup lemon juice and 2 tablespoons of zest, along with the chicken and parsley.

BRAISED TURKEY LEGS WITH LENTILS

Pigs' feet, veal shanks, and other tough cuts of meat always arrived on Maman's table in the form of succulent, slowly braised one-pot dinners. These meats, often overlooked by today's cook, have fibrous connective tissue that is full of taste and nutrition. As the tissue breaks down during braising, the meat becomes velvety tender and the flavors of the meat and other ingredients mingle into a rich broth. I like to use turkey legs, which are inexpensive, readily available year-round, and do not require extensive braising time.

6 SERVINGS

6 turkey legs, halved, with end
    knuckles removed and discarded
    by the butcher
6 tablespoons flour
3 tablespoons olive oil
1 large onion, chopped
3 carrots, trimmed and chopped
2 celery stalks, chopped
1 cup white wine
2 cups chicken stock (see Basics,
    page 375)

One 15-ounce can of tomatoes,
    drained and diced
6 garlic cloves, peeled and minced
6 tablespoons chopped fresh parsley
1 sachet (see Basics, page 374)
3 cups lentils, rinsed
Zest of 1 lemon, grated
Juice of 1 lemon
Salt and pepper

Dredge each turkey leg in flour to thoroughly coat.

Heat the oil in a large pan. Brown the legs on all sides and remove from the pan. Add the onion, carrots, and celery, and sauté until soft but not brown.

Add the wine, swirling in the pan to loosen all the brown bits at the bottom. Bring to a simmer for 5 minutes to reduce by half. Add the stock, tomatoes, garlic, 3 tablespoons of the parsley, the sachet, and lentils. Return the turkey legs to the pan and season to taste with salt and pepper. Bring to a boil, then lower to a simmer and cook over low heat, covered, for approximately 45 minutes. The turkey legs should be tender and pull away from the bones.

Mix the lemon zest, lemon juice, and the remaining 3 tablespoons of parsley. Arrange the turkey legs on a serving platter and spoon the sauce over. Sprinkle the lemon-parsley mixture on top and serve immediately.

VARIATIONS: Lamb shanks or oxtails may be substituted for turkey legs.

- Try seasonal variations when choosing ingredients to go with the meat. For spring, add artichokes and new potatoes, chopped fresh tomatoes in the summer, and root vegetables in the fall.

- Any dried legume may be used instead of lentils.

CRUSHED PEPPER STEAK

Beef was not prevalent in Brittany, so it wasn't until I lived in Paris that I first experienced an excellent steak. It was in a restaurant on the Left Bank, called Steak au Poivre, which literally means "steak with pepper." I can still see the flames putting a burn on the meat as the steak was flambéed in front of me and the cognac sauce finished at the table. Since that night I have prepared my version of pepper steak for hundreds of friends. Each time I serve it and hear the exclamations of delight from my guests, I silently thank the little restaurant in the heart of Paris for introducing me to this exquisite treat.

6 SERVINGS

½ cup crushed black peppercorns
Six 5-ounce New York strip steaks, at
    least 1-inch thick, fat trimmed
1 tablespoon unsalted butter
1 tablespoon olive oil
2–4 tablespoons cognac

4 tablespoons chopped shallots
2 tablespoons lemon juice
2 cups brown stock (see Basics, page
    376)
½ cup cream
2 tablespoons chopped fresh parsley

Firmly press the crushed peppercorns into each side of the meat, then shake off the excess. Wrap in plastic wrap with a piece of waxed paper between each steak and refrigerate overnight, or for at least 2 hours.

Heat a heavy skillet until very hot, then add the butter and oil. Sear the steaks, two at a time, for 2 minutes on each side for rare, 3 minutes for medium. Set aside as the steaks finish. When all are seared, return to the pan, add the 2 tablespoons of cognac and flambé (see Sidenote, page 179). If necessary because of pan size, flambé in 2 batches, adding 2 tablespoons of cognac each time. Set aside.

Discard the excess fat from the pan. Add the shallots, tossing gently for a few seconds before adding the lemon juice and stock. Simmer for 5 minutes to reduce by half. Whisk in the cream and parsley.

Divide the steaks among serving plates and spoon sauce over each steak before serving.

VARIATIONS: A 1-inch-thick fillet of salmon or tuna is a good substitute for meat.

- In the summer, cook the steaks on a grill before flambéing.

HAM AND CHEESE CHAUSSON

During Lent a simple ham and cheese chausson *often replaced the more elaborate lunches we ate during the rest of the year.* Chausson *means "slipper," which is quite appropriate, as the filling in between the two layers of dough are slipped in before baking. It is a fun sandwich to make because the puff pastry can be cut into any fanciful shape your imagination can create.*

4 SERVINGS

2 sheets puff pastry, defrosted
    according to package directions
2 tablespoons Dijon-style mustard

8 slices Swiss cheese
4 slices baked ham
1 egg, beaten

Preheat the oven to 375°F.

Roll 1 sheet of puff pastry into a 12 × 8-inch rectangle. Using a bowl or plate as a guide, cut four 6-inch round pieces. Repeat with the other sheet of puff pastry. Discard the scraps.

On one half of each round, spread a small amount of mustard, then layer with 1 slice cheese, followed by 1 slice ham, and topped with 1 more slice cheese. Fold the other half of the round over the layers. Seal the edges by pressing a fork all around. Brush the chaussons with egg, then with a sharp knife cut a small slit in the top of each to allow steam to escape. Bake for 20 minutes until golden brown.

VARIATIONS: Cooked spinach can also be added, or make a meatless chausson with spinach and cheese only.

- Other cheeses, like Parmesan, blue, goat, or Cheddar, can be used this way.

WINTER POTATOES WITH ITALIAN-STYLE SAUSAGE

The secret to this delicious casserole-style dish is to use end-of-winter potatoes, especially long-stored ones that have started to sprout and wrinkle a bit. These potatoes have a slight give and softness, and the dimples on the surface will have begun filling in with eyes. This indicates a higher moisture than starch content, so the potatoes will be sweeter and have less of a tendency to fall apart when cooking.

6 SERVINGS

½ pound Italian-style sausage, casings removed, cut into ¼-inch pieces

¾ pound celery hearts, cut into ⅛-inch slices

2 leeks, cleaned and coarsely chopped

½ cup chopped fresh celery leaves

1 teaspoon celery seeds, crushed

3 garlic cloves, peeled and minced

1 cup chicken stock (see Basics, page 375)

6 brown baking potatoes, boiled whole for 20 minutes with peel, then peeled and diced

Salt and pepper

Heat a large saucepan and sauté the sausage for 5 minutes. Remove from the pan, then add the celery hearts, leeks, and garlic and sauté for 2 minutes. Stir in the celery leaves, celery seeds, and chicken stock, and bring to a simmer. Mix in the potatoes and sausage, then season to taste with salt and pepper. Cover and simmer for 10 minutes before serving.

VARIATIONS:

- Add fennel in place of the celery when in season.

- Rice can be used in place of potatoes.

CHUNKY SQUASH
AND APPLESAUCE

By the end of January and through February, the apples we harvested in October began shriveling from long winter storage. They had to be used, so it was during this time that Maman always had a pan of baked apples on the table for us to snack on or enjoy with a glass of cider before bed. Inevitably, the apples that didn't get eaten during the day were turned into a thick applesauce to combine with other winter vegetables that had to be eaten as the season of storage came to a close.

6 SERVINGS

2 acorn squash, halved
1 tablespoon canola oil
6 whole Golden Delicious apples or
    winter-stored regional apples,
    unpeeled and cored

2 tablespoons honey
½ teaspoon celery seeds, crushed
Salt and pepper

Preheat the oven to 375°F.

Rub the edges of the squash with oil and place, cut side down, on a large baking sheet. Set the apples next to the squash, then drizzle the apples with honey. Place in the oven for 25 minutes, or until the squash are tender. If the apples soften more quickly, remove from the oven and set aside.

Remove the seeds from the squash and spoon out the pulp, placing it in a mixing bowl. Spoon the pulp from the apples, discarding the peel. Crush the squash and apple together with a fork until well mixed. Mix in the celery seeds and season with salt and pepper to taste. Serve at room temperature.

VARIATIONS: Butternut squash, pumpkin, or other local varieties of winter squash, rutabagas, or turnips may be used instead of acorn squash.

- To turn into a squash-and-apple soup, purée the squash and apples, then mix with 1 quart of chicken stock until smooth. Simmer for 5 minutes to heat through before serving.

JERUSALEM ARTICHOKE BEIGNETS

Fried foods were rarely included in our diet, except for the beloved french fries we so enjoyed during summer festivals. During the endless cold nights of winter, my brothers and sisters and I would talk of the pleasures of warm summer days and long for a taste of those delicious potatoes. Because by that time the winter-stored potatoes had developed their sugar and would not fry properly, Maman occasionally took pity on us and made Jerusalem artichoke beignets, which are reminiscent of french fries because of the crusty breading on the outside and the soft Jerusalem artichoke inside. As soon as we tasted them, all thoughts of french fries disappeared because Jerusalem artichoke beignets stand on their own as a delicious addition to any meal.

6 SERVINGS

2 pounds Jerusalem artichokes,
    peeled and cut into ¼-inch slices
1½ cups water
2 tablespoons unsalted butter
1½ cups flour

2 eggs
¾ cup milk
½ cup apple cider or apple juice
3 cups peanut oil
Salt and pepper

In a saucepan, bring the Jerusalem artichokes, water, and butter to a boil. Cover and let simmer for 5 minutes, or until the Jerusalem artichokes are tender. Drain and season lightly with salt and pepper.

Place the flour in a mixing bowl and make a well in the center. Crack the eggs into the well and begin to mix slowly, adding the milk and cider or juice a few drops at a time to prevent lumps from forming. Mix until all the ingredients are incorporated and smooth.

Heat the peanut oil in a deep pan to 350°F. Dip the Jerusalem artichoke slices into the batter one at a time before submerging in the oil. Do not crowd the pan. Cook for about 5 minutes, or until golden brown. With a slotted spoon, transfer the Jerusalem artichokes to a paper towel to drain. Season with salt and pepper before serving at once.

VARIATIONS: Other vegetables to use can include cauliflower, broccoli, carrots, sweet potatoes, or salsify.

MARINATED PRUNE TART

In our village, as throughout France, we could purchase bread dough made daily from the baker and take it home to bake in our own oven. The dough was turned into tarts, pies, or pizza-shape breads covered with toppings, all cooked on a flat pan over the coals in the fireplace. All of the dishes were easy to do, as Maman took advantage of using fruits and vegetables preserved from the summer, cutting preparation time to almost nothing. Today I try to re-create the convenience of premade dough by making batches of basic yeast dough, dividing it into portions, and freezing it in plastic bags for later use. Here I top a tart with plums preserved at the peak of their freshness in a lovely wine syrup.

8 SERVINGS

1 pound yeast dough, thawed (see
    Basics, page 387)
¼ pound unsalted butter, softened
4 cups plums in wine (see Basics,
    page 392), drained, wine
    reserved

2 cups custard cream (see Basics,
    page 388)
¼ cup powdered sugar

Preheat the oven to 375°F.

On a lightly floured work surface, roll out the dough into a 10 × 12-inch rectangle. Dot the butter over two thirds of the dough. Fold in thirds, letter fashion, roll out again.

In a saucepan, bring the reserved plum wine to a boil. Simmer for 10 minutes to reduce by half, until it is a syrup consistency.

Beat the custard cream in a food processor or with a mixer to soften. Roll out the dough into a 12-inch circle, ⅛ inch thick. Using a fork, prick the dough several times to keep it from rising too much during baking. Spread the cream over the dough to within 1 inch of the edge. Starting in the center of the tart, arrange the plums on top in a circular pattern. Curl up the edge of the tart. Brush the top with the plum wine. Bake for 35 minutes. Serve warm, sprinkled with powdered sugar.

VARIATIONS: This can be done with any cooked fruit, such as currants in wine or apricots in syrup.

ALMOST SPRING ORANGE MOUSSE

By the end of February we feel as if our spirits are running out of steam and we can't wait for the rebirth nature will soon bring. Our bodies are asking for lighter foods, signaling an urgent thrust forward toward spring. Yet the weather is not quite ready to provide our gardens with the foods we crave, so we must use creativity to answer the call of our taste buds. I like to serve orange mousse during the end of February and the first days of March because it combines an end-of-winter fruit that is a symbol of the sun with a mousse as light as spring air.

4 SERVINGS

1 tablespoon unflavored gelatin
¼ cup cold water
Juice of 3 naval oranges
3 egg yolks
Zest of 3 naval oranges, grated

½ cup sugar
1 cup heavy cream
3 egg whites
¼ cup powdered sugar

Sprinkle the gelatin into the water to soften for 10 minutes. Heat the orange juice and gelatin together over low heat until the gelatin dissolves. Do not boil.

Lightly beat the egg yolks together with the orange zest. Beat the sugar into the egg yolks until light and fluffy. Slowly add the orange juice and gelatin, beating constantly for 5 minutes. Refrigerate for 20 minutes until partially jelled.

Beat the cream until soft peaks form, then fold into the orange mixture.

In a separate bowl, beat the egg whites and powdered sugar together until stiff peaks form. Fold into the orange whipped cream.

Turn the mousse into a large serving bowl or individual serving dishes. Refrigerate for at least 2 hours. Garnish with **candied** julienned orange peel, if desired.

VARIATIONS: Grapefruit, lemon, or a combination of the two makes a good citrus mousse.

♥ *Monique's Touch:*

Candied fruit peels make a pretty garnish in winter when fresh flowers and herbs are not available. Peel the skin very thin, taking as little of the bitter white inner skin as possible. Cut the peel into tiny strips about 1/16-inch wide and 1–2 inches long. Heat ½ cup sugar in ¼ cup water until the sugar is dissolved. Cook the peel in the syrup for 5 minutes. Strain and refrigerate until ready to use. For a particularly stunning presentation of the orange mousse, hollow out a halved orange and cook the shell in syrup until candied. Pour the mousse into the shell instead of a bowl and serve.

In the mid-sixties Maman switched from cooking in a fireplace to cooking on a woodburning stove. Here she makes crêpes for the family.

BAVARIAN CRÊPES WITH RASPBERRY SAUCE

The crêpes we ate on La Chandeleur were stuffed with a variety of fillings. My favorite has always been one of Maman's best, a Bavarian cream filling. In this adaptation I have added a delicious, quick, and easy raspberry sauce using frozen raspberries. Using good-quality frozen fruits brings an authentic taste of summer during winter months.

12 SERVINGS

CRÊPES:
1 cup flour
3 eggs
1½ cups milk
4 tablespoons unsalted butter, melted
1 teaspoon vanilla extract

BAVARIAN CREAM:

3 tablespoons unflavored gelatin
½ cup cold water
6 cups custard cream (see Basics, page 388)

RASPBERRY SAUCE:
½ cup sugar
½ cup water
2 cups frozen raspberries, thawed and puréed

In a mixing bowl, make a well in the center of the flour. Crack the eggs into the center. Using a whisk, mix the eggs with the flour slowly to prevent lumps. Whisk in the milk, a few drops at a time. Blend in the butter and vanilla.

Heat a 7-inch nonstick sauté pan or traditional crêpe pan. Sliding the pan off heat, pour ¼ cup of batter into the center of the pan and slowly swirl to **coat** the bottom of the pan. Place back on medium-high heat. Cook for 20 seconds, turn, then cook for 15 seconds more. Set aside and continue. The batter should make about 18 crêpes. Select 7 for the dessert, then freeze the remaining crêpes for later use.

To make the Bavarian cream, soften the gelatin in cold water for 5 minutes. Heat the custard cream until simmering, remove from the heat, and stir in the softened gelatin until dissolved. Set aside.

To assemble the dessert, coat the bottom of a terrine or round mold with ½ cup custard cream sauce. Line the bottom of the mold with crêpes, spoon another ½ cup custard cream sauce on top. Continue layering, ending with the custard sauce. Cover with plastic wrap laid against the surface. Refrigerate at least 2 hours, preferably overnight.

Before serving, make the raspberry sauce. Melt the sugar and water in a saucepan over medium heat and simmer for 3 minutes. Add enough syrup to the raspberries to sweeten according to taste. Pass the sauce through a fine strainer to remove seeds.

To serve, dip the mold in a sink of hot water for 1 minute, or long enough to soften the custard all around. Invert on a serving platter and ladle raspberry sauce over and around.

VARIATIONS: The sauce can be made with the same amount of strawberries, blackberries, or cranberries.

- Chocolate crêpes can be made by adding 2 teaspoons of cocoa powder to the flour. Other flavors may be made by adding flavor extracts or liqueur to the batter.

♥ *Monique's Touch:*

Most crêpe recipes require **coating** the pan with butter before ladling the batter in the bottom, but to save a cooking step, I add the melted butter to the batter during mixing.

MARCH

*Manoir de Kerbiquet. The manoir is registered as
a Historical and Artistic Monument of France;
it was built in the early seventeenth century.*

March is an aptly named month, thundering in and relentlessly advancing across the landscape toward spring. The first pulsing beat of change felt in February is amplified until all of nature is surging to make a final sprint out of the confining, brittle shell of winter into a spring enclosed only by soft air and blue sky. By mid- to late March the change comes, and tattered vestiges of fierce winter give way to a newborn spring.

At the beginning of March our appetites strain against what the weather bitterly tries to impose upon us. The raw chill of early spring seems to demand a smoky fire and hot, slow-cooked meals that bring comfort and steadiness during the cold months. Instead, we rebel against what seems oppressive and dull and allow ourselves to be drawn to what is gentle and cleansing. We are tired of the complicated layering of flavors in long-simmered stews and crave the sharp, clean bite of tender greens. We want to ease away from the thick textures of velvety sauces. The desire is strong for the feel of warm and silky cream soups sliding across our palate. Meat seems too much to ask a body to digest unless it is marinated until fork-tender and served with only a delicate glaze. We turn more to the light weight of fresh steamed fish, seafood, or young chicken. Quick braising with pale cooking liquids, like chicken stock or white wine, takes the place of cooking with brown stocks and red wines. Desserts are less sweet and unadorned. It's as if our bodies are reawakening in concert with the world around us and preparing to receive the new culinary year.

March arrived on the farm and with it the urge to get on with the business of spring. Impatience filled the air as we all waited for the warmer weather to arrive. Papa spent a lot of time outdoors getting ready for the coming season and watching the sky or listening to the weather. He turned the animals out of the barn for the first time in the new year. Each day they spent longer periods in the pasture, becoming a little friskier as the days lengthened and softened. The chickens roughed their feathers and clucked in nervous excitement after Maman shooed them out of the chicken coop into the sunshine.

We children were glad to be outdoors, even if it was mostly to clean out the hedgerows between the fields and to ready the potager for planting. By the middle of the month Papa hoisted a big basket hung by a leather strap onto his shoulders and went into the fields to seed the oats, barley, hay, and wheat. When that was done, he put in the sweet peas and potato plants saved from last year to begin this year's crop. The new leeks also went in while the ground still held the chill of winter. We worked steadily and watched as unforeseen cold winds swept down from the north in the morning before whipping around and becoming warm afternoon breezes.

Then the first true sign of spring happened. The first warm and gentle rainfall fell to earth and brought up all of nature's underground winter work. Immediately after the rain the countryside became a rolling quilt of shades of brown, promising green and pale yellow. The buds emerged across the hills in order of how they would bloom later on—first the Irish broom, then the periwinkle, and last the primaveras. Overhead the sky filled with birds migrating back north. As my father walked down freshly tilled rows broadcasting seed into the soil, the birds swooped behind him, landing to eat their fill before continuing on to Scotland. Inside the house, Maman threw up the windows and opened the doors, inviting the fresh air inside. Everything felt airy and clean. We started looking outdoors once again for seasonal foods to enjoy at the table.

If rain was the harbinger of real spring, it was also a signal that one of the year's favorite seasonal delicacies was about to be enjoyed. As soon as the watercress sprouted along the cold banks of the icy streams, we began to search the fields and bogs for snails. We spent a pleasant day filling burlap sacks with the little mollusks before returning home at dusk. Maman set a box in the corner of the kitchen, and all the snails were dumped in. To make the prison inescapable, tightly woven chicken wire was secured over the top of the box. We paid special care with the chicken wire, as one year the wire was left loose and we awoke to dozens of snails slowly sliming across the kitchen floor. The incarceration of the snails lasted two to three days while they purified themselves by starvation. It was necessary to purge the snails in this manner because they often feed in the wild on plants poisonous to humans. We could hear the snails jostling about in the box, and the nights were punctuated by the sound of snails clinging to the top of the wire until a hunger faint overtook them and they plopped down among their brothers.

At last Maman began the work of cooking the snails. During March the parsley is up, and the garlic in the potager already sprouts green tendrils. The greens have a light taste, a hint of what is to come in April when the bulbs fully form. Maman snipped the greens and mixed them with parsley and sweet butter. After blanching the snails, the lean little creatures were pulled from their shells and the shells filled halfway with garlic butter. The snails were tucked back inside before being topped off by more garlic butter. Pans of snails were set on coals in the fireplace until the butter melted and began to brown. When we finally sat down to eat, we took our time pulling each one sizzling hot from the curved shells with small forks. A delicate snail hung glistening from silver tines momentarily, admired for its buttery plumpness and pungent aroma.

Along with the snails, Maman served braised artichokes in apple cider. The spring artichokes in March wore a bluish cast from being hit by the cold as they emerged. The egg-size globes could be left on the stalk to mature for later eating, but Maman liked to braise some early in the season so we could enjoy the tenderness and crisp green flavor of the new artichokes. Snails and baby artichokes were served only once or twice during the season; then they were gone.

The enjoyment my family experienced with such a simple meal went deeper than satisfying a momentary hunger in the belly. Dishes created by Maman during the seasons told a story whenever we gathered around the table. The story was at once universal and personal. It is the story of how man lives balanced among the seasons. Even today, when most of us need not farm to exist, nature urges us on with our anticipation of the flavors, odors, and colors of each season so that we will live out the rhythms of the year continuously. The other story tells of my family and how we lived our lives each day with traditions that grew out of sharing meals with one another and with our friends. The cook who understands that the stories are one and the same serves a communion between the past and the present. In the end, the hand of the seasonal cook is truly the link between the good earth and family.

MARCH RECIPES

Cauliflower and Walnut Soup with Roquefort Toast

Snails with Parsley-Garlic Butter

Mussels à la Bretonne

Turbot with Nasturtium Capers

Fruits de Mer Cassoulet

Lemon-Stuffed Red Snapper

Coq au Vin

Marinated Flank Steak with Glazed Oranges

Braised Artichokes with Cider

Warm Cabbage Hearts with Crème Fraîche

Spinach and Gruyère Cheese Terrine

Salad of Late Winter Leeks Mimosa

Gâteau Breton

Apple Beignets with Fruit Preserve Coulis

Tropical Fruit Mix Sabayon

GENTLE SPRING SUPPER

Cauliflower and Walnut Soup with Roquefort Toast

Rosé Wine

Turbot with Nasturtium Capers

Spinach and Gruyère Cheese Terrine

Chablis

Apple Beignets with Fruit Preserve Coulis

Café au Lait

CAULIFLOWER AND WALNUT SOUP WITH ROQUEFORT TOAST

By March most of our winter vegetable stores were depleted, so the variety of ingredients in Maman's dishes were minimal. She depended more on single, very early spring vegetables like cauliflower to make soups that were much lighter in flavor than winter soups but still hardy enough to keep us warm and satisfied. The taste of late winter-growing cauliflower is much less intense when it is harvested in March than cauliflower that grows in the heat of summer and is harvested in the fall. To add more depth to her meal, Maman paired it with a strong Roquefort cheese and the last of the winter walnuts.

8 SERVINGS

2 small onions, thinly sliced
1 tablespoon unsalted butter
2 pounds cauliflower, trimmed, florets separated
4 garlic cloves, peeled and minced
6 cups chicken stock (see Basics, page 375)

1 cup crumbled Roquefort cheese
½ French baguette, cut on the bias into 16 thin slices, toasted
½ cup walnut pieces, lightly toasted and crushed
Salt and pepper

Place the onions and butter in a saucepan and cook, covered, over low heat for 2 minutes, or until the onions are soft. Do not brown. Mix in the cauliflower and garlic, and continue cooking, covered, for 5 minutes more.

Stir in the chicken stock and bring to a boil. Lower to a gentle simmer and cook for 20 minutes, or until the cauliflower is soft. Remove about ½ cup cauliflower and set aside for garnish.

In a food processor, purée the soup until smooth. Pass through a fine strainer to remove any remaining fiber so that it is velvety in texture. Adjust the seasoning with salt and pepper. Return to the pan and keep warm.

Reserving 3 tablespoons of cheese for garnish, spread the rest on the toast slices. Sprinkle with walnuts.

Divide the reserved cheese and cauliflower among serving bowls. Ladle the soup into the bowls and serve with the cheese toast.

VARIATIONS: A combination of broccoli and cauliflower or broccoli by itself can be used.

- At the end of winter, adding peeled, diced pear and apple with the cauliflower gives the soup a fresh flavor.

- Vary the cheese flavor by using Gorgonzola, Stilton, or goat cheese.

SNAILS WITH PARSLEY-GARLIC BUTTER

It is difficult to hunt snails unless you live in the country and know where to look. Today fresh snails are hard to find, though they are being farm-raised in some parts of the country. Likewise, fresh garlic greens are rarely found in the market. I have adapted Maman's recipe to the reality of the difficulties often encountered by today's cooks. By using good-quality canned snails and substituting gently flavored young garlic from a farmers' market for fresh greens, you can create a contemporary but deliciously seasonal spring favorite. The recipe serves six as an appetizer or three as a main course.

6 SERVINGS

36 snail shells
1 cup unsalted butter
4 garlic cloves, minced
3 tablespoons chopped fresh parsley

¼ cup bread crumbs
36 canned snails, rinsed under cold
    running water and drained
Salt and pepper

Preheat the oven to 450°F. Have ready 6 grooved metal or ceramic **snail dishes.**

Place the shells in a pot of boiling water for 1 minute. Rinse under cold running water and drain.

In a food processor, combine the butter, garlic, and parsley. Pulse until well blended, then season with salt and pepper to taste.

Insert ¼ teaspoon of the butter mixture inside each shell. Stuff 1 snail in each shell. Fill the shells to the top with the remaining butter.

Dip the top of each shell in the bread crumbs and arrange, top side up, in the snail dishes. Place in the oven for 5 minutes, or until the butter is bubbly and brown. Serve immediately.

VARIATIONS: Snails served inside their shells are an elegant presentation, but for a simpler preparation, sauté the snails for 3 minutes in ½ cup melted unsalted butter combined with the garlic, parsley, and bread crumbs. Divide among 6 heated plates and serve immediately.

- To make a delicious main course, sauté the snails as above and serve over freshly cooked, hot fettuccine.

♥ *Monique's Touch:*

Snail dishes are inexpensive and can be found easily in most cities. However, if unavailable, use this alternative method for baking the snails: Spread 2 cups of coarsely ground sea salt in the bottom of a baking pan large enough to hold all the shells. Place the stuffed shells, top side up, in the salt, which will keep the shells from tipping or rolling. Proceed as directed. The salt may be reused after baking.

MUSSELS À LA BRETONNE

In March and April the mussels in Brittany are sweet and in great abundance. Not too long ago it was said one should not eat mussels and other shellfish in months not spelled with the letter "R" because they enter the reproduction stage during the summer. Shellfish become soft, their liqueur cloudy, which people equate with being unsafe. More accurately, the heat made shellfish difficult to transport without spoiling in the summertime. Because we went without mussels in the months ahead, my family ate them often in March, especially at the celebration of La Mi-Carême *to mark the halfway point in the season of Lent. Today quick cold-storage transportation eliminates many spoilage problems, making shellfish bought in the market safe any time of the year. In my home I still serve mussels à la Bretonne come March as a pleasant way to mark the natural seasonality of this delicious food from the living sea.*

8 SERVINGS

1 quart water
1 tablespoon flour
8 artichoke bottoms
4 cups white wine
6 tablespoons chopped shallots
3 garlic cloves, peeled and minced
6 tablespoons chopped fresh parsley

4 pounds mussels, cleaned and
  bearded
1 egg yolk
1 cup crème fraîche (see Basics, page
  379)
Salt and pepper

Bring the water to a boil. Dilute the flour in a small amount of cold water to make a paste. Add the paste with the artichoke bottoms to the boiling water to **prevent discoloration.** Reduce to a simmer and cook for about 15 minutes, or until the artichokes are tender. Drain and keep warm.

In a large saucepan, combine the wine, shallots, garlic, and 4 tablespoons of the parsley. Bring to a boil, then lower to a simmer. Place the mussels in the pan, cover, then cook for 8 minutes, or until all the mussels have opened. Discard any unopened mussels. Remove the mussels before straining the broth through a fine strainer lined with cheesecloth. Return the broth to the saucepan. Shell the mussels, reserving a few in their shell for garnish. Set aside and keep warm.

Reduce the broth by one half by simmering for 5 minutes. In a mixing bowl, blend the egg yolk and crème fraîche together, then slowly add to the simmering broth. Do not let the sauce boil or it will curdle. Adjust the seasoning with salt and pepper, then stir in the remaining 2 tablespoons of parsley and the shelled mussels.

Place an artichoke bottom on each plate, then ladle the mussels evenly over the artichokes. Serve immediately.

VARIATIONS: Instead of serving the mussels over the artichoke bottoms, slice the bottoms thin, then blend with the mussels in the sauce. Serve over fettuccine, rice, or couscous.

- For a dramatic presentation, cook the artichokes whole, with the choke removed. Serve the mussels inside the artichoke hollow.

♥ *Monique's Touch:*

Artichoke color is very delicate and tends to turn brown when exposed to air or gray when cooked in water. To **prevent discoloration** during preparation, I always rub the cut edges of the artichokes with a lemon half. To counteract color change while cooking, I dilute 1 tablespoon of flour in a small amount of cold water to make a paste, then add it to the boiling water. The flour will lightly coat the artichokes (as does the lemon juice), preventing oxidization, which causes discoloration.

SIDENOTE:

To prepare a whole artichoke for cooking:
1. Using a sharp knife, trim the stem even with the base. 2. Slice off the top inch of leaves. Rub the exposed areas with a lemon half. 3. Cut off the top ½ inch of remaining leaves with kitchen shears to remove the prickly points. Rub the exposed areas with a lemon half. 4. Pull off any withered or tough leaves on the bottom. Rub the exposed areas with a lemon half. 5. Scoop out the center hairy choke with a melon-baller, teaspoon, or sharp knife. Squeeze lemon juice into the hollow.

To prepare artichoke bottoms:
1. Trim the stem off the base of the artichoke. 2. Holding the artichoke bottom up, bend each leaf until it snaps, then gently peel back, leaving the meat at the bottom of the leaf attached to the bottom of the artichoke. Continue around the artichoke until about 1 inch of leaves from the bottom have been removed. 3. Using a sharp knife, cut off the remaining cone of leaves. Rub with a lemon half. 4. Scoop out the center hairy choke with a melon-baller or sharp knife. Squeeze lemon juice into the hollow.

TURBOT WITH
NASTURTIUM CAPERS

Turbot is a delicate fish whose season begins during very late winter and early spring. Maman liked to prepare turbot simply poached without smothering it with complicated sauces. She often used the nasturtium capers pickled the summer before, as turbot takes well to the slightly sour taste of the capers.

6 SERVINGS

1 tablespoon unsalted butter
3 tablespoons minced shallots
Six 5-ounce turbot fillets
1 cup dry white wine
1 tablespoon tomato paste
2 teaspoons cornstarch
2 teaspoons cold water
¼ cup crème fraîche (see Basics, page 379)

2 tablespoons nasturtium capers, crushed (see Monique's Touch, page 213)
2 tablespoons mixed chopped fresh chives and parsley
Salt and pepper

Preheat the oven to 350°F. With the butter, coat the inside surface of a 15 × 9-inch non-aluminum baking pan that can be used on top of the stove. Cut a piece of waxed paper slightly larger than the pan.

Sprinkle the shallots on the bottom of the pan, then arrange the fillets on top. Pour the wine around the fillets. Set the pan on a burner and bring to a simmer for 2 minutes. Remove from heat and lay the waxed paper against the fish and finish in the oven for 10 minutes, or until the fish flakes easily with a fork. Transfer the fillets to a serving platter and keep warm.

Set the pan over medium heat. Stir in the tomato paste. Dilute the cornstarch with the water and mix to make a smooth paste. Stir into the sauce, along with the crème fraîche and capers. Heat until warm, stirring constantly. Adjust the seasoning with salt and pepper.

Spoon the sauce over the fillets and sprinkle with chives and parsley before serving.

VARIATIONS: Use other fish, like sole, flounder, snapper, talapia, or sea bass.

- Green peppercorns instead of capers add a sharper taste.

FRUITS DE MER CASSOULET

Fruits de mer, or fruits of the sea, is the lyrical phrase the French use for shellfish. Maman used assorted fruits de mer left from the large traditional seafood platter she served on special occasions to make this wonderful stew the next day. The fish that went into it varied each time, but usually included shrimp, mussels, oysters, clams, sea scallops, and crab. Often bits of firm fish, like halibut, monk fish, salmon, or bass, found their way into the pot. It is a wonderful way to turn extra fish into an appetizer for an elegant dinner or, when served with bread, to create a simple supper.

6 SERVINGS

2 tablespoons unsalted butter
3 tablespoons chopped shallots
1½ pounds assorted shellfish, cleaned and shelled
1 egg white

Pinch of salt
2 egg yolks
2 teaspoons Dijon-style mustard
½ cup bread crumbs
White pepper

Preheat the oven to 450°F.

Heat the butter in a pan and sauté the shallots for a few seconds until warm. Do not brown. Add the shellfish and sauté for only 5 minutes, tossing once or twice each minute. Remove from the heat.

In a bowl, beat the egg white and salt until soft peaks form. In a separate bowl, cream together the egg yolks and mustard. Fold in the egg white and season with white pepper. Gently fold in the shellfish.

Turn the mixture into a ceramic baking dish or divide among 6 individual ramekins. Sprinkle with the bread crumbs and bake for 5 minutes, or until golden brown. Serve immediately.

LEMON-STUFFED RED SNAPPER

By mid-March, Maman had almost used up her stored herbs, and she was looking for other ingredients to flavor her early spring dishes. It was the time of year to look forward to lightening up food, to anticipate moving from dried to fresh herbs. Still, in March the only available fresh herb was parsley that may have lingered through a mild winter. Parsley, combined with a small amount of dried herbs, was not potent enough to be satisfying, especially when used with a flavorful fish like snapper. To compensate, lemon—strong, tart, and cleansing— found its way into late winter and early spring menus.

6 SERVINGS

6 tablespoons unsalted butter
½ cup chopped shallots
1 tablespoon plus ¼ cup olive oil
2 cups bread crumbs
Zest of 3 lemons, grated
Juice of 3 lemons, plus 1 lemon cut
    into 6 wedges, for garnish

1 cup chopped fresh parsley
6 small whole red snapper, cleaned
1 cup white wine
1 teaspoon dried thyme
2 tablespoons chopped fresh parsley
Salt and pepper

Preheat the oven to 350°F. Dot the bottom of an 11 × 16-inch baking pan with 3 tablespoons of butter. Season the bottom with salt and pepper. Cut a piece of parchment paper the size of the pan.

Sauté the shallots in 1 tablespoon of olive oil until soft but not brown.

In a mixing bowl, combine the shallots, bread crumbs, lemon zest and juice, the ¼ cup of olive oil, and the parsley. Divide the stuffing and fill each snapper. Skewer a toothpick along the edge of the fish to close the cavity. Place the snapper in the pan, making sure the sides of the fish don't touch to ensure even cooking. Pour the wine over the fish and sprinkle with thyme and parsley. Dot the top of the fish with the remaining butter. Cover with parchment paper and bake for 20 to 25 minutes until flaky.

Remove the fish from the pan and arrange on a serving platter. Over high heat bring the wine to a boil. Simmer until reduced by half, about 5 minutes. Adjust the seasoning with salt and pepper. Spoon the sauce over the snapper and serve.

VARIATIONS: Six 4-ounce snapper fillets may also be used. Using a small, sharp knife cut a small pocket horizontally into the fillet. Stuff the pocket and proceed as directed.

- The sauce can be thickened by stirring in ¼ cup of cream after the reduction and then simmering for 3 additional minutes.

- Other fish well suited for this recipe are catfish, trout, salmon, halibut, grouper, or bass.

COQ AU VIN

In the spring, when Maman decided to make her coq au vin, or chicken in wine, my siblings and I knew we had a long morning ahead of us. Among the flock of around fifty chickens that roamed freely throughout the courtyard and barn area, Maman picked out exactly which hen she wanted to go into the pot. It was always an old hen, too old to lay eggs but ripe with rich flavor that would seep into the sauce as it cooked. Once Maman marked her quarry, it was up to us children to capture the hen before lunch. The chase was on as we tried to distinguish the honored dinner guest from her scattering sisters, every chicken taking off in separate directions to avoid being caught. Woe to the child who tried to pass off a substitute hen from the one Maman wanted! Inevitably, after a morning of scrambling up haystacks or crawling through the woodpile to find the hiding place, the old hen was caught and brought to her just reward. Our just reward came the next day, as a pot of savory coq au vin proudly took center stage on the dinner table.

4 SERVINGS

One 3-pound chicken, cut into 8 pieces

4 garlic cloves, peeled and crushed

2 carrots, sliced

1 leek, trimmed and coarsely chopped

½ pound mushrooms, quartered

1 medium onion, halved, one half diced

3 cloves

1 large bay leaf

1 teaspoon dried thyme

4 cups red wine

1 tablespoon unsalted butter

4 strips bacon, diced

3 tablespoons flour

1 cup chicken stock (see Basics, page 375)

2 tablespoons chopped fresh parsley

Salt and pepper

Place the chicken, garlic, carrots, leek, mushrooms, and diced onion in a nonaluminum pan. Stud the remaining half of the onion with the cloves. Add to the pan, along with the bay leaf and thyme. Pour the wine over all, cover, and refrigerate overnight, or for at least 2 hours.

Drain the marinade from the pan and reserve. Remove the cloves from the onion and dice the onion, then add the diced onion to the vegetables. Set aside.

In a large pot, melt the butter with the bacon until hot, remove the bacon, and reserve. Brown the chicken on all sides. Set aside. Add the **reserved vegetables** and sauté for a few minutes until their aroma begins to develop. Place the chicken back in the pot. Add the flour and toss gently until well coated. Stir in the reserved marinade and simmer for 5 minutes. Add enough stock to cover the chicken and add the bacon. Season with salt and pepper before bringing to a boil. Lower to a simmer, cover, and cook gently for 1 hour, or until the chicken is tender. Adjust the seasoning with salt and pepper, and sprinkle with parsley before serving.

VARIATIONS: This recipe can be done with duck, 2 Cornish hens, or 3 chicken breasts.

- White wine can be substituted for red wine. The flavor and appearance of the dish will be lighter.

- Any seasonal mushroom can be used in coq au vin. If dried mushrooms are used, reconstitute them by soaking them in enough warm water to cover for 30 minutes. The soaking liquid can replace part of the chicken stock, if desired.

- Adding 1 cup of drained and diced tomatoes will give the coq au vin a richer amber color, and the acid in the tomatoes will help tenderize the meat.

Monique's Touch:

Traditional coq au vin does not include vegetables, but I always add back the **reserved vegetables** used in the marinade. I learned this from Maman, who rarely threw any food away but instead found ways to make a meal go further. The vegetables add flavor and a nice texture as well.

MARINATED FLANK STEAK WITH GLAZED ORANGES

March was a very busy month in our family, as preparations began in the garden for the coming warm spring. Maman didn't have time to spend in the kitchen after a day of garden work. She marinated the meat during the day so it would be ready for a quick sauté in the evening. Orange juice added to the marinade not only flavored it, but the acid in the juice helped tenderize the meat, making a slow-braising process unnecessary for tougher cuts of meat.

6 SERVINGS

3 tablespoons red wine vinegar

1 tablespoon cracked black peppercorns

Zest of 1 orange, grated

Juice of 1 orange

1½ pounds flank steak, trimmed and scored

¼ cup sugar

2 naval oranges, sectioned, juice reserved (see Sidenote, page 294)

1 cup brown stock (see Basics, page 376)

1 tablespoon olive oil

1 tablespoon unsalted butter

2 medium onions, thinly sliced

1 cup crème fraîche (see Basics, page 379)

2 tablespoons chopped fresh parsley

Combine the vinegar, peppercorns, orange zest, and orange juice in a nonaluminum pan. Coat both sides of the steak with the marinade and let rest in the pan, refrigerated, overnight, or for at least 2 hours. Drain, reserving marinade. Cut the steak on the bias into ⅛-inch strips, 4–5 inches long.

In a sauté pan, melt the sugar until it begins to form a syrup, about 3 minutes. Lay the orange segments in a single layer in the pan and brown for 2 minutes on each side. Set aside. Add the stock to the pan and simmer for 2 minutes to reduce by half.

In a heavy sauté pan, heat the oil and butter until hot but not smoking. Sear the steak strips on all sides until brown, then set aside on a plate. Add the onions, stirring constantly for 1 minute. Add the marinade, the glazing syrup, and any drippings from the steak that have accumulated on the plate. Simmer for 2 minutes to reduce to ¼ cup. Stir in the crème fraîche and add the steak back to the pan. Heat for just 2 minutes. Transfer to a serving platter, sprinkle with parsley, and garnish with glazed orange sections.

VARIATIONS: Venison and buffalo meat are an unusual and delicious substitute for steak.

- The oranges may be omitted for a simpler variation.

BRAISED ARTICHOKES WITH CIDER

Artichokes, large, fat, and flavorful, were treated almost like a braised roast by Maman. Slow braising retains all the flavor the artichoke has developed over the long winter. Doused with a soup plate full of braising liquid and served with a piece of bread and slices of cheese, artichokes became the centerpiece of our meal. I still like to cook them this way because they keep well in the refrigerator and reheat quickly for lunch the next day.

4 SERVINGS

4 artichokes, stem trimmed, 1 inch cut off the top, cut surface rubbed with lemon juice
3 tablespoons unsalted butter
1 leek, trimmed and coarsely chopped

3 shallots, chopped
2 cups apple cider
3 tablespoons chopped fresh parsley
Salt and pepper

Preheat the oven to 350°F. Cut a piece of parchment paper the size of a pan large enough to hold the artichokes close together.

Heat the butter in the pan until hot, then sauté the leeks and shallots until soft. Do not brown. Add the cider and artichokes. Spoon some of the leeks and shallots over the artichokes, then season with salt and pepper. Place the **parchment paper** lightly on top of the artichokes. Cover, bring to a boil, then lower to a simmer. Immediately place in the oven and braise for 35 minutes, or until a center leaf pulls out easily. The time will depend on the size of the artichokes.

Remove the artichokes from the pan and place on a work surface. Gently press down on the top of each artichoke to expose the center. Remove the center leaf, then with a spoon remove the hairy choke and discard. Place on a serving plate and ladle some of the braising liquid on each. Sprinkle with parsley and serve.

VARIATIONS: Fresh fennel bulbs make a delicious substitution for artichokes.

- This can be done with brown stock instead of cider.

❤ *Monique's Touch:*

Placing the **parchment paper** over the artichokes provides a close environment for the braising liquid to create steam. However, artichokes have a tendency to float and turn upside down when cooking. If this should happen, place a plate the same size as the inside of the pan over them as a weight to keep the artichokes immersed. Continue cooking as directed.

SIDENOTE:

Artichokes are actually the bud of a thistle, belonging to the daisy family. They come in sizes ranging from hen eggs to softballs, depending on the type and maturity. Look for artichokes with firm, tight leaves and a plump bottom. The stem should be cut no shorter than 1 inch, as it is the stem that helps retain moisture that keeps the heart fresh during transport. Freshness can be determined by gently squeezing the globe and listening for a crisp sound when the leaves rub against each other. Artichokes have two seasons, spring and fall. The spring artichokes are prized for their full flavor, acquired by a slow growing season in the cold of winter.

WARM CABBAGE HEARTS
WITH CRÈME FRAÎCHE

Cabbage leaves are endlessly versatile as a wrapping for stuffing or when used in a number of soups. What is left of the cabbage after the leaves are gone is the heart, sweet and tender. Maman liked to serve the hearts simply dressed in crème fraîche and served warm. Should there be any left—a rare occurrence—the hearts were added later in the week to soup.

6 SERVINGS

2 quarts water
2 small heads green cabbage, outer
  leaves removed to the heart,
  hearts quartered and thinly sliced
½ cup chopped fresh parsley

1 large onion, thinly sliced
1½ cups crème fraîche (see Basics,
  page 379)
Salt and pepper

In a deep saucepan, bring the water to a boil, then lower to a simmer. Immerse the cabbage hearts and blanch for 5 minutes. Remove, drain, and cool for 5 minutes.

In a serving bowl, combine the cabbage hearts, parsley, onion, and crème fraîche. Toss until the hearts are coated. Season with salt and pepper, and serve while warm.

VARIATIONS: Scallions or red onions may be added for color and variety.

- Two tablespoons of dill adds additional flavor.

- The hearts of Napa cabbage, which is part of the savoy cabbage family, make a delicately flavored variation from stronger-flavored green cabbage hearts.

SPINACH AND GRUYÈRE CHEESE TERRINE

Maman used to call this "quiche without a border," as it doesn't have a crust. Occasionally she didn't have time to make a pie shell and found it easy to cook the terrine over the fire in a hot-water bath, which does not require the constant attention a piecrust does to keep from burning. This is a versatile supper dish that can be presented as an appetizer, a main course, or a salad.

8 SERVINGS

1 tablespoon unsalted butter
2 tablespoons olive oil
2 small onions, chopped
2½ pounds fresh spinach, stems
    removed, rinsed, and reserved in
    cold water
1 cup grated Gruyère cheese

CUSTARD:
3 whole eggs
2 egg yolks
1 cup milk
1 cup cream
2 tablespoons chopped fresh chives
Salt and pepper
Freshly ground nutmeg

Preheat the oven to 350°F. Lightly butter a 2-quart ceramic terrine mold.

In a large pan, heat the olive oil, then sauté the onions until transparent but not brown. Taking a handful of spinach at a time, shake off the water and add it to the pan. Cook for 2 minutes, or until the spinach is wilted and soft. Set aside 12 leaves. Transfer to a strainer and drain as much liquid as possible out of the spinach, squeezing if necessary. When thoroughly drained, chop coarsely.

To make the custard, lightly beat together the whole eggs, egg yolks, milk, and cream. Stir in the chives. Season with salt and pepper and nutmeg.

Line the terrine with the reserved spinach leaves. Pour one third of the custard in the bottom before adding one third of the spinach. Sprinkle with ⅓ cup Gruyère cheese. Repeat the layers, ending with the cheese. Place the mold in a hot-water bath (see Monique's Touch, page 32) and bake for 45 minutes, or until a toothpick in the center comes out clean.

To serve, invert on a plate and slice.

VARIATIONS: Mix in a small amount of fresh sorrel with the spinach.

- The custard can be flavored with curry, chopped garlic, or fresh summer herbs, like basil or oregano.

- In the summer, diced roasted red pepper adds a deeper flavor.

- Serve cold with the basic vinaigrette (see Basics, page 381) spooned over each slice.

- The terrine can be done in individual ramekins and served as an appetizer. Cook for 25 minutes.

- To make a quiche, mix the spinach and cheese together with the custard and pour into an unbaked pie shell. Bake in a preheated 375°F oven for 35 minutes.

SALAD OF LATE WINTER LEEKS MIMOSA

The mimosa shrub comes into bloom on the northern coast of Brittany in the very early spring, just as the last of the mature winter leeks, so full of flavor, give way to the next generation of milder-flavored leeks shortly to come. The mimosa shrub is covered with tiny yellow spring buds, and this dish is named for it because the pressed egg yolk sprinkled over the leeks always reminded us of the flower. I like serving this salad because it is like putting a bit of spring on your plate.

6 SERVINGS

6 large leeks, trimmed to 7 inches in
    length, halved lengthwise
2 tablespoons unsalted butter
2 cups water
3 eggs, hard-boiled, with white and
    yolk separated

1 tablespoon chopped fresh parsley
¾ cup basic vinaigrette (see Basics,
    page 381)
2 teaspoons Dijon-style mustard
Salt and pepper

In a large saucepan, place the leeks closely together. Add the butter and water, season with salt and pepper. Cut a piece of parchment paper the same size as the pan and lay against the leeks. Bring to a boil, lower to a gentle simmer, cover, and cook for 15 minutes. Cool in the pan.

Chop the egg white and mix with the parsley. Spread on the bottom of a serving platter, then arrange the leeks on top. Mix the vinaigrette and mustard, then pour over the leeks. Gently **press the yolks** through a small-holed colander while holding it over the leeks. Chill before serving.

VARIATIONS: This can also be done with celery hearts or halved fennel bulbs.

- The first spring asparagus is traditionally served this way. Cook the asparagus gently, according to the thickness of the stalk.

♥ *Monique's Touch:*

Gently **pressing the yolks** through the colander makes tiny balls of yolk that look like mimosa, but if the yolk is not cooked hard enough, the result will be vermicelli-like strands. To make sure the egg is cooked hard all the way through, place the egg in a pan with 1 teaspoon of salt. Cover with 1 quart of cold water and bring to a boil. Turn off the heat and let the egg stand in the water for 45 minutes. Rest the egg in cold running water for 5 minutes before peeling.

GÂTEAU BRETON

During the transitional month of March, neighbors in our village began venturing farther afield as the weather warmed. In the winter, visiting was confined to family and those who lived close by, but the gentle stir of early spring air enticed housewives to wander into each other's kitchen to exchange seeds and gossip, and the animals being born gave the men an excuse to stop by "just to lend a hand." Almost every day Maman would make an extremely fast and easy gâteau Breton to welcome her unexpected visitors and the lovely spring season that brought them to her.

12 SERVINGS

2 cups flour

1 cup sugar

1 cup cold unsalted butter, cut into small pieces

6 egg yolks, lightly beaten, 1 tablespoon reserved

1 tablespoon rum (optional)

Preheat the oven to 350°F. Line an 8-inch cake pan with parchment paper.

In a mixing bowl, blend together the flour and sugar. Add the butter, a few pieces at a time, using your fingers to work the dough into a sandy texture. Make a well in the center and add the **egg yolks** and rum, if desired. Work with your hands until a soft, semi-sticky dough is formed. Press the dough into the cake pan, smoothing the top with a spatula. Brush with the reserved yolk. Dragging the tip of a fork across the dough, mark the top in a grid pattern. Bake for 50 minutes, or until golden brown and a toothpick in the center comes out clean. If browning too quickly, turn the oven down to 325°F and continue baking. Cool in the pan to room temperature and unmold before cutting.

♥ *Monique's Touch:*

Often recipes call for the addition of only **egg yolks,** leaving the cook with extra egg whites. Freeze extra whites and use later to make egg white omelets, meringue, angel food cake, or a soufflé. To freeze, place in an 8-ounce container. Cover, date, and place in the freezer. The first whites will keep for 6 months. Add egg whites whenever you have them until the container is full. It will hold 7 egg whites, which is the number called for in many cake or soufflé recipes. Another method is to place each egg white in a section of an ice-cube tray. When the tray is full, unmold the egg white cubes and store in a food-storage zip-lock plastic bag for up to 3 months.

APPLE BEIGNETS WITH FRUIT PRESERVE COULIS

Americans are most familiar with beignets in the Deep South, where they were first served in Louisiana Cajun family kitchens. Cajuns were originally French people from the northwest coast of Brittany and Normandy who immigrated to North America. Eventually they made their way down the Mississippi River to the bayous surrounding New Orleans, bringing the cooking traditions of their French homeland with them. I enjoy traveling to New Orleans, where I can always get a fresh beignet and a café au lait to remind me of home.

6 SERVINGS

1½ cups flour
1 tablespoon sugar
¼ teaspoon freshly ground nutmeg
3 egg yolks
1 cup milk
1 teaspoon vanilla extract
3 egg whites

6 medium Golden Delicious or Granny Smith apples, peeled, cored, and cut into ½-inch dice
2 quarts peanut oil
½ cup powdered sugar
2 cups apricot or peach preserves

Combine the flour, sugar, and nutmeg in a mixing bowl. Make a well in the center and add the egg yolks. Slowly mix in the dry ingredients, then slowly add the milk, stirring constantly to prevent lumps. Add the vanilla extract. Mix until well blended.

Beat the egg whites until soft peaks form. Fold into the batter. Gently stir in the apples.

Heat the preserves to soften. Pass through a fine strainer, pushing through as much pulp as possible. Set aside.

In a deep pan, heat the peanut oil to 350°F. Carefully drop the batter, in 1-tablespoon measures, into the oil. Cook until golden on all sides, remove, and place on a paper towel to drain. Sprinkle with confectioners' sugar and serve hot, with the preserves on the side for dipping.

VARIATIONS: Other fruits, like pears, bananas, peaches, or berries, can be used instead of apples.

- Cider or beer can replace half of the milk. Both act as a leavener, making the dough lighter, and give the beignets a nuttier flavor.

- Instead of vanilla, cinnamon or almond extract may be used to flavor the batter.

TROPICAL FRUIT MIX SABAYON

This is a versatile dessert that entirely relies on market availability for variation. March has little in the way of fresh regional fruits or nuts to offer seasonally in most parts of the country. However, the late winter tropical fruits are a wonderful way to begin lightening up heavy winter fare as we look forward to the brighter tastes of spring. As the fruits available at market move through the natural growing seasons, they can be mixed into the custard base for a salad that reflects the time of year in which it is served.

6 SERVINGS

1 naval orange, peeled, segmented, and juice reserved (see Sidenote, page 294)

1 pink grapefruit, peeled, segmented, and juice reserved

1 quart water

4 egg yolks

2 tablespoons sugar

2 tablespoons Grand Marnier liqueur

1 banana, peeled and sliced

½ pineapple, peeled and cut into ½-inch dice

1 kiwi, peeled and sliced

Measure out enough of the reserved orange and grapefruit juice to equal ¼ cup combined. Reserve the remainder for another use.

In the bottom of a double boiler or in a 2-quart saucepan, bring the water to a boil. Meanwhile, combine the orange juice and grapefruit juice, yolks, sugar, and liqueur in the top half of the double boiler or a glass or stainless steel mixing bowl large enough so that the bottom fits into the saucepan without touching the water. When the water reaches the boiling point, remove from the heat and place the bowl over the water. Beat the mixture with an electric mixer until it triples in volume and becomes fluffy, about 3 minutes.

Combine the orange and grapefruit segments, banana, pineapple, and kiwi. Divide among 6 champagne flutes. Fill each glass to the top with custard. Serve at room temperature or chilled.

VARIATIONS: Any combination of seasonal fruit may be used, like raspberries, strawberries, papaya, mango, peaches, or poached pears.

- Other flavoring liqueurs or extracts may be substituted, like lemon, vanilla, kirsch, Madeira, or Marsala.

- Instead of individual glasses, mix the fruit in a large glass or trifle bowl. Pour the custard over and serve from the bowl.

Basics

RECIPES

Sachet

Chicken Stock

Brown Stock

Fish Stock

Vegetable Stock

Court Bouillon

Crème Fraîche

Monique's Mayonnaise

Basic Vinaigrette

Short Pastry Dough

Sweet Short Pastry Dough

Puff Paste

Basic Yeast Dough

Custard Cream

French Buttercream

Applesauce

Plums in Wine

SACHET

A sachet is a bag of aromatics used in stocks, soups, or cooking liquids to add flavor to the dish. It is also sometimes referred to in recipes as a "bouquet garni," or simply as a bundle of herbs and seasoning. Below is the recipe to make one sachet, but I usually make several at a time and store the extras in a freezer bag until I need them.

1 SACHET

4 large sprigs parsley, chopped
1 teaspoon dried thyme
1 large bay leaf
10 whole black peppercorns, cracked
1 large garlic clove, crushed

Cut a piece of cheesecloth into a 3 × 3-inch square.

Place all the ingredients in the center of the cheesecloth. Gather up the 4 corners of the cloth and secure with kitchen twine. Sachet ingredients may also be placed in a metal tea ball, if desired. Use as directed in recipes.

STOCKS

There are many conveniences I use in my kitchen to save time, but one handmade item I always try to have in my freezer is a quantity of stocks. Stocks are very easy to make, as they need little preparation or attention while simmering. They give a depth of flavor and personality to soups, stews, and sauces that just can't be found in canned stocks (a few of which I keep on hand to use in a pinch). When making stock, much depends on the size and gelatin content of the bones and the age of the vegetables used. Hence, the wide variation in cooking times. A good rule of thumb is to remember the more cooking time, the richer the flavor of the finished stock. This does not apply to delicate fish stock, which should be simmered gently and briefly.

Chicken Stock:

4 QUARTS

4 pounds chicken bones, cooked, uncooked, or mixed (do not use livers),
rinsed
6 quarts cold water
1 sachet
2 onions, studded with 2 cloves each
2 carrots, coarsely chopped
1 leek, white part only, coarsely chopped
2 large celery stalks, coarsely chopped

Place the bones in a large stockpot and cover with water. Bring to a boil, then lower to a simmer. Cook for 20 minutes, occasionally skimming off the foam that rises to the top.

Add the sachet, onions, carrots, leek, and celery. Bring back to a boil, then immediately lower to a simmer. Cook, uncovered, for 4 hours. Skim any foam rising to the top.

Strain into a stainless steel or plastic container through a colander lined with cheesecloth. Let cool to room temperature, then refrigerate. When completely cool, remove any solid fat from the top. Freeze in covered containers or zip-lock freezer bags in 8-ounce portions.

SIDENOTE:
When making stock, always begin with cold water to allow enough time as the liquid comes to a boil and during simmering for all the flavor of the ingredients to leach out. This ensures the final stock will be full-bodied and flavorful.

Brown Stock:

8 pounds beef or veal bones, or mixed

6 tablespoons olive oil

5 carrots, coarsely chopped

3 onions, coarsely chopped

6 celery stalks, coarsely chopped

1 white turnip, coarsely chopped

¼ cup tomato paste

1 leek, coarsely chopped

1 large onion brûlé

1 sachet

1 dozen whole black peppercorns

10 quarts cold water

Preheat the oven to 450°F.

Spread the beef or veal bones in a large roasting pan so that they are not crowded. Drizzle with oil, then roast in the oven for 1 hour until the bones are very brown but not scorched. Transfer the bones to a large stockpot.

Place the carrots, onions, celery, turnip, tomato paste, and leek in the roasting pan. Roast until caramelized, about 20 minutes. Do not scorch. Add to the bones.

Cover with water, adding more if necessary to bring the water level to at least 3 inches above the bones. Add the **onion brûlé,** sachet, and peppercorns. Bring to a boil, then lower to a simmer. Skim the foam as it rises. Simmer for 6 hours.

Strain into a stainless steel or plastic container through a colander lined with cheese-cloth. Let cool to room temperature, then refrigerate. When completely cool, remove any solid fat from the top. Freeze in covered containers or zip-lock freezer bags in 8-ounce portions.

♥ *Monique's Touch:*

Onion brûlé simply means burnt onion and is used as a flavoring and coloring ingredient in classic French cooking. It adds a deeper flavor to sauces and stocks, and I prefer onion brûlé to using bottled caramel coloring to give soups, stocks, and some sauces a golden-brown color. To make 1 onion brûlé, cut an onion in half and brush lightly with canola oil. Place the halved onion, cut side down, in a very hot flat-bottomed pan. Sear until almost burned to caramelize the natural sugar in the onion.

Fish Stock:

2 tablespoons unsalted butter
1 medium onion, coarsely diced
1 cup sliced mushroom stems
1 celery stalk, coarsely chopped

3 pounds lean fish bones, such as red snapper, bass, or grouper (do not use salmon), rinsed
1 cup dry white wine
1 sachet

In a large, stainless steel pot, melt the butter, then sauté the onion, mushrooms, and celery lightly for 1 minute. Add the bones, wine, and sachet.

Cover with water to 3 inches above bones and bring to a boil, then lower to a simmer. Simmer gently for 30 minutes.

Strain into a stainless steel or plastic container through a colander lined with cheesecloth. Set the container in a sink filled with ice water. Stir frequently. When completely cool, remove any solid fat from the top. Freeze in covered containers or zip-lock freezer bags in 8-ounce portions.

Vegetable Stock:

3 tablespoons olive oil
1 cup coarsely chopped onion
1 cup coarsely chopped leek
½ cup coarsely chopped celery
½ cup coarsely chopped cabbage
½ cup coarsely chopped carrot
½ cup coarsely chopped turnip
½ cup coarsely chopped parsnip

½ cup coarsely chopped tomato
4 garlic cloves
1-inch piece of ginger, peeled
2 cloves
1 teaspoon dried fennel
1 teaspoon celery seeds, crushed
6 quarts cold water
1 sachet

In a large pot, heat the oil, then add the onion, leek, celery, cabbage, carrot, turnip, parsnip, tomato, garlic, ginger, cloves, fennel, and celery seeds. Sauté for 5 minutes, tossing gently a few times.

Add the water and sachet. Bring to a boil, then lower to a simmer for 45 minutes.

Strain into a stainless steel or plastic container through a colander lined with cheesecloth. When completely cool, remove any solid fat from the top. Freeze in covered containers or zip-lock freezer bags in 8-ounce portions.

Court Bouillon:

1½ quarts cold water
¼ cup cider vinegar
1 cup white wine
1 cup coarsely chopped onion

1 cup coarsely chopped celery
1 sachet
2 teaspoons salt

Combine all the ingredients in a large pot. Bring to a boil, then lower to a simmer, uncovered, for 20 to 45 minutes. The longer it simmers, the more concentrated the flavor. Strain before using. Stock simmered for less time should be used to poach fish, chicken, and shellfish. Stock simmered for 30 minutes or more should be used for making sauces.

CRÈME FRAÎCHE

Crème fraîche is a cultured heavy cream that thickens and develops a tangy taste as it sits. It is similar to sour cream, but less bland with a creamier texture. Crème fraîche is easy to make and is more versatile than regular sour cream because it can be boiled without separating. Crème fraîche keeps for 2 to 3 weeks in the refrigerator.

2 CUPS

2 cups heavy cream
½ cup buttermilk

Whisk the cream and buttermilk together in a saucepan over low heat. Bring to 80°F (do not let temperature rise higher), then transfer to a glass container. Cover with cheesecloth and let stand at room temperature overnight. Cover and refrigerate.

MONIQUE'S MAYONNAISE

Mayonnaise is not difficult to make at home, and it's one of the simplest ways to add a professional taste to dishes served to the family. Older mayonnaise recipes called for using uncooked eggs, which today raises health questions about bacterial contamination. In the version I have developed, this concern is eliminated because the temperature of the mayonnaise is raised with the addition of hot white sauce, killing any bacteria from the eggs. The mayonnaise will have a thinner consistency than commercial mayonnaise, which contains gum emulsifiers as a thickening agent.

2 CUPS

3 tablespoons unsalted butter
3 tablespoons flour
1 cup milk
1 tablespoon Dijon-style mustard

2 tablespoons lemon juice
3 egg yolks
¼ teaspoon white pepper

In a saucepan, melt the butter, then stir in the flour, mixing constantly as the mixture cooks over medium-low heat for 1 minute. Taking the pan off heat, slowly stir in the milk, blending well. Place back on medium-low heat, stirring constantly until thickened.

In a food processor, blend together the mustard, lemon juice, egg yolks, and white pepper. With the processor running, add the hot white sauce in a steady stream. Continue processing a few seconds longer until all the ingredients are combined. Store in the refrigerator for 1 week.

BASIC VINAIGRETTE

A good basic vinaigrette, made up in advance, is a must for cooks short on time. Endless variations can be made from this version, making it easy to create dressings appropriate to the seasonal ingredients you have on hand. In addition, I sauté ingredients in hot vinaigrette when I don't have time to marinate. The vinaigrette contains the oil I need to cook with, and the great flavors from the garlic and herbs give meats and vegetables a wonderful taste.

1 QUART

4 tablespoons chopped shallots
3 garlic cloves, chopped
4 tablespoons chopped fresh parsley

4 tablespoons Dijon-style mustard
1 cup red wine vinegar
3 cups safflower, peanut, or olive oil

In a food processor, blender, or mixing bowl, combine the shallots, garlic, parsley, mustard, and vinegar. Blend well.

With the processor or blender running, or while briskly hand-whisking, slowly add the oil in a steady stream. Mix for a few minutes until the dressing is emulsified and thick.

Place in a container and refrigerate for up to 2 weeks. If olive oil is used, it will solidify with refrigeration. Bring to room temperature before using.

SHORT PASTRY DOUGH

The absence of sugar makes this dough perfect for savory pies, as well as for dessert pies and tarts when less sweetness is desired. Note that if made by hand, the butter should be room temperature, but if made in a food processor, it should be very cold.

1 RECIPE

1½ cups flour
½ cup unsalted butter, cut into ½-inch
    pieces
½ teaspoon salt
1 tablespoon ice water
1 egg yolk

BY HAND:

In a mixing bowl, combine the flour, butter, and salt. Work with your fingers, making sure the palms of your hands do not touch the dough, until the mixture looks crumbly but dry and the butter is the size of dry oatmeal.

Mix the ice water and egg yolk. Add to the flour and quickly work the dough until it just begins to mass.

BY FOOD PROCESSOR:

Combine the flour, butter, and salt in the bowl of a food processor fitted with the metal blade. Pulse 5 or 6 times until the mixture looks crumbly but dry and the butter is the size of dry oatmeal.

Mix the ice water with the egg yolk and add all at once. Pulse the processor on and off until the dough just begins to mass.

FINISH FOR BOTH METHODS:

Turn the dough onto a floured work surface. Gather into a ball. Roughly, with the heel of your hand, push the dough away from you in 3 clumps, making a 6-inch smear across the work surface each time. Gather the dough into a ball and repeat 3 times, each time turning the ball one-quarter turn.

Pat into a 6-inch disk and wrap tightly with plastic wrap. Let rest in the refrigerator at least 20 minutes. At this point the dough can be left refrigerated overnight or frozen for later use.

When ready to use, remove the dough from the refrigerator and let come to room temperature. Place on a floured work surface. Roll 1 inch larger than pan size needed.

Pick up the dough by rolling it up with the rolling pin, then unrolling it on top of the pan. Press the dough evenly all around the inside of the pan. Trim the edge, or to add strength to the edge, turn the excess dough under itself and press into the sides of the pan. Chill for 15 minutes. Fill and bake as directed.

For recipes calling for a partially baked or blind-baked shell, preheat the oven to 375°F. Proceed as above through chilling. After chilling, line the shell with aluminum foil and fill with professional pie weights or substitute rice, beans, or glass beads. Place in the preheated oven and bake for 20 to 30 minutes, or until a very pale golden color. Carefully remove weights and foil before using as directed.

VARIATION: Butter adds flavor and color to pastry, but for a less expensive, lower-fat alternative, substitute lard or vegetable shortening in the same quantity.

SWEET SHORT PASTRY DOUGH

This dough is used for delicate, sweet pastries, such as tarts, tartlets, and pies.

1 RECIPE

> 1½ cups flour
> ¼ cup sugar
> Pinch of salt
> ¾ cup unsalted butter, cut into ½-inch
>   pieces
> 2 large egg yolks, broken

Sift the dry ingredients together.

BY HAND:
Place the dry ingredients in a mixing bowl. Add the butter and work with your fingers until the dough looks mealy but still dry. Add the egg yolks and blend quickly, letting the dough gather naturally in big lumps without pressing it together with your fingers. After it gathers, use your knuckles to press the dough into a mass.

BY FOOD PROCESSOR:
Place the dry ingredients and butter in the bowl of a food processor fitted with the metal blade. Pulse 5 or 6 times until the dough is mealy-looking but dry. Add the egg yolks and pulse until the dough gathers into a mass.

FINISH FOR BOTH METHODS:
Turn the dough onto a floured work surface. Gather into a ball. Roughly, with the heel of your hand, push the dough away from you in 3 clumps, making a 6-inch smear across the work surface each time. Gather the dough into a ball and repeat 3 times, each time turning the ball one-quarter turn.

Pat into a 6-inch disk and wrap tightly with plastic wrap. Let rest in the refrigerator at least 20 minutes. At this point the dough can be left refrigerated overnight or frozen for later use.

When ready to use, remove from the refrigerator and let come to room temperature. Place on a floured work surface. Roll 1 inch larger than pan size needed. Pick up the dough by rolling it up with the rolling pin, then unrolling it on top of the pan. Press the dough evenly all around the inside of a 10-inch tart pan or six 3-inch tartlet pans. Trim the edges, or to give the edge extra strength, turn the excess dough under itself and press into the sides of the pan. Chill for 15 minutes. Fill and bake as directed.

For recipes calling for a partially baked shell, preheat the oven to 375°F. Proceed as above through chilling. After chilling, line the shell with aluminum foil and fill with professional pie weights or substitute rice, beans, or glass beads. Place in the oven and bake for 20 to 30 minutes until a very pale golden color. Carefully remove weights and foil before using as directed.

VARIATIONS: For a butter cookie–like texture, increase the sugar to ½ cup. With the additional sugar the dough becomes extremely soft and delicate and must be molded in the pan by hand instead of rolled out.

PUFF PASTE

This dough is used to make cream puffs, eclairs, croquembouche, Paris-Brest, and other desserts, or it can be used to hold such savory fillings as chicken or tuna salad.

24 PUFFS

1 cup water
4 tablespoons unsalted butter
Pinch of salt
Dash of nutmeg
1 cup flour
5 eggs
1 tablespoon milk

Preheat the oven to 425°F.

In a saucepan, place the water, butter, salt, and nutmeg. Bring to a hard boil until the butter completely melts and becomes foamy. Add the flour all at once and immediately remove from the heat and mix with a wooden spoon until it resembles very dry mashed potatoes. Cool to room temperature, about 15 minutes. (Puff paste may be frozen for up to 4 weeks at this point. To use, defrost and proceed as directed.) After cooling, add 4 eggs, one at a time, blending well after each addition.

To make the puffs, fill a pastry bag fitted with a ½-inch tip with puff paste and pipe 1-inch mounds of dough onto a baking sheet lined with parchment paper. Beat the remaining egg and mix the milk. Using a pastry brush, brush the top of each puff with the egg wash, rounding off the top of the puff.

Bake for 15 minutes, or until golden brown and almost double in size. Turn the oven off and let the puffs stand inside with the door ajar for about 20 minutes so the moisture will evaporate. After cooling, the puffs may be stored for up to 5 days in a container covered with a towel. Do not store in plastic or in a sealed container, as the puffs will become soft.

BASIC YEAST DOUGH

Nothing is more welcoming than the smell of freshly baked bread. This versatile recipe can be made in advance and frozen so that fresh bread or tart or pizza crust is available with little planning.

1 LOAF OR 2 TART OR PIZZA CRUSTS

3 cups flour
1 teaspoon salt
1 tablespoon yeast or 1 packet dry yeast
1 cup warm water, 90°–100°F

Combine the flour and salt in a bowl. Sprinkle the yeast over the water and wait a few minutes for it to dissolve. Make a well in the center of the flour and slowly add the water while mixing with a wooden spoon or your hand. Transfer to a floured work surface when the dough begins to form a ball.

Knead by rapidly and vigorously folding the dough over on itself, then push it away with the heels of your hands. Continue for 5 minutes until the dough is smooth. Place in a lightly oiled bowl, cover with plastic wrap, and let rest at room temperature (80°–90°F) for about 45 minutes, or until double in size. The dough is now ready to use as a tart or pizza crust.

TO MAKE BREAD:
Punch down and knead as above for 2 minutes. Shape into a loaf pan and let rise about 35 minutes, or until double in size. Bake in a preheated 450°F oven for 20 minutes.

TO FREEZE FOR LATER USE:
Punch down and wrap in plastic wrap, then secure in a zip-lock bag. Can be formed into a loaf, tart, or pizza shape beforehand. To use, defrost in the refrigerator overnight. Proceed as above for bread or use immediately for tart or pizza crust.

CUSTARD CREAM

Custard cream, or pastry cream as it is also known, is a thick custard sauce flavored with vanilla. It is often used as a filling in a pastry in place of whipped cream, which can soften quickly and make the puff soggy.

3 CUPS

2 cups milk	¼ cup cornstarch
1 vanilla bean, split in half lengthwise	6 egg yolks
½ cup flour	½ cup sugar

Place the milk and vanilla bean in a saucepan and heat until scalding, just below a simmer. Sift together the flour and cornstarch.

In a mixing bowl, beat the egg yolks and sugar until thick and pale yellow. Whisk in the flour and cornstarch until well blended. Remove the vanilla bean from the milk. Slowly add the milk to the egg mixture, blending well.

Rinse the film of milk from the pan and pour the custard into the saucepan. Heat over medium flame, constantly stirring gently so the custard does not stick to the pan. Stir until thickened. Do not boil. If the custard becomes lumpy, remove from heat and beat hard until lumps are gone. Then heat again to thicken, if necessary.

The custard can be used immediately. To store, place in a bowl and dot with 1 tablespoon butter. Lay a piece of plastic wrap against the surface and let come to room temperature for 20 minutes before refrigerating. When ready to use, bring to room temperature, then beat with a whisk to loosen.

VARIATIONS: Chocolate cream can be made by adding 1 cup melted semisweet chocolate after thickening.

- Mocha cream can be made by simmering 1 cup of coffee until reduced to ¼ cup, then adding after the custard thickens.

- Praline cream can be made by stirring in 1 cup ground praline after thickening.

FRENCH BUTTERCREAM

True buttercream is an exquisite indulgence that once experienced will forever change the way you taste commercial frostings made of vegetable shortening. Nothing compares to it, and it is well worth the effort, especially at holiday time or whenever the occasion calls for a special dessert.

4 CUPS

6 egg yolks
4 whole eggs
1 pound sugar
¾ cup water

3 teaspoons vanilla extract
1½ pounds unsalted butter, cut into
  small pieces

Combine the egg yolks and whole eggs in the bowl of an electric mixer fitted with a wire whisk.

In a saucepan, heat the sugar and water to 238°F.

Turn the mixer on high speed while quickly adding the sugar water. (To prevent splatters, lay a large cotton towel over the mixer, draping it down the sides of the bowl.) Beat until the eggs have doubled in volume and are light and fluffy. Cool to room temperature.

Add the vanilla to the egg mixture. Using the highest speed, beat continuously while gradually adding the **butter** a few pieces at a time. Beat until all the butter is incorporated and the buttercream is smooth and light.

Transfer to a container and cool before using, or refrigerate up to 2 days. Bring to room temperature and beat lightly before using.

VARIATIONS: Chocolate buttercream can be made by adding 6 ounces of melted bittersweet chocolate to the egg mixture.

- Mocha buttercream can be made by adding approximately 3 ounces of strong coffee or espresso to the egg mixture. Be careful of how much coffee is added or the buttercream will taste bitter.

♥ *Monique's Touch:*

The temperature of the **butter** is very important to attaining the right consistency of the buttercream. If the buttercream begins curdling while the butter is added, the butter is too cold. Place a hot towel under the bottom of the bowl and continue adding the butter. If the buttercream is thin, the butter is too warm. Place a zip-lock bag of ice and water underneath the bowl and continue adding the butter.

Maman and Papa surrounded by nine of the ten children, 1945. My youngest brother, Albert, was born a few months later. On the left *my sister Mimie holds me.*

APPLESAUCE

Whenever Maman made apple tarts during the fall, she saved the peels to make applesauce. I do the same thing when I peel apples or pears for other uses. I always freeze the peels and cores in a plastic bag to save for the day I make applesauce. The extra peels thicken the texture of applesauce because they contain pectin, and they also heighten the apple flavor in the sauce. Applesauce has many uses in my kitchen. We mix it with hot cereal, spread it on toast, or serve it as a condiment with game or pork. A delicious chutney may be made simply by adding raisins and nuts.

1 QUART

2 pounds assorted regional seasonal apples or Golden Delicious, Granny Smith, and McIntosh apples, washed in cold water, each cut into 8 pieces

1 cup cold water
1 vanilla bean, halved lengthwise

Place the apples in a large, nonaluminum pan. Add the water and vanilla bean. Cover, place over medium heat, and simmer for 30 minutes, or until the apples are soft.

Remove the vanilla bean, rinse, pat dry, and set aside for another use.

Process the apples through the medium blade of a food mill. Transfer to a container or zip-lock bag before refrigerating. Can be frozen for up to 6 months.

VARIATIONS: Add cinnamon to taste for a spicier applesauce.

- Pear-apple sauce is an especially good combination. When pears become overripe and brown, freeze them until it's time to make applesauce. Proportion the pears and apples according to taste and proceed as above.

PLUMS IN WINE

Fruit preserved in wine can be used in a variety of recipes or served on their own. For those who are interested in putting food up for the winter, plums in wine is an easy recipe to start with. In Brittany most homes have a couple of jars of pretty fruit on display on the mantel, and guests are offered a little glass of the fruit liqueur, or the fruit is given away as gifts at holiday time.

2 QUARTS

2 pounds Italian plums, halved, seeds removed
1 cup water
2 cups red wine

½ cup red wine vinegar
2 cups sugar
1 vanilla bean, halved lengthwise

In a large bowl, combine all the ingredients. Let stand overnight in the refrigerator.

Strain the liquid into a large saucepan. Bring to a boil and let simmer for 25 minutes until the syrup is reduced by one half. Add the plums and bring to a boil. Skim any foam from the top. Remove from heat.

Pack the plums and syrup into 2 quart-size or 4 pint-size sterilized Mason jars, filling each jar to the neck. Screw the lids on tightly. Place the jars in a large pot filled with cold water at least 3 inches above the jars. Bring to a boil for 25 minutes. Remove and let stand until the domes on the lids retract. Store in a dry place until ready to use.

VARIATIONS: Other fruits, like peaches, apricots, and cherries, may be used.

- Instead of canning the fruit, store in zip-lock bags after cooking. Can be frozen for up to 6 months.

Basic Necessities

A well-stocked pantry and a kitchen fitted with several pieces of good cooking equipment can go a long way toward making time in the kitchen more enjoyable. Below are several items I have come to rely on when using the kitchen on a daily basis. They reflect my tastes and needs, so you should adjust your pantry according to your own cooking style. Do not let the list overwhelm you, especially if you are just starting out. Build the inventory slowly, like a long and valued friendship.

PANTRY:
Salt
White pepper
Whole black peppercorns
Potato starch
Arrowroot
Baking powder/soda
Sugar/powdered sugar
Yeast
Tea
Instant coffee
Vinegars: balsamic, red wine, rice
Oils: olive, canola, peanut,
    safflower, sesame
Worcestershire sauce
Soy sauce
Hot pepper sauce
Honey
White and red wine
Dry vermouth
Sherry wine
Brandy or cognac
Shallots
Onions
Potatoes

REFRIGERATOR:
Milk
Eggs
Mayonnaise
Variety of cheese: Parmesan, Swiss,
    Cheddar, etc.
Maple syrup
Peanut butter
Horseradish
Ketchup
Mustard: plain, Dijon-style
Lemon juice
Salsa
Apricot Preserves
Chutney
Parsley
Scallions
Celery
Carrots

FREEZER:
Variety of pestos
Egg-roll wrappings

Phyllo dough
Unsalted butter

Bacon
Chopped summer herbs
Bag of grated mixed cheeses

Variety of stocks
Assorted summer berries

HERBS/SPICES:
Dry mustard
Paprika
Curry
Cumin
Cayenne pepper
Dried thyme
Dried oregano
Dried dill
Dried rosemary
Dried sage
Bay leaves

CAN/DRY GOODS:
Whole and diced tomatoes
Tomato paste
Low-sodium chicken broth
Garbanzo beans
Pickles
Capers
Artichoke hearts
Olives
White and wild rice
Assorted pastas
Dried beans: red kidney, black, great
    northern white, lentils
Couscous
Dried mushrooms
Semisweet baking chocolate
Vanilla beans and extract
Garlic

COOKING EQUIPMENT:
Sharp knives: 10-inch chef, 6-inch utility, several paring
1 set heavy, lined stainless steel pans: 1-, 2-, 4-quart saucepans, 8-quart soup pot,
    16–20-quart stockpot, 9-inch sauté pan, 12-inch sauté pan, 10–14-inch straight-
    side sauté pan w/lid
8–10-quart cast-iron Dutch oven w/lid

Sharpening steel
Flex/wire whisks (stainless)
Pastry brush/bag/tubes
Skimmer
1 set measuring cups
1 set measuring spoons
Kitchen scissors/twine
Small/large cutting boards
Wooden spoons, assorted sizes
Cooling rack

Vegetable peeler
Rolling pin
Ladles, assorted sizes
Oven thermometer
1-quart measure
Ounce/gram scale
Small, nonelectric juicer
Rubber/metal spatulas
Tart/cake pans, assorted sizes
Sifter

3 mixing bowls, assorted sizes
Roasting pan
½-size sheet pan
Colander
Food mill
Food processor
Bottle opener

Baking dish
Nonstick omelet pan
Fine-mesh strainer
Fine/coarse graters
Pepper mill
Electric mixer
Cheesecloth

Harvest Chart

The harvest chart includes all the fresh produce used in recipes in this book. The availability months refer to dates the items should be available at farmers' markets in their indigenous growing area. It is only a guide. The best way to determine what is fresh and available is to ask questions and get to know the purveyors at your local produce market.

	MIDWEST	EAST	SOUTH	WEST	N. WEST
Apples	Sep–Oct	Sep–Nov	Aug–Sep	Aug–Oct	Sep–Nov
Apricots	Jul–Aug	Jul	Jun	Jun–Jul	Jul
Artichokes				Mar–May Sep–Oct	
Arugula	Apr–May	Apr–May		Mar	Apr
Asparagus	May–Jun	May–Jun	Feb–Mar	Mar–Jun	May–Jun
Beans, Green	July–Sep	July–Sep	Mar–May	Jun–Sep	June–Sep
Beets	Jun–Sep	Jun–Oct	Dec–Feb	May–Sep	May–Oct
Blackberries	Aug	Aug		Aug	Aug–Sep
Blueberries	Aug	Jul–Aug		Jun	Aug–Sep
Broccoli	Aug–Oct	Aug–Oct	Feb–Apr	Jan–May	Aug–Nov
Brussels Sprouts	Oct–Nov	Oct–Nov		Jan–Mar	Oct–Dec
Cabbage	Aug–Nov	Aug–Nov	Jan–Mar	Apr–May	Aug–Nov
Carrots	Aug–Oct	Jul–Sep	Dec–Apr	Jan–Jun	Jul–Oct
Cassis/Currants	Jul	Jul			Jul
Cauliflower	Sep–Oct	Sep–Oct	Dec–Feb	Mar–May	Aug–Nov
Celery	Jul–Oct	Aug–Nov	Jan–May	Oct–Dec	Jul–Nov
Celery Root (Celeriac)	Aug–Sep	Aug–Sep		Aug	Sep–Oct
Cherries	Jul–Aug	Jul		Jun–Jul	Jul
Chestnuts	Nov				Oct–Nov
Corn	Aug–Sep	Aug–Sep	May–Jun	Jun–Aug	Aug–Oct
Cranberries	Oct	Oct–Nov			Oct–Dec
Cucumbers	Jul–Sep	Jul–Sep	Apr–May	Jun–Sep	Aug–Sep
Eggplant	Jul–Aug	Jul–Aug	Jan–Apr	Jun–Sep	Jul–Sep
Endive	Sep–Oct	Sep–Nov	Mar–Apr	Oct–Jan	Sep–Nov
Fava Beans	Jun–Jul	Jun–Jul	May–Jun	May–Jun	Jun–Jul
Fennel	Sep	Sep	Jun	May–Jun	Sep
Figs			Aug	July–Aug	

	MIDWEST	EAST	SOUTH	WEST	N. WEST
Gooseberries	Jul–Aug	Jul–Aug			Jul–Sep
Grapefruit			Nov–Apr	May–Aug	
Grapes	Sep–Oct	Sep–Oct	Aug–Nov	Jun–Oct	Sep–Oct
Horseradish	Sep				
Jerusalem Artichokes	Nov	Nov	Dec–Jan	Feb–Apr	Nov
Leeks	Sep–Nov	Sep–Nov	Nov–Jan	Feb–Apr	Sep–Dec
Lemons			Apr–Aug		
Lettuce	Jun–Sep	Jun–Sep	Dec–Apr	Mar–Sep	Jun–Sep
Lima Beans	Jun–Jul	Aug	May	Mar–Jul	Jun–Sep
Mushrooms:					
Chanterelles	Sep	Sep			Sep–Oct
Morels	May	May			Apr–May
Nuts:					
Walnuts/ Pecans	Sep–Oct	Sep–Nov			Oct–Dec
Almonds				Aug–Oct	
Hazelnuts					Sep–Oct
Onions	Aug–Oct	Sep–Nov	Apr–Aug	May–Sep	Aug
Peaches	Jul–Aug	Jul–Sep	Jun–Jul	Jun–Aug	Jul–Aug
Pears	Aug–Oct			Aug–Oct	Sep–Nov
Peas	May–Jul	May–Jul	Dec–Feb	Mar–Jun	May–Jul
Peppers	Aug–Sep	Jul–Sep	Nov–May	Jul–Oct	Jul–Sep
Plums	Aug–Sep	Aug–Sep		Jun–Aug	Aug–Sep
Potatoes:					
New	Jun–Aug	May–Jun	May–Sep	Jun–Aug	Jun–Jul
Mature	Sep–Oct	Sep–Oct	Nov–Jan		Sep–Oct
Pumpkins	Oct	Oct	Oct–Nov	Nov	Oct
Radishes	May–Jul	May–Aug	Mar–May	Mar–Jun	May–Jul
Raspberries	Jun–Sep			Apr–Jul	Jul–Aug
Rhubarb	May–Jun	May–Jun	Feb–May	Mar–Jun	May–Jun
Salsify	Oct–Nov	Oct–Nov			Oct–Jan
Sorrel	Apr–Jun	Apr–Jun	Jan–Feb		Apr–Jun
Spinach:					
Spring	Apr–Jun	Apr–Jun	Jan–Mar	Feb–Apr	Apr–May
Fall	Sep–Oct	Sep–Oct			Sep–Nov
Strawberries	Jun–Jul	Jun–Jul	Nov–Apr	Apr–Jul	Jun–Jul

	MIDWEST	EAST	SOUTH	WEST	N. WEST
Summer Squash:					
Yellow/					
Zucchini	Jul–Sep	Jul–Sep	Nov–Apr	May–Nov	Jul–Oct
Sweet Potatoes			Oct–Dec	Nov–Dec	
Tomatoes	Jul–Sep	Jul–Sep	Dec–May	Jul–Nov	Jul–Sep
Root Vegetables	Sep–Nov	Sep–Nov			Oct–Dec
Watercress	Apr–May	Apr–May	Dec–Feb	Jan–Mar	Apr–May
Winter Squash:					
Butternut/					
Acorn	Sep–Nov	Sep–Nov	Oct–Dec		Oct–Nov

Index

Entries for ingredients list recipes in which the ingredient may be substituted or added as well as recipes that feature the ingredient. Titles of featured recipes are capitalized and given in full; those based on variations or substitutions are lowercased and may be reworded to reflect the change in ingredients.

roast
Braised Pork Roast with Carrots and Plums, 181
with grapes, 204
scaloppine, 179, 295–96
tenderloin
grilled, with gooseberries, 113
medallions, with oranges and cracked pepper, 293
Pork Tenderloin with Tomato Relish, 146–47
with Portobello mushrooms, 237
Seared Pork Tenderloin Oriental, 79–80
See also bacon; ham
Potage of Fresh Peas with Mint, 70
potager. See kitchen garden
potato(es), 83, 305
baked
Baked Potato with Capers and Olives, 213
in Belgian Endive au Gratin, 243
stuffed with Wild Mushroom Fricassee, 173
Bastille Day "Pommes Frites" French Fries, 120
caneles, 83
chips, 120
chowder ingredient, 71
Country-Style Cod with Browned Potatoes and Onions, 328
cutting, 306
harvest chart, 397
mashed
with Cider Sausage, 148
Shepherd's Pie crust, 182–83
new, 83
cleaning and peeling, 84
en cocotte variation, 51
harvest chart, 397
New Potato Salad with Lovage, 84–85
omelet filling, 44
Potato Cakes with Ham and Ricotta, 81–82
Risole New Potatoes, 83
selecting, 84
Three Greens Omelet variation, 44
Warm New Potatoes with Camembert, 58–59
peeled, keeping in cold water, 82
Potato-Leek Tourte, 241
Potato Lyonnaise, 305–6
Pumpkin au Gratin variation, 211
in root vegetable purées, 200
salad, 84–85
with shrimp and fennel, 144
in soups, 8
Cream of Vegetable Soup, 319
with Tomato Fondant, 156
Winter Potatoes with Italian-Style Sausage, 335

Winter Roasted Vegetables, 242
See also sweet potatoes
pot-au-feu, 286
Le Pot-au-Feu à la Sauce Piquante, 299–300
potée, 303
Smoked Meat Potée with Cabbage and Chestnuts, 303–4
Poulet Princess, 19–20
praline
in custard cream, 34, 388
for Mother's Day Cake, 60–61
preserving foods, 166–67, 168
fruits in wine, 391
mushrooms, 174
nuts, 249
pickling, 146, 168
tomatoes, 184
Proust, Marcel, 312
prunes
with braised pork roast, 181
Breton Pudding, 164
Marinated Prune Tart, 338
pudding, Breton Pudding, 164
puff paste, 386
pumpkin, 195, 211
and applesauce, 336
harvest chart, 397
Pumpkin and Spice Roulade, 247–48
Pumpkin au Gratin, 211
Pumpkin Custard with Butterscotch Caramel Sauce, 250–51
pumpkin pecan pie, 249
with quince, 307
seeds, toasted, 211
Purée of Butternut Squash with Roasted Hazelnuts, 201
Purée of Grilled Eggplant, 119

quail
Grilled Butterflied Quail with Gooseberries, 112–13
roasted, 113
quatre-épices, 261–62
quiche fillings
spinach and cheese custard, 367
squash purée, 201
quince, 307
Rutabaga and Quince Mash, 307

rabbit, 235
in Calvados, 297–98
country paté, 261–62
Rabbit Braised with Mustard and Chestnuts, 235–36
radishes, 26
harvest chart, 397
Snow Pea and Radish Salad, 26–27
ragout, Pheasant Ragout with Morels and Chives, 75

raisins
Breton Pudding, 164
Grated Carrot Salad variation, 126
in stuffing, 234
raspberries
Bavarian Crêpes with Raspberry Sauce, 341–42
harvest chart, 397
Strawberry-Rhubarb Compote variation, 64
vinaigrette, 24, 91
ratatouille, 157, 158
Mediterranean Ratatouille, 157–58
ravigote sauce, 104–5
ravioli
Herb Ravioli with Shrimp and Fennel, 144
with Spring Green Sauce, 56
squash purée filling, 201
Red Lentils with Crème Fraîche, 274
relishes, 246
Cranberry-Pear Relish, 246
Pork Tenderloin with Tomato Relish, 146–47
rémoulade, Celery Root Rémoulade, 151
réveillon, 255
rhubarb, 64
harvest chart, 397
Strawberry-Rhubarb Compote, 64
rice
to bind root vegetable purées, 200
with Italian-style sausage, 335
with roasted garlic and mushrooms, 272
salad, 214–15
vegetable stuffing, 154–55
See also wild rice
rillettes, 263
Duck Rillettes, 263
Risole New Potatoes, 83
Roast Beef and Pesto Sour Cream Sandwich, 118
Roast Chicken with Tarragon, 17–18
Roasted Beets, 185
Roasted Fillet of Turbot with Caramelized Onions, 49
Roasted Hazelnut and Mixed Green Salad, 216
Roasted Thanksgiving Turkey with Sage, 232–33
roasting, 233
Roast Leg of Lamb with Garlic, 21–22
Roast Salmon with Cider-Apple Cream Sauce, 175–76
Rock Cornish Game Hen en Cocotte, 50–51
root vegetables, 242
caramelizing, 185
earliest, 151
grating, 321
harvest chart, 398